Gender, Society & Development

Advancing women's status: women and men together?

Acknowledgements

The editorial team in the Information, Library and Documentation Department
would like to acknowledge with thanks the assistance of Rita Joldersma and Dia
Timmermans in reviewing the papers; the contribution of KIT Press staff throughout
the publication process; and André van den Dungen for his technical wizardry.

Royal Tropical Institute
KIT Press
Mauritskade 63
1092 AD Amsterdam
The Netherlands
Tel. (20) 5688272

Material in this book has been compiled and edited by staff of the Information, Library and
Documentation Department of the Royal Tropical Institute, Amsterdam. The editorial team
comprised: Maria de Bruyn, Sarah Cummings, Henk van Dam, Erwin van Delden, Johan
Roelfsma and Minke Valk.

CIP-DATA KONINKLIJKE BIBLIOTHEEK, DEN HAAG

Advancing

Advancing women's status: women and men together? : critical reviews and a selected
annotated bibliography / Maria de Bruyn (ed.). - Amsterdam : Royal Tropical Institute. -
(Critical reviews and annotated bibliographies. Gender, society & development,
ISSN 1382-4686 ; 1)
With ref.
ISBN 90-6832-630-9
NUGI 661
Subject headings: women ; developing countries

© 1995 Royal Tropical Institute – Amsterdam
Cover Design: Ad van Helmond
Printing: ICG Printing, Dordrecht
ISBN 90 6832 630 9

Advancing
women's status:

Gender, Society & Development

women and men
together?

CRITICAL REVIEWS AND ANNOTATED BIBLIOGRAPHIES SERIES

Royal Tropical Institute (KIT)
Amsterdam, the Netherlands

Contents

General information

I. A description of the records in the annotated bibliography

The annotated bibliography is divided into five sections: four of these reflect the themes of the critical reviews and have abstracts; while the final one lists publications and resources without abstracts. The different sections can be identified using the contents page. Within each section, the records are listed alphabetically by author. Subject, author and geographical indexes provide a means of rapidly locating records on specific topics. Two examples of typical records are shown below:

1,2 **089 Persistent inequalities : women and world development**
3,4 TINKER, IRENE. Equity Policy Center,
5 Washington DC, USA. Oxford University Press, New York, xi, 302 p. 1990 [EN] Bibliogr.:p.
7,8 257-291. Includes index ISBN 0-19-506158-6
9 Despite an improved understanding about women and development, women remain faced with persistent inequalities. Past and current debates in the field of women-in-development that have challenged many earlier assumptions about development and the reality of women's work and lives within and outside the household are highlighted. The politics of the women-in-development approach are addressed from a variety of perspectives, including feminist and gender perspectives. The impact of intrahousehold distribution and control on individual household members, and women in particular, is examined. Empirical data from the Philippines and Sri Lanka indicate that behaviour within the household can be modified by improving women's economic opportunities outside the household.
10 KIT, Amsterdam   [N 90-1847]

1,2 **009 Women's roles and gender gap in health and survival**
3 BASU, ALAKA MALWADE. - In: *Economic and*
6 *Political Weekly* 28(1993)43 p.2356-2362, [EN]
7,8 ill. 39 lit.refs ISSN 0012-9976
9 Gender differences in health and mortality in India are examined by analysing the health risks women face in their productive/economic, domestic and reproductive roles, relative to the risks men face. Determinants of women's health are divided into determinants affecting exposure to illness, and determinants affecting the outcome of illness. Male mortality is also compared with female mortality. A general finding is that where women are economically active, not restricted to the domestic domain and not defined primarily by the number of children they bear, the gender gap in health and survival is smaller than it is for women who are economically inactive, imprisoned in the domestic world, and dependent on their reproductive success for their status.
10 KIT, Amsterdam   [B 3057-28(1993)43]

1
Record number.

2
Original title.

3
All authors are listed and entered in the Author Index.

4
Affiliation (professional address) of the first author is given.

5
For monographs, the publisher, place, number of pages and year of publication are given.

6
The reference includes the journal title in full (in italics), the volume number, year of publication (in brackets), issue number, inclusive page numbers as stated in the original document.

7
Language of the text is given in square brackets. Summaries, glossaries, indexes, illustrations and literature references are also noted.

8
The bibliographic data conclude with the ISSN or ISBN (if available) of the original document.

9
Abstract

10
The shelf-mark of the book or journal in the library of the Royal Tropical Institute is given in square brackets at the end of each record. Please state this shelf-mark number in your photocopy request.

II. The following acronyms can be found in the text:

ADB	Asian Development Bank
AIDS	acquired immunodeficiency syndrome
CEDAW	Convention on the Elimination of All Forms of Discrimination Against Women
CEPAL	Economic Commission for Latin America
ECA	United Nations Economic Commission for Africa
ECLAC	Economic Commission for Latin America and the Caribbean
FAO	Food and Agriculture Organization
GEMINI	Growth and Equity through Microenterprise Investments and Institutions, USA
GDP	gross domestic product
HIV	human immunodeficiency virus
IDS	Institute of Development Studies, UK
ILO	International Labour Organization
INSTRAW	International Research and Training Institute for the Advancement of Women
IPPF	International Planned Parenthood Federation
KIT	Royal Tropical Institute
MRG	Minority Rights Group
NGO	non-governmental organization
OECD	Organization for Economic Cooperation and Development
UN	United Nations
UNCRD	United Nations Centre for Regional Development
UNDP	United Nations Development Programme
UNESCO	United Nations Economic and Social Commission
UNFPA	United Fund for Population Activities
UNICEF	United Nations Children's Fund
UNIFEM	United Nations Development Fund for Women
UNU	United Nations University
USAID	Agency for International Development, USA
VENA	Women and Autonomy Centre, the Netherlands
WHO	World Health Organization
WIDER	World Institute for Development Economics Research, Japan
STDs	sexually transmitted diseases

Preface

I am pleased to introduce this book as the first in a new series on Gender, Society and Development, produced by the Information, Library and Documentation Department of the Royal Tropical Institute. The series focuses on gender relations, namely the social, economic, political and legal roles of women *and men* in society. Rather than addressing women's concerns in isolation, it sets out to explore an approach to development in which women and men together are striving to bringing about change. This focus is derived from the growing recognition that singling out women as a special group can marginalize women and their concerns from their rightful place in the mainstream of development. Each publication in the series will include state-of-the-art literature reviews, plus an annotated bibliography identifying key literature in the field. In practice, the series' emphasis on women and men will mean that authors of review articles will be asked to integrate men into their discussions and recommendations, while a special effort will be made to include publications in the bibliography which consider how women and men together are participants in the development process. The series will be based on gender expertise within KIT, as well as including articles from selected outside authors.

Advancing women's status: women and men together? was produced to coincide with the Fourth World Conference on Women, held in Beijing during September 1995. Four of the main themes of the conference are addressed in critical reviews on women's status and rights, education and training, economic participation, and sexual and reproductive health. The annotated bibliography has been selected to reflect these themes.

N.H. Vink
Director General
Royal Tropical Institute

Introduction

A gender-based approach to advancing women's social status and position

Maria de Bruyn

In September 1995, the UN Fourth World Conference on Women discussed women's needs and concerns, assessing changes in women's health, education, employment, family life, politics and human rights over the past decade. Taking that conference as a starting point, this book employs a gender-based perspective to review current knowledge and recent experiences related to four areas which are in the forefront of international and national discussions concerning women and development. These comprise:

- women's status and rights: ensuring gender equity in social status and equal respect for women's and men's human rights through appropriate policies and programming, social security measures and legislation;
- programme planning and gender training: ensuring that development programmes are gender sensitive by including a gender-based perspective in educational policies and training of policymakers and project implementers;
- economic participation: assessing the effect of structural adjustment programmes on women's economic participation and ensuring equal access of women and men to employment and income opportunities in the formal/informal and agricultural sectors; and
- sexual and reproductive health: advocating equal access of women and men to sexual and reproductive health care as well as equally shared participation in and responsibility for family planning and prevention of sexually transmitted diseases (STDs), including HIV infection.

These interrelated areas are highlighted in the four sections of this book. Each section begins with a critical review article, providing an overview of the current situation and proposals concerning how gender-based policies can be translated from theory to practice. Each article is followed by an annotated bibliography of relevant, up-to-date literature related primarily to developing countries. The abstracts provide information on regional and national level research and programmes, with occasional case studies at the community level illustrating salient points. The fifth section of the book concludes with a list of useful reference publications, such as review documents, directories and manuals. The book will serve as a background document and resource guide for policymakers, programme planners and implementers, project staff and researchers.

Why talk about gender instead of women and development?

For many years, governments, UN agencies, the World Bank and non-governmental organizations (NGOs) have used women-in-development (WID) approaches to involve women and girls in programmes which aim to combat poverty and generally improve the overall standard of living of the poorest sectors in society. In recent years, WID approaches have been criticized, however, because they mainly concentrate on increasing the efficacy and efficiency of projects through women's participation instead of improving women's overall status and position. Critics also argue that many WID programmes are inadequate because they neglect women's position and activities in the domestic sphere and do not sufficiently analyse the causes of and processes leading to female subordination.

Accordingly, policymakers and researchers now propose that programmes be based on the concept of gender. Whereas the term 'sex' refers to male and female biological attributes, the term 'gender' can be defined as *socially-ascribed meanings given to the categories man and woman*. Gender refers to widely-shared ideas and expectations (norms) about women and men. The ideas include our beliefs about 'typical' or 'appropriate' feminine and masculine characteristics and abilities. The expectations are what we think about how women and men should behave in various situations. Such ideas and expectations are learned from families, friends, opinion leaders, religious and cultural institutions, schools and the media. They determine the status, economic and political power and roles which women and men are granted in society. Examples of gender-based norms/values noted in various societies include:

- 'Motherhood' as the primary validation of a woman's status and rights to entitlements (MacFadden 1994): while most societies also value 'fatherhood', male status is not mainly dependent on producing and caring for children;
- 'Motherism' to denote women's perceived need to assist and take care of men (Lewis 1992): women are expected to have a 'maternal instinct' which makes them singularly adapted to caring for others while men are viewed as lacking such inclinations; and
- 'Womanism', a concept focusing on the power which women can wield but which ignores the low societal status accorded to women (ibid.).

The concept of gender can be utilized in two ways: descriptively and analytically (Krishnamurthy 1994: 21). A descriptive gender approach concentrates on describing and explaining how socially-ascribed differences between women and men change over time and vary with class, caste, ethnicity, religion and age. An analytical approach examines how socially constructed power relationships between women and men lead to female subjugation.

In comparison to the WID approach, a gender-based development approach focuses on both male and female social roles as well as gender inequalities so that programmes and projects can take these into account and thereby contribute to equality between the sexes and empowerment of women. Unfortunately, as much of the literature cited in this volume shows, there is still a long way to go before this approach really takes root. Many so-called gender-based programmes implicitly equate 'gender' with 'women', concentrating mainly or exclusively on female consciousness-raising and education, and increasing women's access to health care, social services and participation in income-generating schemes. Moreover, some development workers (including women) resist using a gender-based perspective because they feel it challenges long-held cultural values and practices which should not be changed to comply with Western concepts. In these cases, the dynamic nature of culture should be emphasized; cultures have changed throughout history and continue to do so. Advocating women's empowerment is a universal rather than a Western goal.

Status and rights

'Wife beating is an accepted custom...we are wasting our time debating the issue': comment made by a parliamentarian during floor debates on wife battering in Papua New Guinea (Heise et al. 1994).

'Women should wear *purdah* [head-to-toe covering] to ensure that innocent men do not get unnecessarily excited by women's bodies and are not unconsciously forced into becoming rapists. If women do not want to fall prey to such men, they should take the necessary precautions instead of forever blaming men' (comment by a member of the Malaysian parliament during debates on the reform of rape laws) (ibid.).

'The child was sexually aggressive' (reason given by a Canadian judge for suspending the sentence of a man who had sexually assaulted a 3-year-old girl) (ibid.).

Violence against women is found in societies everywhere in many forms, including domestic verbal and physical abuse, rape and sexual assault, incest and female genital mutilation (circumcision). Unfortunately, it is often considered acceptable behaviour and/or women themselves are blamed for inciting men to engage in it. Violence against women thus provides one of the most graphic illustrations of the low position and status which women are accorded in many countries.

Societal norms and values provide the framework within which status and position are ascribed. The literature clearly demonstrates that women are generally disadvantaged in comparison to men in terms of status and rights at all levels of society. The extent of inequality is further determined by other factors, such as age, stage in the life-cycle, ethnicity, and religion.

Within most families, women and girls have less decision-making power yet they are held responsible for bearing and nurturing children; this role is extended to providing care and services for the entire family so that female household members carry out most household tasks. Men, on the other hand, are considered the primary income earners (even when they do not, in fact, provide the majority of household earnings) and they are trained for and entrusted with tasks relating to production and dealings outside the household arena. Family elders therefore often give preference to male family members and offspring when deciding which children attend school and to what level, who controls the household finances, who engages in subsistence or cash crop farming and who participates in community projects. A distinction thus arises at the household level which has ramifications at higher levels: women's primary role is seen as belonging to the domestic or reproductive sphere, while men are expected to assume responsibility for the public or productive sphere (Du Guerny and Sjöberg 1993). The status ascribed to these two spheres differs substantially.

At the community level, although lip-service may be paid to the participation of women in communal decisions and activities, their contributions are often not actively sought out or taken into account. At the national level, there may be a lack of regulatory measures, legislation and supportive mechanisms to provide a frame-work for ensuring that women's rights are respected and met.

Changes in men's and women's status and position are needed as a basis for ensuring gender equality in relation to, for example, education, economic participa-tion and sexual/reproductive health. To achieve this, norms and values concerning male and female social roles must be challenged at the household and community levels. Awareness-raising interventions must not only target men but women as well, since women play a major role in socialization processes which keep the norms in place that implicitly and/or explicitly grant women secondary status. For example, some women's loyalties in the Middle East are primarily to their kin and families and this causes them to act in ways which reinforce rather than challenge female subordination (Al-Mughni 1993).

To create a supportive environment for gender-based programmes, policies and legislation must be enacted to offer women and men the opportunities to assume new roles and exercise their rights without bias. In some cases, this means that conflicts between written and customary laws must be resolved. In Uganda and other African countries, for example, customary laws grant a widow's in-laws her husband's (and their communally acquired) property, even though constitutional law guarantees her the right to at least a small percentage of the inheritance (Ars 1995). Laws and measures are needed to ensure women's access to workers' benefits, pensions and social services, even when they are self-employed or working in the informal sector (M.A. Singamma Sreenivasan Foundation 1993). Laws which, at first sight, seem protective of women must be re-assessed. For example, restrictions on women working at night, which are intended to protect them from physical assault, and legal provisions for maternity leave may also make women less attractive job applicants for employers (Young 1993: 80-81). Women must also be made aware of the legisla-tion which grants them certain rights so that they can seek legal recourse if neces-sary. Legal literacy programmes around the world, in which community-based workers are trained to make the law accessible to women, provide an example of how this can be accomplished (Schuler et al. 1992).

In addition to the judicial system, sensitization of those working in various societal institutions which support important norms and values is necessary. These institutions include the media, religious organizations and law enforcement agencies.

Women's organizations can play a vital role in this regard, especially if they link up with wider social movements to prevent marginalization of gender issues (Young 1993: 164).

Programme planning and gender training

'"If a pregnant woman is found to have AIDS she should be killed so that AIDS ends with her," said a Zimbabwean member of parliament during a debate on legalising abortion. He opposed terminating pregnancies on the grounds that abortion had no place in local traditions. Moreover, he said, "the women would still continue to spread AIDS"' (Death 1994).

Even people at the highest levels of society continue to espouse ideas which designate women as irresponsible or incapable of controlling their own behaviour. As a consequence, women's freedom of movement and action is more closely regulated than that of men. Concomitantly, women face more restrictions in influencing policies, gaining access to education and income-earning opportunities, and deciding about their own and their families' health. Societies as a whole lose out because valuable contributions to development by half of their population are prevented.

Incorporation of a gender perspective into programme planning is therefore essential. Massiah suggests that programmes use a 'visibility framework' which can provide ways of signalling gender gaps that development initiatives must address (Massiah 1993: 26-29). The framework includes different types of visibility:
• conceptual visibility: external observers' perceptions that men and women are subject to gender-related disadvantages;
• subjective visibility: individuals' recognition of the effects of gender domination on their own attitudes, behaviour and situation;
• theoretical/statistical visibility: identification of trends and patterns of gender domination which help explain how systems maintain gender inequalities;
• socio-economic and political visibility: identification of the power resources available to men and women, and the legal and political barriers to equity; and
• domestic visibility: gender relations at the individual and household levels.

Based on these categories, programmes can develop indicators for both descriptive and analytical gender-based assessments. Such indicators can relate to human, physical and economic resources, the status of women and men as well as legal provisions.

Formulating appropriate policies and programme frameworks is only a first step, however. These frameworks then have to be implemented. It is insufficient to simply institute special 'women's' programmes and units within organizations because the danger remains that gender issues will not be integrated into wider planning and programmes. Ultimately, both men and women in all walks of life and occupations must become advocates for changes in norms, values, policies and laws which will lay the foundations for gender equity.

Gender training can be a useful tool for motivating both men and women to become such advocates. Offering special gender training courses for participants from different sectors is one strategy; another is to implement gender training for specific groups, such as businesspersons, farmers, entrepreneurs and trainers themselves. Gender training can help create an environment which will contribute to the initiation and maintenance of policies and programmes intending to achieve gender equality. Because 'gender' is so often equated with 'women', however, this type of training is frequently seen as a women's issue or activity. Both governmental and NGO employers tend to send female rather than male staff to such courses, a tendency which needs to change.

The benefits of gender training can be multiple, depending on the approach taken. Informative courses which explain the gender concept and how it can be used to assess policies and programmes provide policymakers and programme implementers with a sound knowledge base. Programmes focusing on attitudinal change go a step further by tackling participants' norms and values which keep inequalities in place. For example, an NGO in the Philippines, HASIK, has developed a gender training programme for men which aims to act as a catalyst and transform participants at both individual and organizational levels (Constantino-David 1994: 55). Through games, song, dance, reflection and discussions, the male participants listen to women's voices and concerns to help them understand female subordination and gender roles. The game of 'feminist poker' and various exercises encourage participants to articulate their own ideas about why women are oppressed. They are then assisted in envisioning a better future by addressing issues such as women's work burden and how to change the institutions which construct gender roles. Action planning at the conclusion of the course helps the men translate what they have learned into organizational/professional goals and schemes.

Increasing women and girls' overall access to educational opportunities is, of course, vital. Female literacy in countries around the world lags behind that of men. Levels of educational attainment continue to differ considerably, with more men benefiting from secondary and tertiary schooling as well as vocational training. When women do benefit from higher education, they still tend to be directed towards learning skills which will relegate them to occupations reflecting their 'reproductive role', such as care and service professions. If male and female access to and participation in higher education and occupational training becomes more equal, perhaps this will contribute to equalizing the status accorded to different educational achievements and subsequent employment.

Economic participation

Economic power and independence can enable women and men to care better for their health; conversely, healthy people can achieve more politically and economically. Male and female economic participation are strongly influenced, however, by the educational levels, status and position of men and women in any given society and/or community. Norms and values once again play an important role. They determine women's mobility, affecting their opportunities for training, and influence which types of work are considered 'proper' for women and men. Various reports indicate, for example, that implicit and explicit 'gender stereotyping' of technology and technological skills cause women and men to choose different occupations; it also means that their capabilities are assessed differently (Wajcman 1994: 220; Young 1993: 71, 74). Conversely, those with more economic power and a higher occupational status are in a better position to advocate gender-equal policies and programmes.

The extent of women's economic participation is not yet known in many countries, partly because of the difficulties of defining economic activity. This is reinforced by the fact that women continue to be seen primarily as wives, mothers and homemakers, and there is no official (and statistical) recognition of their work in the domestic sphere (Tassawar 1993; Yudelman 1993). A review of the literature indicates that women's overall participation in the labour force is characterized by lower wages, limited contractual and labour protection, no job security, concentration in certain sectors and industries, and poor working conditions (Naylor 1994; Rajagopal 1993; Young 1993: 74, 79). In addition, self-employed women and those employed in the informal or agricultural sectors often work in small enterprises, which provide them with little access to the credit and information needed to manage and market their products effectively (Young 1993: 94-96). The literature indicates that two strategies are of special importance for increasing women's economic participation: increasing their access to credit and capacity-building regarding organizational and work skills, together with information provision (Ehui 1994; M.A. Singamma Sreenivasan Foundation 1993: 287).

The impact of economic stabilization and structural adjustment programmes is an important factor to consider when examining women's economic participation. Although the overall effects of adjustment policies on women are difficult to distinguish because women in different sectors are affected differentially, it is slowly becoming clear that women are working longer hours in an effort to reduce the effects of rising food prices and cuts in social services (Massiah 1993: 12; Rocha 1989; Young 1993: 37-38).

Sexual and reproductive health

'"The female condom will increase immorality among women and single mothers," said Father Ndikaru wa Teresia of Thika parish. "It is worse than the male condom, giving women the opportunity to do what they want. We are going to preach against these condoms; the church cannot condone their use"'(Muhindi 1993: 3).

'"Right now I'm pregnant. It was an accident, I was planning to go to the clinic but my husband took away my card. He wanted more children so I became pregnant"' (Marres 1992).

While women are generally held responsible for family planning and prevention of HIV/STD transmission, their ability to do so is severely restricted. To increase shared responsibility between women and men and enable women to gain more decision-making power in this sphere, some programmes have shifted their focus from family planning and fertility control to reproductive health. The reproductive health approach focuses on a wider range of health problems than family planning, including contraception, abortion, genital mutilation, morbidity related to the reproductive organs, HIV/STDs and perinatal care. Given this emphasis on morbidity and mortality, however, the reproductive health approach may unnecessarily 'medicalize' these issues. More recently, therefore, the reproductive health concept has been broadened to include sexual health, paying attention to sex education, relationships, sexual orientation, parenting, health throughout the life-cycle (including puberty and menopause), sexual abuse and violence. Such a broadening of scope covers women and men of all ages, rather than only focusing on women of childbearing age.

There are many links between sexual health and male/female status, education and economic participation. Three examples can be given. First, norms and values related to male and female status may impede men and women from taking and sharing responsibility for various aspects of sexual health. Neither young unmarried and childless women nor men may be welcome at family planning centres. Men feel that they cannot visit these centres because they are perceived to deal with 'women's business'. Further, women do not attend STD clinics because having an STD could mark them as 'immoral' and damage their reputation. For many men, on the other hand, having an STD is viewed as proof that they are 'real men'. Men have more decision-making power in relationships so they control whether HIV/STD prevention measures such as condom use are employed. Second, given limited access to education and income, women and men do not have the same type of access to health services. Illiterate women cannot, for example, benefit from printed AIDS/STD prevention materials. Men control the household finances and have wider access to radio and television so they receive more information about sexual health services. Third, when income opportunities are limited, women may feel forced to barter sex for money and basic necessities, a survival strategy which places them at greater risk of HIV/STD infection. Concomitantly, norms condoning and even encouraging men to have multiple partners contribute to a greater demand for commercial sex.

Sexual and reproductive health programmes need a gender-based focus if they are to improve men's and women's wellbeing. The factors which will help motivate and encourage men to take responsibility for their own and their partners' sexual health should be determined. Programmes which make women more explicitly aware of how male domination affects their options in this sphere may also motivate them to change norms and practices which prevent them from safeguarding their own and their families' health. Services must further be re-oriented to better meet men's and women's specific concerns and needs. This includes improving the accessibility and acceptability of family planning and STD services, as well as promoting research which will enable both women and men to have a broader range of options for birth control and HIV/STD prevention.

Conclusion

Since the First World Conference on Women in 1975, interest in women's issues has increased considerably. Reflecting this interest is the accumulation of data relating to women's position throughout the world. Although numerous problems are unresolved, statisticians are now beginning to collect gender-disaggregated data which will constitute baseline information against which to measure progress.

In the policy sphere, the establishment and signing of the UN Convention on the Elimination of All Forms of Discrimination against Women has been one advance. Another has been the establishment of women's ministries and special units within ministries, development institutions and programmes. The great increase in women-focused organizations, working in fields ranging from credit provision to community organization, as well as increased networking among them in order to facilitate sharing of experiences and expertise, is also welcome.

Nevertheless, a great deal remains to be accomplished before a true gender-based perspective, as opposed to only a women-based perspective, is incorporated into policies and programmes worldwide. Advocating strategies to raise male consciousness regarding the benefits of gender equality might stimulate thinking in this field. It may then become possible to talk about changes in women's status coming about as a result of women and men working together.

Bibliography

Al-Mughni, H., *Women in Kuwait: the politics of gender*. London, Saqi Books, 1993.

Ars, B., 'Alice erfde alleen de ziekte van haar overleden man'. *Internationale Samenwerking*, vol. 10, no. 2 (1995), pp. 2-3.

Constantino-David, K., 'A model for gender training for men'. In: A. Rao et al. (ed.), *Reflections and learnings: gender trainers workshop report*. Amsterdam, Royal Tropical Institute, 1994, pp. 58-61.

Du Guerny, J. and E. Sjöberg, 'Inter-relationship between gender relations and the HIV/AIDS epidemic: some possible considerations for policies and programmes'. *Aids*, vol. 7, no. 8 (1993), pp. 1027-1034.

Ehui, M.M.K., 'Politiques et moyens d'intervention pour améliorer l'accès des petits paysans au crédit: le cas de la femme dans les mécanismes de crédit en zone rural'. *Food and Agriculture in Africa,* vol. 5 (1994), pp. 1-25.

'Death sentence'. *World*AIDS, no. 33, May (1994), p. 3.

Heise, L.L., J. Pitanguy and A. Germain, *Violence against women: the hidden health burden*. Washington, D.C., 1994.

Krishnamurthy, R., 'Gender concepts in training and planning'. In: A. Rao et al. (ed.), *Reflections and learnings: gender trainers workshop report*. Amsterdam, Royal Tropical Institute, 1994, pp. 21-25.

Lewis, D., 'Theorising about gender in South Africa'. *Southern Africa*, vol. 5, no. 12 (1992), pp. 42-44.

M.A. Singamma Sreenivasan Foundation, 'Integrating women in development planning: the role of traditional wisdom'. In: J. Massiah (ed.), *Women in developing economies: making visible the invisible*. Paris, UNESCO, 1993, pp. 280-300.

MacFadden, P., 'Motherwood [sic] as a choice'. In: *Southern Africa*, vol. 7, no. 9 (1994), pp. 40-41.

Marres, D., 'AIDS and childbearing: an explorative study among Kenyan women'. (M.A. thesis, University of Limburg, Maastricht, 1992.)

Massiah, J., 'Indicators for planning for women in Caribbean development'. In: J. Massiah (ed.), *Women in developing economies: making visible the invisible*. Paris, UNESCO, 1993, pp. 11-134.

Muhindi, B., '"Immoral" female condom'. *World*AIDS, no. 28, July (1993), p. 3.

Naylor, R., 'Culture and agriculture: employment practices affecting women in Java's rice economy'. *Economic Development and Cultural Change*, vol. 42, no. 3 (1994), pp. 509-535.

Rajagopal, 'Fibre cooperatives for rural women: an analysis of organisational and management aspects'. *Journal of Rural Development*, vol. 12, no. 6 (1993), pp. 597-615.

Rocha, L., *The invisible adjustment: poor women and the economic crisis*. Santiago, UNICEF, the Americas and the Caribbean Regional Office, Regional Programme Women in Development, 1989.

Schuler, M. and S. Kadirgamar-Rajasingham (ed.), *Legal literacy: a tool for women's empowerment*. New York, PACT Communications, 1992.

Tassawar, S.I., 'The cultural context of women's productive invisibility: a case study of a Pakistani village', *Pakistan Development Review*, vol. 32, no. 1 (1993), pp. 101-125.

Wajcman, J., 'Technology as masculine culture'. In: *The Polity reader in gender studies*. Cambridge, UK, Polity Press, 1994, pp. 216-225.

Young, K., *Planning development with women: making a world of difference*. New York, St. Martin's Press, 1993.

Yudelman, S.W., 'Women farmers in Central America: myths, roles, reality'. *Grassroots Development*, vol. 17, no. 2 (1993), pp. 2-13.

1 Women's status and rights

A critical review of women's status and rights

Neil Thin

Defining status and rights

In 1948, three years after adoption of the UN Charter, the Universal Declaration of
Human Rights recognized the principle of equality between women and men. Nearly
half a century later, the inadequate implementation of this principle is widely
regarded as one of the most pressing problems of our age and one of the most
embarrassing blots on the development landscape.

Three things must be observed before embarking on a discussion of changes in
women's status and rights. First, both of these are relational concepts which concern
relations between women, relations between men, as well as between women and
men. Debates about women's status and rights are debates about gender and therefore about the fabric of society rather than just debates about women. Second, since
debates about social inequalities and injustice have historically paid insufficient
attention to gender inequalities and gender injustice, our understanding of social
inequality and injustice (and associated concepts such as poverty, needs, vulnerability, ethics and welfare) will be enriched by putting gender into the picture (Phillips
1991). Conversely, effective understanding of women's status and rights demands
analogies and cross-references between gender and other forms of difference based
on such factors as age, class and ethnicity. Third, the concepts of status and rights
have evolved in debates dominated by men. Throughout most of their history, these
concepts have normally been used with reference to relations among men or among
groups rather than to gender relations. They must therefore be applied with caution
to gender relations and modified to suit this new purpose. Promotion of women's
rights may be another case of trying to move women into a men's domain rather than
challenging the nature of androcentrism itself. As Tinker puts it, 'by asking for equal
rights with men *as if they were men*', women may be denying their own values, and
'*by using men as their measure*', women may be ensuring that they are always
second class (1990: 51-52; emphasis in original).

Rights entail not only relations, but responsibilities. The use of the male concept
of rights to promote women's emancipation may be a double-edged sword. If women
are to acquire men's rights and responsibilities, there needs to be a complementary
move of men into women's domains. If women's status is to change, so must men's.
Both the concepts of status and rights of women are contentious. Bearing these pro-
visos in mind, development planning depends on contrasts between better futures
and unacceptable present conditions. To plan improvements in women's lives and

social improvements in gender relations, we need an understanding of the status quo and current gender wrongs.

Theory, research and analysis

Theories about the causes of gender inequality are crucial in shaping policy and practice. When influential theorists attribute primacy to one cause rather than another, this affects both budgetary allocations for research and the policies guiding practical interventions. For example, some theorists explain the dramatic regional variations in female survival across India in terms of lower female contribution to the production of exchange values in northern India, whereas others see this economic factor as a more superficial cause than gender ideologies which are rooted in cultural histories (Harriss and Watson 1987: 94). Those who favour an infrastructural explanation would be likely to try to bring about improvements in women's wellbeing by changing their reproductive roles, whereas those who favour cultural explanations would put more emphasis on cultural interventions designed to change attitudes. Practices of performance measurement implicitly embody theories about causation, typically assuming development to be led by the monetized, non-domestic parts of the economy.

Generalizations about the 'position of women' are flawed on at least two counts. First, there is no such thing as a position held constantly by any one woman let alone all women in any region or country. What is needed is some understanding of the various positions that women of different classes and ethnic groups find themselves in at various times in their day and throughout their lives. Second, women are 'positioned' both vis-à-vis men and vis-à-vis other women. Without comparable discussions on the 'position of men', generalizations about the 'position of women' are unhelpful (Rogers 1980: 29). The importance of the relational aspect of status is brought out emphatically by Jeffery and Jeffery's analysis of relations within the household in northern India, where 'mothers-in-law are just as important as husbands as restrictors of women's autonomy' (1993: 73). Their book also highlights an important point about the social status of traditional birth attendants (*dais*) in this area, who are so socially degraded that attempts to improve their effectiveness through provision of short training courses are likely to prove futile.

It is also helpful to distinguish a variety of contexts to which status is relevant. A change which improves women's status in one context may not improve it in another. Vlassoff (1994) shows how economic developments associated with agricultural growth in Maharashtra, India, have enabled families to withdraw female labour from the fields, thereby enhancing both family prestige and women's status within the family. However, their confinement to the domestic arena actually reduces women's autonomy and power in wider society.

Such contradictions arise not only from contextual differences but also from differences between interpretational levels. It has, for example, been argued that the ideological inferiority of women in Muslim societies sometimes works to the material advantage of cash-earning women. The same Muslim ideology forces men to take responsibility for the financial support of their family, giving women the right to use their own marketing profits as they choose (UN 1986: 177). The same set of gender relations looks different when interpreted in ideological or material terms.

Planners find their field of operation more effectively clarified by looking at the visibility and audibility of women rather than at their status or rights (though of course these are aspects of status, and women have a right to be seen and heard). Massiah, for example, has pointed out that in the Caribbean both women and women's concerns are 'invisible' to planners because of their macroeconomic focus and their assumption that women will be beneficiaries of welfare and trickle down rather than participants in structural change (1993: 14). 'Visibility' is not so much about the availability of information about women's lives and work, but rather about the availability of political will to recognize women's lives and work and about the availability of realistic plans and budgets to bring about helpful transformations. There is no shortage of idiot's guides to gender inequality, but there is a worrying lack of analysis of the reasons why available information about gender inequalities is not translated into fairer practice (Goetz 1994: 28).

Policy, bureaucratic structures and legal measures

Currently the main mechanism for both promoting and monitoring national policies and legislation on women is the reports regularly submitted by signatories of the 1979 UN Convention on the Elimination of All Forms of Discrimination Against Women (CEDAW). By January 1995, 139 States had ratified the Convention. Within the UN, the United Nations Development Fund for Women (UNIFEM) has been bringing women's needs to the attention of national and international decision-makers. For example, during a 1993 global campaign for the protection of women's rights, UNIFEM ensured that violence against women was addressed in international debates on human rights. In Africa, UNIFEM supported the instruction of 300 trainers in community-based legal rights education.

Mainstreaming

The key policy issue, debated endlessly, is that of 'mainstreaming': how to bring about equal participation of women and men in the mainstream of development without resorting to separatist means which perpetuate the marginalization of women. In his message to mark International Women's Day on 8 March 1994, James Gustave Speth of the UNDP criticized the continued separation of gender issues from mainstream planning, arguing that 'the integration of women in development has received much attention in the past few decades. Yet women's development is still regarded as a separate issue, not as an integral part of all development' (speech made available by UNDP through Internet, 1994).

One major set of outcomes from the UN Decade for Women has been the establishment in most governments and in many development, research and training agencies of some kinds of separate bureaucratic structures to address either 'gender issues' or 'women's issues', such as women's bureaus and ministries, commissions on the status of women, and gender studies units. There are vital debates about whether these outputs are bringing about the achievement of the objective of gender equality, not least because ultimate objectives remain ill-defined. The existence of women's divisions, as in the UN itself, paradoxically emphasizes the continued divisions and asymmetries between women and men. On the women's side of the division there is social security and welfare, on the men's side, the economy. There is, as Moser says, 'a fundamental contradiction between the UN Decade's objectives for machineries to improve the status of women by ensuring their full integration into national life, and the welfarist objectives of social welfare ministries' (1993: 119).

Interventions for gender equality

Another key issue is the level at which interventions for gender equality are most effectively pitched. It is an uncomfortable fact that women's power, autonomy and perceptions of their own situation are to a large extent circumscribed by the family structures in which they live. Policies defined at state level are unlikely to have significant impact unless translated through agencies that both understand and have access to the internal workings of households and families. Thus, in most parts of the world, a policy promoting women's right to reproductive choice is unlikely to succeed if promoted mainly through women's clinics since it fails to address the roles of husbands and mothers-in-law in influencing a woman's reproductive options.

Arguably the single most important issue in gender planning is the need to disaggregate the household, to identify different stakeholders within the household, acknowledging both their divergent and convergent interests, both their conflicts and forms of cooperations. One of the more sophisticated arguments about households is provided by the economist Amartya Sen (1990), who discusses the peculiar 'cooperative conflicts' which mean that households can neither be regarded as units nor as class-divided. Household members behave according to bargains struck in view of potential 'breakdown scenarios' which would happen if members did not cooperate. The form of cooperation is not necessarily the ideal solution for mutual benefit but it is distorted by the members' perceptions of the relative value of each member's contributions and their respective interests. Both women and men often undervalue women's contributions, and women often prioritize the good of the family over their own individual interests. Policies which treat households as undifferentiated cooperative units are therefore likely to perpetuate existing inequalities within households.

Cultural interventions

Just as the household has often been regarded as an inner sanctum into which the state should not venture, so too 'culture' tends to be regarded as a sacred entity beyond the manipulation of policy and legislation. Although many academics, especially anthropologists and cultural theorists, have had important debates concerning the balance between international consensus on women's emancipation and respect for cultural diversity, it is often remarkable how little attention is paid to multiculturalism in policy formulation. Yet cultural plurality often results in major contradictions between different sets of precepts. India, for example, has a civil legal system which is contradicted, often to the detriment of women's rights, by a plural set of religious laws pertaining to the cultural traditions of eight religious categories (Haksar 1986). In India, as in many other parts of the world, modern reinterpretations of Islamic traditions have exaggerated or invented Islamic doctrines promoting gender inequality precisely in order to make public affirmations of the cultural distinctiveness of Islam in the face of Western cultural imperialism (Moghadam 1993: 25-26).

As with women's status and rights, it is essential to recognize that culture and tradition are adapted in relation to other cultures and traditions. Would-be homogenizers of global norms ignore this fact at their peril. However, just as a separatist approach to 'women's issues' risks essentializing women (inventing or exaggerating universal 'natural' properties of women) and providing exaggerated, static definitions of needs, a cultural relativist approach to multiculturalism runs the risk of essentializing cultures, and particularly religious ideologies, portraying them as more fixed and independently influential than they really are. A recent publication based on a workshop on Islam and gender warns of the 'danger of culturalism', whereby sociological issues are explained solely in terms of religious ideology; many other issues are at stake and, in any case, ideologies, even written versions, are diverse (Thijssen 1994: 19).

Women's economic participation

A frequent criticism of policies designed to promote women's emancipation has been that they over-simplify the gains to be made by promoting women's access to employment in the public arena. Tinker (1990), for example, has pointed out that women-in-development policymakers assume that work enhances status, yet women's work opportunities often mean longer working days with no commensurate improvement in status. Moser suggests that gender planning has evolved in stages matching general development policy: the evolution from modernization and growth-focused policies in the 1960s, through basic needs and redistribution in the 1970s, to structural adjustment in the 1980s has been matched by an evolution from a 'welfare' approach to women, to an 'equity' approach, to an 'efficiency' approach in which women's involvement in development is seen as a convenient means for making efficiency gains. What is needed, she argues, is a new focus on empowerment (1993: 8).

A key debate alluded to in the 'efficiency' approach is whether planners see women's participation (in the paid workforce, education, decision-making, community management) as a means or as an end in itself. It would be unfortunate if Moser's disparagement of the 'efficiency' approach were used to support arguments against advertising the advantages to all of society, and to national economies, of women's emancipation. For example, a key component of nation-building is an effective education system. If governments promote gender equality in access to education and educational advancement, it is more important that they simply do so than that they debate whether they are doing so in the interests of women's rights or in the interests of nation-building, strengthening the economy through building a more highly-skilled workforce, or stabilizing population by reducing the number of children. It may make little difference to policy whether an equity or an efficiency approach is being followed (Klasen 1993: 7). As Chalker puts the case for women's rights: 'It is a matter of justice. But it is also downright practical common sense. Removing discriminatory barriers and enhancing opportunities of 50% of the human race results in stronger economic growth, improved child survival and helps conserve the environment' (1994: 3-4).

The inverse of promoting women's programmes with a view to macroeconomic benefits is attempting to tailor macroeconomic policies to ensure that their impact on women is beneficial. This has proved exceptionally difficult with structural adjustment programmes. There is now widespread agreement that while the 1980s were a decade of rapidly heightening international awareness of gender issues in planning, they were a 'lost decade' in development terms because of the exacerbation of poverty caused by international debt and structural adjustment. Despite occasional benefits to women from new employment opportunities brought about by economic liberalization, not only have women borne the brunt of poverty increases, they have also suffered more than men from cutbacks in social services, welfare provision and education (Palmer 1991).

Perhaps the most difficult policy issue of all is the challenge of engineering attitudinal change. Just as it may be assumed that the state has no role to play within the household, so too some might argue that the state cannot shape the way people think. Yet even here there are policy measures and legislation that can promote gender equity by requiring media representations which avoid gender-stereotyping and promote more positive images of women as agents with a wide range of opportunities. The first UN review and appraisal of the Nairobi Forward-looking Strategies in 1990 recommended that governments should complete the revision of textbooks by 1995 to eliminate sex-biased presentations.

Translating policy into practice

Policies and legislation reflect theories about how society might be. These are useless unless complemented by strategies to bring about their realization. The next three sections focus on three sets of issues in the translation from theory to practice. These by no means exhaust the key issues and are intended as examples of some of the more important practical issues in reducing gender inequalities.

Violence

Violence against women merits special attention in the analysis of gender planning not only because of its sociological importance and factual prevalence worldwide, but because it illustrates important difficulties in the interface between the state and the household and between laws and practical outcomes. Goetz notes that it is only recently that international development agencies and governments have begun to take domestic violence and extra-domestic sexual harassment seriously as development issues (1994: 27). Their exclusion from policy was due to the perception that issues concerning intimate interpersonal relations, whether within the household or between women and men at work, were at least beyond the reach of development planning and legislation, if not actually irrelevant. The growing recognition of the role of gender-based violence as a constraint on political development and a threat to the health of women and children provides an important illustration of why the scope of development planning must be redefined if it is to become gender aware.

Even something as basic as violence is subject to widely varying cultural interpretations. The UN Declaration on the Elimination of Violence against Women (General Assembly resolution 48/104 of 20 December 1993) includes 'female genital mutilation and other traditional practices harmful to women' under the category of 'physical, sexual and psychological violence occurring in the family'. By doing so, it questions the sanctity of cultural traditions to which both men and women subscribe. Although most readers will agree that this is morally desirable, pragmatism dictates that little is likely to be achieved by simply telling practitioners of female genital mutilation that they are wrong and that this aspect of their culture is morally corrupt.

Perhaps the most important lesson from the study of violence is that it is one of the most difficult aspects of behaviour to target directly, and that indirect methods of bringing about cultural change are more likely to have the desired impact. To give just one example, the Bangladesh Rural Advancement Committee has reported that male violence against women has been reduced in villages where women's saving and credit organizations have been established (cited in Chalker 1994).

Women as individuals, women in groups, women as a category

A key strategic issue is the balance of emphasis on promotion of individual or collective empowerment of women. Viswanath's (1991) analysis of two NGOs in southern India contrasts the approach of one NGO, whose emphasis on individualistic development has prevented the development of collective self-help and collective consciousness, with that of another whose emphasis on team-building has assured lasting commitment to furthering collective goals. Others, however, have argued that if women's projects promote collective action and men's projects promote individual entrepreneurship, opportunities for development of economically profitable women's small enterprises may be limited.

The issue of collective versus individual interest is closely linked to the distinction between practical or immediate interests and strategic or long-term interests. For example, an Indian woman who aborts her female foetus following amniocentesis may well be acting rationally in pursuit of her (and her family's) practical need for physical, social and economic wellbeing, even if by so doing she perpetuates a system which denigrates women and denies girls the right to life. To take another extreme example, in contexts where female genital mutilation is the norm, a mother who imposes this on her daughter, or a girl who chooses voluntarily to undergo such an operation, may be acting rationally in the interest of the girl's status and marriage prospects.

The notion of the 'tragedy of the commons' may help in explaining why victims of social injustice participate in perpetuating it. Unless social transformers facilitate enlightened collective self-interest for sufficiently large numbers of people, both male and female individuals will continue to perpetuate forms of injustice which impose costs on present and future generations. They will do so, rationally, so long as they perceive that they alone will bear the cost of questioning the system, while the long-term benefits of such questioning accrue to other people. Social transformation requires either collective, enlightened self-interest or martyrs. It usually occurs through a combination of the two, but collective action can be part of the planning process, whereas martyrdom cannot.

Implementation strategies are most likely to be flawed when the theories that inform them are unstated. One pervasive but often unstated set of theories underpinning many 'women's development' projects is a set of assumptions about common characteristics of women as a category in contrast to men. These often come close to biological reductionism as, for example, in recently popularized assumptions about the special relationships between women and their natural resources (e.g., Ofosu-Amaah and Philleo 1992; Shiva 1989; for a good critique see Joekes, Leach and Green 1995). Such assumptions are not only theoretically naive and guilty of perpetuating gender divisions and gender stereotypes, they support 'women's projects' which take for granted women's willingness and capacity to increase their unpaid responsibilities for management of natural resources.

Mainstreaming and men's involvement: a new consensus?

The concept of mainstreaming women's issues in development planning has been around since the 1980s (Anderson 1993). The key questions, though, are who is to be brought into whose mainstream, why, and in what ways should the mainstream be modified by this process? Most analysis of gender and development focuses on the fact that the mainstream is controlled by men but that this is unfair both because it affects women and because women's contributions to the mainstream are under-recognized. Women should therefore be brought into the mainstream both because this would be more fair (equity) and because development will be helped as a result (efficiency). Far less attention is paid to the ways in which this male-dominated mainstream ought to be changed by the processes of promoting greater gender equity in development.

The UN Draft Platform for Action, which has been further discussed and ratified at the Fourth World Conference on Women, 'requires immediate action to create a peaceful, developed and just world, based on the principle of equality for all peoples of all ages and from all walks of life, built on the strength of women's knowledge, energy, creativity and skills *in partnership with men*' (emphasis added). It also calls for a 'radical transformation of the relationships between men and women'. In January 1995, CEDAW affirmed that the sensitization of men to the benefits of gender equality, which would accrue to both men and women, was essential. There has emerged in recent years a dramatic shift of emphasis towards a less gender-segregated approach to understanding and changing gender inequalities; this means both understanding women in relation to men as well as identifying strategies which involve men, both separately and together with women, in addressing gender inequalities.

The exclusion of men
These important messages about gender relations and collective benefits are still contradicted by numerous messages that focus on women and exclude men from the picture. The Beijing conference, though it will involve men, is still 'on women' not on 'gender'. The UN Bulletin *Women on the Move* refers to 'women's struggle for equality' and pays little heed to men's roles, supportive or antagonistic, in such a struggle. Anderson's paper, revealingly entitled 'Focusing on women', portrays UNIFEM's mainstreaming efforts as unsuccessful because they almost entirely censor out images of men as agents in this process.

Small wonder, then, that 'men sometimes abdicate their responsibilities in what they now conceive as a 'women's' concern' (Phillips 1991: 166). Even Moser, whose book studiously puts 'gender' rather than 'women' into its heading and most of its chapter titles, nonetheless writes primarily about women and ends up providing a paradoxically gender-blind definition of gender planning as 'a means by which women, through a process of empowerment, can emancipate themselves' (1993: 190). And in a mildly amusing example, which nonetheless reflects the reality of countless gender-blind, women-only contraceptive promotion projects, Young is able to refer without a hint of irony to 'the feminist demand for women's reproductive autonomy' (1989b: 101). The need for greater freedom of reproductive choice, misrepresented as a world of man-free sexual reproduction, translates into misguided projects that seek to exclude men from processes of reproductive choice and thereby promote gender inequalities in reproductive responsibility and reproductive cost.

The same author, however, highlights the danger of woman-centred development planning by acknowledging that 'for the vast majority of women independence from husbands is a precarious business, one that is bought at the price of being permanent-ly on the edge of economic disaster' (Young 1989a: xii). Powerful examples of this are provided by Pryer's (1989) account of how both governmental and NGO health programmes in Bangladesh typically target only or mainly women and children, ignoring the important relation between the incapacitation of male breadwinners and nutritional status of the rest of the family.

The great challenge of gender-aware development planning is to put women into the picture without censoring men from the plans. To support women's transforma-tive action independent of men creates role models with important rhetorical effects. As the Secretary-General of the Fourth World Conference on Women, Gertrude Mongella, put it: 'the image of women as strong players and managers of change is crucial in order for us to take actions which will make sure that obstacles hindering women from decision-making and effective participation in development activities are removed' (*Women on the Move*, Issue No. 1). But the interests of both women and men may be harmed by an excessively gender-segregated promotion of women's empowerment.

Gender planning
Moser suggests that the shift in emphasis from women to gender has occurred 'principally in academic research'; development strategies need to be informed by gender-aware rather than simply woman-aware theories. She acknowledges that there is such a thing as gender planning which 'differs fundamentally from planning for women-in-development'. The former is more confrontational with its 'fundamental goal of emancipation' and its 'integrative' approach which addresses women in relation to men. The women-in-development approach, addressing women in isolation, is more popular because less threatening and is an add-on rather than an integrative approach (1993: 2-4).

In one of the most significant developments linking academic theory with development policy and practice, Moser has adapted Molyneux's (1985) distinction between 'practical and strategic gender interests into one between practical and strategic gender needs' (1993: 40). In Molyneux's distinction, the practical interests of women concern immediate needs dictated by a particular form of gender relations, whereas strategic interests concern the more radical possibilities for social transformation. Moser translates this distinction into one between planning which addresses women's immediate needs and planning which challenges gender norms. To this we should add that radical gender planning challenges not only gender norms but the paradigms of mainstream development planning.

In both formulations, however, several vitally important issues are conspicuously absent. First, the concept of 'interest' is naive in its neglect of perception and available information: a woman may not perceive an interest which someone else, on the basis of different perception and information, may think she ought to perceive. A concept of informed interest, like the legal concept of informed consent, is needed in gender planning. Second, the concept of gender interest is blind to context: interest, like status and rights, is relational so that a woman has different interests as a mother-in-law than she does as a daughter-in-law, for example. Gender interest must be contextualized. Third, both Molyneux and Moser more or less censor men's interests from the picture except insofar as they are barriers to the achievement of women's needs; the fact that men have strategic and practical interests which may or may not coincide with those of women is hardly recognized in either theory or planning. However, since men have interests and are powerful, gender planning must be as explicit about men's interests as it is about women's interests, and it must address both gender conflicts and gender complementarities.

Gender planning can only achieve social progress and address the three weaknesses mentioned above if it is based on *informed social interests* (whether practical or strategic). In other words, gender planning must find contextualized win-win solutions to gender inequalities which both men and women perceive as being in their combined interest. The questions concerning the benefits or otherwise of involving and targeting men along with women force planners to make explicit the relative emphasis on conflict and consensus in their planning models. So-called radical planners see conflict as the necessary dynamic for bringing about social transformation; they force other planners, who by the nature of their profession are optimistic and seek to emphasize synergies and win-win solutions, to pay attention to trade-offs and policy conflicts (Jackson 1993). Reformist planners assume that consensus, especially across power divisions, is desirable and essential if socially beneficial and lasting transformation is to be brought about.

There would still be an equity argument against the exclusion of men from gender struggles even if it were practically possible to solve gender inequalities without the equal participation of men: why should women as researchers, policymakers, planners and implementers do all the work of solving problems created to a large extent by men?

Assessing progress

Although the UN Decade for Women undoubtedly brought about massive increases in the amount of attention paid to gender issues in planning, and in the amount of information about women's status and roles in development, the tools for assessing progress towards internationally-agreed goals of women's emancipation (such as those set out in CEDAW) are still rudimentary. Popular indicators of women's status include life expectancy, mortality of women and children, fertility, income, education, political participation, economic production, legal rights, age at marriage, residence after marriage, place in kinship system, suicide rates, divorce and records of domestic violence. But there is no agreement on how these various indicators ought to be prioritized, related to one another, and packaged to produce policy-relevant assessment of results.

Setting targets

As noted above, many of the mechanisms of international policy dialogue and research promotion are also mechanisms for monitoring change at national, regional and global levels. The UN has provided member governments with a list of the most significant indicators of women's advancement to be assessed in the national reports submitted to the UN. These indicators are linked with the critical areas of concern identified in the Platform for Action. The UN keeps a Women's Indicators and Statistics Data Base (WISTAT).

One of the main advantages of international agencies which promote women's equality is that they facilitate not only dialogue but also target-setting and monitoring. However, there is a real danger that macrolevel, aggregated target-setting will become a symbolic activity divorced from the realities of most countries. All planners know that unrealistic targets are discouraging. It most important to distinguish rhetorical declarations of vision from pragmatic targets. It is one thing to declare as a global human rights' goal 'the eradication of all forms of discrimination on grounds of sex', quite another to set specific milestones towards the achievement of such a goal. It may be realistic to forecast universal ratification of a convention by a certain date, but targets for translation of a convention's rhetoric into empirical realities must be at least country-specific and based on sound assessment of what is achievable within particular contexts. Such realistic targets are rarely set.

Striking examples of unrealistic targets which have rhetorical status but little practical value are the WHO's slogan 'Health for All by 2000', and UNESCO's target for all governments to increase the proportion of women in leadership positions to at least 30% by 1995, with a view to achieving equal representation between women and men by the year 2000. The latter could only be regarded as achievable by the loosest interpretation of 'leadership'. Women still occupy only 13% of senior management jobs within the UN itself (UN A/49/349, 30 August 1994). Targets and rights are similar in their status as icons of intent which may or may not have significant effects on reality. As Cook puts it: 'International human rights relevant to women's health are worth little where there are no enforceable duties to make them effective' (1994: 51).

The relationship between poverty and gender inequality

Another difficult policy assessment issue concerns the balance of emphasis on poverty and gender inequality. These two sets of questions are of course closely linked. As the 1990 UNDP *Human development report* noted, 'poverty has a decisive gender bias'. But is it more important to assess women's welfare and power vis-à-vis men or to assess everyone's welfare? Whereas, as noted above, women's status and rights are relational, many of the indicators by which women's wellbeing is measured are not. If women's welfare (measured in terms of mortality, nutrition and health) vis-à-vis men is better in sub-Saharan Africa than in most other developing countries (Klasen 1993: 20), both women and men there are worse off than people in most other parts of the world.

Women may 'advance' over a given period in a given country in terms of welfare indicators, but during the same period their 'status' may decline. A particular change may be viewed positively or negatively, depending on whether poverty or women's autonomy is emphasized. Thus, for example, an increase in the percentage of female-headed households may be seen as an indicator of the increasing impoverishment of women and children through abrogation of male responsibility, or as a step towards the dismantling of patriarchy. Female-headed households may be produced as part of an 'advancement strategy' or as part of a 'survival strategy imposed by dire need' (Lewis, 1993: 23).

In an ambitious attempt to promote an international ranking system for women's advancement, Ahooja-Patel (1993) proposes an Index of Women's Advancement based on an aggregate unweighted score for seven indicators: real GDP per capita, maternal mortality, infant mortality, female life expectancy at birth, female post-secondary educational enrolment, female share of labour force, and female participation in parliament. Endless arguments about the usefulness of such a system are possible, and the author admits that this is a rough and ready system which 'may seem like adding elephants and chickens'. What is most significant is that only three of the seven indicators proposed imply a comparison with men in the countries concerned; the scale acknowledges the importance to women of absolute welfare rather than just relative deprivation.

It is now widely acknowledged among planners that gender-disaggregated data are needed at all levels, including within the household. There is a danger, though, that gender-segregation of development assessment misses out on a vast range on factors affecting women for better or worse. Thus, Moser claims that 'in the UN agencies, less than 4% of project budget allocation benefit [sic] women' (1993: 112) with no attempt to assess whether women benefit directly or indirectly from the remaining 96% of UN funds.

Finally, we must acknowledge that assessment of overall development performance, rather than just indicators of women's status, has to change, paying greater heed to women's roles in development. Assessment of national economic performance is still woefully inadequate worldwide because of the narrow definition of 'economic' which excludes the vital non-monetized economic roles of women. As Elson puts it, 'a basic communication failure occurs in the way that the economy is defined' (1993: 7). Only when it is recognized that social reproduction and community management are vitally important economic activities, whether monetized or not, can development assessment hope to give a true picture of change.

Conclusion

There are few development objectives more closely synonymous with social progress than the notion of the 'advancement of women', which the UN Fourth World Conference on Women was convened to assess. In other words, there is widespread global agreement that by bringing about improvements in the lives and survival chances of half of the world's population, planners will be doing a favour to all of the world's population now and in the future. The Conference on Women was thus in effect a conference on social progress.

The Conference and its associated activities comprised debates about the nature of social progress. By enhancing women's contributions to the analysis of social progress, this should lead to a more balanced view of progress than the productivist views that have dominated international development planning so far. Young has argued that women, because of their domestic roles, tend to be people-oriented rather than thing-oriented. Their position at the interface between social reproduction and the production of things means that they are better placed than men to propose holistic forms of development which avoid the reductionism of a development paradigm that mistakenly sees 'growth' (narrowly defined in male economistic terms) as an end in itself (Young 1989a: xx).

It is in precisely this kind of radical questioning of the inadequacy of male models of society that the greatest potential of feminist development analysis and planning lies. To understand why these potentials may not be realized if this analysis focuses on women rather than on gender and society, it is worth bearing in mind the two principles of justice proposed by Rawls (1972): the 'fairness' principle which maximizes equality, and the 'average utility' principle which says that inequality should be optimized to achieve greatest benefit for everyone. With respect to debates about women's status and rights, according to the first principle it is essential to dismantle the inequalities that subordinate women and prevent them from realizing their potential. According to the second, we must recognize the benefits to society of a balanced approach to undoing injustice. We must also bear in mind that, unlike Rawls' theory which imagines an 'initial position' of equality, planners in the real world start from an ongoing position of inequality.

Bibliography

Ahooja-Patel, K., 'Gender distance among countries'. *Economic and Political Weekly*, Feb 13 (1993), pp. 295-305.

Anderson, M., *Focusing on women: UNIFEM's experience in mainstreaming*. New York, UNIFEM, 1993.

Chalker, L., 'Women's status in developing countries: British aid and human rights policy.'(Speech at Queen Elizabeth House, Oxford) Unpublished paper, 1994.

Cook, R.J., *Women's health and human rights: the promotion and protection of women's health through international human rights law*. Geneva, World Health Organization, 1994.

Elson, D., 'Gender relations and economic issues'. *Focus on Gender*, vol. 1, no. 3 (1993), pp. 6-12.

Goetz, A.M., 'From feminist knowledge to data for development: the bureaucratic management of information on women and development'. *IDS Bulletin*, vol. 25, no. 2 (1994), pp. 27-36.

Haksar, N., *Demystification of law for Women*. New Delhi, Lancer Press, 1986.

Harriss, B. and E. Watson, 'The sex ratio in South Asia'. In: J.H. Momsen and J. Townsend (ed.), *Geography of gender in the Third World*. London, State University of New York Press/Hutchinson, 1987, pp. 85-115.

Jackson, C., 'Questioning synergism: win-win with women in population and environment policies?' *Journal of International Development*, no. 5 (1993), pp. 651-668.

Jeffery, R. and P.M. Jeffery, 'A women belongs to her husband: female autonomy, women's work and childbearing in Bijnor'. In: A.W. Clark (ed.), *Gender and political economy: explorations of South Asian systems*. New Delhi, Oxford University Press, 1993.

Joekes, S., M. Leach and C. Green (ed.), 'Gender relations and environmental change'. *IDS Bulletin*, vol. 26, no. 1 (1995).

Klasen, S., *Gender inequalities and development strategies: lessons from the past and policy issues for the future*. (International Employment Policies Working Paper no. 41) Geneva, International Labour Office, 1993.

Lewis, D.J., 'Going it alone: female-headed households, rights and resources in rural Bangladesh'. *European Journal of Development Research*, vol. 5, no. 2 (1993), pp. 23-42.

Massiah, J. (ed.), *Women in developing economies: making visible the invisible*. Oxford, Berg/UNESCO, 1993.

Moghadam, V., *Modernizing women: gender and social change in the Middle East*. Boulder, Colorado, and London, Lynne Rienner, 1993.

Molyneux, M., 'Mobilization without emancipation? Women's interests, state and revolution in Nicaragua'. *Feminist Studies*, vol. 11, no. 2 (1985).

Moser, C.O.N., *Gender planning and development*. London, Routledge, 1993.

Ofosu-Amaah, W. and W. Philleo, *Women and the environment: an analytical review of success stories*. Washington, DC, United Nations Environment Programme/WorldWIDE Network, Inc., 1992.

Palmer, I., *Gender and population in the adjustment of African economics: planning for changes*. Geneva, International Labour Organisation, 1991.

Phillips, A., *Engendering democracy*. Cambridge, Polity Press, 1991.

Pryer, J., 'When breadwinners fall ill: preliminary findings from a case study in Bangladesh'. *IDS Bulletin*, vol. 20, no. 2 (1989), pp. 49-57.

Rawls, J., *A theory of justice*. Oxford, Oxford University Press, 1972.

Rogers, B., *The domestication of women*. Discrimination in developing societies. London, Tavistock, 1980.

Sen, A.K., 'Gender and cooperative conflicts'. In: I. Tinker (ed.), *Persistent inequalities: women and world development*. New York and Oxford, Oxford University Press, 1990, pp. 123-49.

Shiva, V., *Staying alive: women, ecology and development*. London, Zed Press, 1989.

Thijssen, H. (ed.), *Women and Islam in Muslim societies*. (Poverty and Development Series no. 7) The Hague, Ministry of Foreign Affairs, Development Cooperation Information Department, 1994.

Tinker, I., 'The making of a field: advocates, practitioners, and scholars'. In: I. Tinker (ed.), *Persistent inequalities: women and world development*. New York and Oxford, Oxford University Press, 1990, pp. 27-53.

United Nations, *World survey on the role of women in development*. New York, UN Department of International Social and Economic Affairs, 1986.

Viswanath, V., NGOs and women's development in rural South India: a comparative analysis. Boulder, Colorado, Westview Press, 1991.

Vlassoff, C., 'From rags to riches: the impact of rural development on women's status in an Indian village'. *World Development*, vol. 22, no. 5 (1994), pp. 707-719

Young, K., 'Introduction'. In: K. Young (ed.), *Serving two masters*. Ahmedabad, Allied Publishers Ltd, 1989a, pp. ix-xxiv.

Young, K., 'Not the Church, not the State'. In: K. Young (ed.), *Serving two masters*. Ahmedabad, Allied Publishers Ltd, 1989b, pp. 101-128.

Annotated bibliography

Women's status and rights

001   Researching women in Latin America and the Caribbean
ACOSTA-BELÉN, EDNA; BOSE, CHRISTINE E.
Westview, Boulder, CO x, 201 p. 1993 [EN]
Includes lit.refs, index ISBN 0-8133-8465-6

The book provides a comprehensive critique of research on women in Latin America and the Caribbean. The contributors evaluate scholarship on women and gender in specific disciplines and topical areas. A brief overview is provided of issues and trends that have emerged in the study of women's participation in mixed social, political, women's and feminist movements in Latin America. A theoretical framework and a review of the most relevant literature on women in the development process with reference to Latin America and the Caribbean is presented. Concentrating on Mexico and Central America, and to a lesser extent on South America, major areas of research in anthropology and related social sciences which have emerged during the 1980s and 1990s are discussed, including the change from women's studies to gender studies; the relation between gender, class and ethnicity; and women's participation in social and popular movements. Trends in migration research on Latin American and Caribbean women are identified, research directions and priorities in the area of women's writings are reviewed, and some of the most significant research produced by women's groups and organizations is considered. An outline of some of the main theoretical issues confronting women's studies and ethnic studies is provided, together with and key areas in which they can benefit from each others' conceptual approaches.
KIT, Amsterdam   [N 94-642]

002   Women in the Middle East : perceptions, realities and struggles for liberation
AFSHAR, HALEH. St. Martin's Press, New York, NY xiii, 250 p. 1993 [EN] Includes lit.refs, index ISBN 0-312-07921-4

This collection of 12 essays compares the realities of women's lives in the Middle East with the descriptions found in Western writing about them. The introductory chapter discusses the problems and shortcomings of culture-bound, Westernized perceptions of women and Islam. Two case studies of Islam and revivalism are concerned with the institution of marriage and the way in which women in Iran have used religious rituals to improve their public and private status. The following two chapters concentrate on women's activities in the labour market, indicating that progress in this sphere has not always been beneficial to women. The second section of the book deals with political struggles at national and international levels. The wider political arena is first examined, followed by liberation in the context of Arab patriarchal systems and Muslim women's difficult position during political struggles. Israeli and Palestinian women's joint resistance activities during the Intifada (a Palestinian uprising in 1987) are discussed, as well as the experiences of the left in Iran in the period leading up to the revolution. The use of networking as an empowering process is also considered.
KIT, Amsterdam   [N 93-3200]

003   The girl child : an investment in the future
AIDOO, AGNES AKOSUA; SOHONI, NEERA K.
UNICEF. Program Publications, New York, NY 45 p. 1991 [EN] ill., graphs, tabs. Includes lit.refs ISBN 92-806-1003-1

Girl and boy children are compared using indicators of health, nutrition, education and workload. Special initiatives for girls are reviewed and recommendations are suggested. The girl child has a lower status and enjoys fewer rights, opportunities and benefits than the boy who has first call on family and community resources. The state of deprivation of girls and women is illustrated with statistics on life expectancy, age of first marriage, literacy rate, school enrolment, immunization, and mortality rates from 131 countries. Together with policy recommendations, priority areas for change and development are suggested: equal health, equal nutrition, workload reduction and equal education for the girl child. Gender equality needs to be a clear objective and a measure of childhood development in developing countries. Sustained political will and action are required to ensure equality of status and opportunity for the girl child in the 1990s. Policy initiatives for governments, international organizations and private groups are recommended, including: adopting political, legislative and development policies that eliminate gender disparity and discrimination in childhood; undertaking specialized research and investigation into the status of the girl child; creating data bases on girls and women by collecting data disaggregated by gender and age; and formulating targets and concrete actions to improve the basic health, nutrition, education and social status of the girl child.

KIT, Amsterdam   [Br U 92-108]

004   Women in Kuwait : the politics of gender
AL-MUGHNI, HAYA. Saqi Books, London 174 p. 1993 [EN] Includes lit.refs, glossary, index ISBN 0-86356-199-3

A portrait of women in Kuwait is provided, based on personal experience and on research into women's organizations. A wide range of issues are discussed in terms of their impact on the role of women: class, tribe and politics; the oil boom; the growth of the state; the emergence of women's organizations in a male-dominated society; the recent Islamic revival; and the future prospects for women's participation in society. Analysis of the political role of women's organizations demonstrates that upper and middle class women have very little interest in promoting feminist issues and they neglect, to the extent of denying, the many problems women face in a society exclusively controlled by men. The elite still has a critical interest in controlling female sexuality, promulgating laws on morality, and defending the family and the traditional role of women within it. It is concluded that Middle Eastern women are partly responsible for their own oppression: women's loyalties are primarily to their families and kin, and they act in ways which reinforce rather than challenge female subordination. The education of women and their access to prestigious professions have resulted in class consolidation rather than social mobility. Both patriarchy and the social system thus impede the development of a female solidarity movement which has considerable implications for women in low income groups, because it is these women who suffer most from the discriminatory welfare policies of the state and from patriarchal structures, whether in the form of male violence or male religious discourse. The basis for female solidarity should be sought in an informal organization of women.

KIT, Amsterdam   [N 94-600]

005   Focusing on women : UNIFEM's experience in mainstreaming
ANDERSON, MARY B. UNIFEM, New York, NY iii, 28 p. 1993 [EN] Includes lit.refs

The concept of mainstreaming, which emerged from the women-in-development (WID) movement in the 1980s, implies strengthening of women's active involvement in development and interfacing women's capabilities and contributions with macroeconomic development issues. Mainstreaming began as an effort to increase the impact and effectiveness of WID programmes in incorporating women and women's issues into development policies and programmes. Based on evidence and on learning that has been derived both from the field and the centres of development activity, the concept and practice of mainstreaming have undergone important changes since 1985. UNIFEM has been an effective innovator in promoting mainstreaming and a leader in developing the concept and strategies for mainstreaming. The thrust of mainstreaming is now, more than ever before, on achieving equality between women and men and on furthering basic and sustainable economic, social and political development for everyone.

KIT, Amsterdam   [Br U 94-200]

006   Images of women in Philippine media : from virgin to vamp...
AZARCON-DELA CRUZ, PENNIE S.; RAMOS-SHAHANI, LETICIA; COSETENG, ANNA DOMINIQUE M.L. Asian Social Institute, Manila ix, 136 p. 1988 [EN] ill. Includes lit.refs ISBN 971-8543-09-0

The book considers the ways in which women are institutionalized in various local media in the Philippines. The media under study are: radio advertisements and serials, television advertisements and shows, newspapers, tabloid newspapers, different kinds of magazines, and movies. The treatment of women and women's issues in 1975 is compared to news and headlines on women in 1985. Women are generally portrayed in the media as either housewives, mothers or domestic workers, or as secretaries, models or mistresses. Men, on the other hand, are portrayed as being strong, brawny, aggressive and ruthless, and as without tender feelings. Women reporters are still assigned to the secondary or 'soft' fields of health, education, and life-style sections. Although some women occupy key positions in the media as television producers, editors and publishers, the media remains largely a male-dominated field as far as policies and top-level decisions are concerned. This may explain why women's issues are largely ignored. However, a few initiatives to raise awareness of women's representation in the media may contribute towards an improved and more realistic image of women and women's issues. The scrutiny and eventual liberation of women from rigid media characterizations can also lead to freedom for men from the male stereotypes with which they are confronted.

KIT, Amsterdam   [N 94-1979]

007   Bigger than men? : gender relations and their changing meaning in Kipsigis society, Kenya
BÜLOW, DORTHE VON - *Africa* 62(1992)4 p.523-546 [EN] ill., maps 53 lit.refs. With French summary ISSN 0001-9720

Kipsigis women in Kericho District, Kenya, appear to be strong and independent, despite their increased subordination under colonization and commoditization. The changes that have occurred in gender relations and in production relations between pre-colonial and colonial times, on the one hand, and contemporary society (1985-1986), on the other, are examined. During this period, Kipsigis society has changed from being a classless, decentralized society to one with class differentiation and radical changes in gender relations and meanings attributed to gender. Men's and women's separate economic and political spheres have undergone a process of disintegration and restructuring into a patriarchy in which men control the means of production and are the formal heads of households. Women, contrary to their former status as heads of households, are now jural minors in their husbands' households. The respect, complementarity and reciprocity between women and men in the past have been replaced by women's structural economic dependence on men and men's fear that women may 'try to be bigger than men'. Conceptions of female and male are being redefined and reinterpreted to match a changed reality. In this process, women find support in shared customary ideas about separate female and male spheres and women's autonomous status as heads of household.

KIT, Amsterdam   [A 1671-62(1992)4]

008   Projects for women in the Third World : explaining their misbehaviour
BUVINIC, MAYRA - *World Development* 14(1986)5 p.653-664 [EN] 32 lit.refs ISSN 0305-750X

The economic objectives of many income generation projects for poor women in developing countries, designed during the UN Decade for Women (1975-1985), have evolved into welfare projects during implementation. The prevalence of welfare interventions can be explained. First, particular project characteristics define the typical interventions for women and facilitate the achievement of social rather than production aims. Second, these characteristics are a result of the expertise in the welfare sector of women-based institutions that execute women's

projects. Finally, the choice of women-based implementing agencies and the more generalized preference for welfare action are determined by the comparatively lower financial and social costs of implementing welfare initiatives compared with economic-based projects.

KIT, Amsterdam   [E 1271-14(1986)5]

009   Changing socio-economic conditions of women in Africa in the context of the Nairobi Forward-Looking Strategies for the Advancement of Women : sectoral analysis of political participation, education, employment and law
ECONOMIC AND SOCIAL COUNCIL. UN. ECA, Addis Ababa [39] p. 1991 [EN] ill., tabs. Includes lit.refs

Changes in the socio-economic conditions of women in Africa during 1985-1990 within the context of the UN's Forward-Looking Strategies for the Advancement of Women are reviewed. The conceptual framework of the long-term objectives of the strategies, namely equality, development and peace, is described. Following an analysis of women's political participation and decision-making, an overview is provided of the situation of women in education, employment and industry. Issues in the field of law and legislation are also considered. Progress made at the international level is outlined. The economic conditions of the 1980s, by restricting growth and reducing national capacity to mobilize the public sector for social and economic change, are found to have lessened the likelihood of rapid progress towards achieving the objectives of the strategies. In Africa, economic stagnation, continued population increase, the prolonged international debt crisis, and the structural adjustment policies designed to mitigate it have constrained the activities of women as individuals, as carers and providers for family and household, and as participants in the practical development of their countries. Accordingly, inequality between men and women in health, nutrition, levels of literacy and training, access to education and economic opportunities, and in participation in decision-making at all levels has sometimes been exacerbated both by the crisis itself and by the policies adopted to cope with it. Women's technical skills, education and training in science and technology, and supportive policy and legal measures need to be improved.

KIT, Amsterdam   [U 92-435]

010   Widows and health in rural North India
CHEN, MARTY; DREZE, JEAN - *Economic and Political Weekly* 27(1992)43/44 p.WS81-WS92 [EN] ill., tabs 48 lit.refs

The lives of widows in Northern India are examined using an earlier study of single villages in Gujarat, Uttar Pradesh and West Bengal, undertaken in 1983-1989, and an ongoing 1991 study of two villages each in Bihar, Rajasthan, Uttar Pradesh and West Bengal. The position of widows is influenced by a set of practices that govern gender relations as a whole. The vulnerability and dependence of widows is caused by restrictions on residence, inheritance, ownership, remarriage and employment which place them in a situation of acute economic dependence. The majority of widows live with one or more sons, and this living arrangement is the main form of community support they receive. Widows typically receive very little support from persons other than their own children, and even when living with one or several adult sons may be vulnerable to neglect. Their ability to engage in income-earning activity is severely restricted due to various patriarchal norms such as patrilineal inheritance and the gender division of labour. The consequences of this social and economic marginalization are manifest in poor health and high mortality levels. Marginalization is consistent with the traditional Hindu perception of widows as guilty and inauspicious women. The most effective way of ensuring the social protection of widows is to recognize their contribution to the household economy.

KIT, Amsterdam   [B 3057-27(1992)43/44]

011   Gender and political economy : explorations of South Asian systems
CLARK, ALICE. Oxford University Press, Delhi viii, 375 p. 1993 [EN] Includes lit.refs, index ISBN 0-19-563170-6

The relations between gender and the political economies and societies in South Asia are the foci of 9 papers contained in this book. The papers provide an overview of current perspectives on women and gender in the region by presenting data which have been recently collected or re-analysed. Three topics are addressed: (1) relations of production/reproduction in Bijnor and Rajasthan, India; (2) class and gender relations and the effect of modernization, including agricultural intensification in Andhra Pradesh, India, and urban class formation in Bangladesh; and (3) women's movements and organizations, including interest groups, in Bangladesh, Bombay and Sri Lanka. The different conditions and roles of women and men in urban and rural areas are considered. The effects of economic and technological change on the gender roles of production and reproduction, and on women's role, status and conditions are discussed.

KIT, Amsterdam   [N 93-6077]

012   Convention on the Elimination of All Forms of Discrimination Against Women
Yearbook of the United Nations (1979)33 p.889-899 1982 [EN]

The thirty-third session of the UN General Assembly adopted and opened for signature, ratification and accession, the Convention on the Elimination of All Forms of Discrimination Against Women. The assembly asked the Secretary-General to present the text to the 1980 International Conference of the UN Decade for Women for its information and to submit a report to the Assembly in 1980 on the status of the Convention. Discrimination against women is defined in Part I, article 1. Part II provides for women's right to full political and public life on equal terms with men. Part III provides for elimination of discrimination against women to ensure them equal rights with men in education, employment, health care and other economic and social areas. The articles in Part IV ensure women equality with men before the law and the absence of discrimination in matters relating to marriage and family relations. The annex provides documentary references, voting details and the original text of the resolution.

KIT, Amsterdam   [K 1106-(1979)33]

013   Women's health and human rights : the promotion and protection of women's health through international rights law
COOK, REBECCA J. WHO, Geneva vii, 62 p. 1994 [EN] ill., tabs. Includes lit.refs ISBN 92-4-156166-1

The relevance of international human rights to the promotion and protection of women's health is examined. A framework is suggested for future analysis and for cross-fertilization and collaboration among organizations concerned with human rights and women's health. A review is made of the health risks women face at different points in their life-cycle. Indicators to measure state compliance with international treaty obligations for human rights are developed. Mechanisms for protection of women's health at international, regional and national levels, and current initiatives to enhance women's health through the law of human rights are described. At national level, health care associations are providing legal services to women to educate them about their legal rights and to advance legal protection of their health and wellbeing. Internationally, medical associations are developing programmes to promote the role of medical ethics in the protection of human rights and to educate their members in the role of medical ethics in practice and research. Other actions to be undertaken include education of health professionals in the law of human rights and education of human rights' advocates in how to acquire and interpret health data and extract the elements that are legally significant. Health professionals and human rights' advocates should inform advocacy with health data by employing their knowledge of prevailing and achievable practices and the goals

of international treaties on human rights. These proposals would stimulate the development and effective implementation of the principles for the promotion and protection of women's health, and particularly address health status factors, health service factors and conditions affecting the health and wellbeing of women. On the basis of such principles, efforts could be made towards the development of specific guidelines for the legal promotion and protection of women's health.
KIT, Amsterdam   [U 94-329]

014   Women and conflict
EL-BUSHRA, JUDY - *Focus on Gender* 1(1993)2. Oxfam, Oxford vi, 58 p. 1993 [EN] Includes lit.refs ISSN 0968-2864 ISBN 0-85598-222-5
This issue concentrates on gender issues in situations of military and civil strife in Afghanistan, Brazil, Chad, Guatemala and Sri Lanka, as well as in Asia. It examines the effect of armed conflict on women's lives and livelihoods and the situation in which many women refugees and displaced persons find themselves. In all countries, women suffer daily infringement of their basic rights as human beings, and live with the ever present threat of physical and sexual violence. Violence against women is used to keep them in their place, to limit their opportunities, and to hamper their ability to organize. Patriarchy is analysed as an ideology which fosters discriminatory treatment and sanctions violence as a legitimate instrument to maintain the status quo. A number of articles draw attention to the gender-related impact of war on women; others emphasize the psychological and social impact of conflict situations. Physical and sexual violence against women does not only occur at times of war: domestic violence occurs across all social groups. Women are, however, not passive victims of struggle and conflict.
KIT, Amsterdam   [D 3030-1(1993)2]

015   Les droits de la femme dans la charte africaine des droits de l'homme et des peuples
ELMADMAD, KHADIJA - *Afrique 2000* (1993)14 p.21-37 1993 [FR] 21 lit.refs ISSN 1017-0952
Although women are often regarded as important for the future of Africa, article 18 of the African Charter on Human Rights still categorizes women's rights among the rights of vulnerable and incapable groups. Even in the formulation of human rights, women are implicitly considered unequal to men. A critical review is presented of the ambiguity of modern and traditional norms, and the contradictions in the formulation of human rights' declarations. In a so-called new international order, it is impossible to maintain formulations that ignore the human rights of the majority of the people, namely women.
KIT, Amsterdam   [A 2829-(1993)14]

016   Social change and life planning of rural Javanese women
GERKE, SOLVAY - *Bielefelder Studien zur Entwicklungssoziologie* 51. Breitenbach, Saarbrücken 217 p. 1992 [EN] ill., graphs, tabs. Includes lit.refs, glossary ISSN 0171-7537 ISBN 3-88156-563-9
Based on extensive research, censuses and interviews, the impact of social change on the lives of rural women in Busuran village of Yogyakarta Province, Indonesia, is examined. Indonesian development ideology, including the role assigned to women in the development process, is described. Following an overview of the province under study, the social and economic changes that have taken place during the last decades are discussed, including the introduction of contraceptives, the family planning programme, and increased formal education opportunities. Middle class and younger women have actively used the changes to gain more control over their lives, including family planning. Women have integrated these changes into their daily lives but not in a homogeneous way. Older women welcome family planning on a theoretical plane as a way to reduce hardship; married women are planning a better life for their children, based on education; and unmarried women strive for a better future for themselves which they perceive to be possible as a result of birth control. Although marriage and having children are still the undisputed aims of women in Javanese society, all of the interviewed women would like some economic independence, whilst none of them considers confinement to the role of housewife and mother as her ideal. The modernization process in the village is not only typical of many villages in the province but also an example of the way in which all Javanese villages are likely to develop in the near future.
KIT, Amsterdam   [E 2341-(1992)51]

017   Engendering China : women, culture, and the state
GILMARTIN, CHRISTINA K. - *Harvard Contemporary China Series* 10. Harvard University Press, Cambridge, MA xiii, 454 p. 1994 [EN] Includes lit.refs ISBN 0-674-25331-0
This book is based on a conference of the same name which was held in Harvard, USA, during February 1992. The conference grew out of the recognition that Western feminist theory could not provide a standard theory for analyzing women in China. Covering the 16th Century to the present, the papers presented take up gender issues from a variety of disciplinary perspectives. Four essays show that in addition to traditional networks (family, household, kinship), women have also been involved in networks such as poetry societies, formally recognized

extrafamilial relations, and work relationships. Historically specific meanings associated with bodies, female bodies in particular, and sexuality and reproduction are explored in various papers. Nation-building and the construction of gender in the 20th Century are the concern of papers tracing how gender has been essential in shaping the contours of the socialist state. The policy of the state party has merely brought women into the sphere of socially productive labour. Women have been made more subject to state domination as exemplified by birth control policies. The role of the state in shaping women's image and status, and images of women in contemporary Chinese fiction are explored. Analyses in the final section reveal an increased focus on women and gender differences in state policy and literary production in the post-Maoist period.

KIT, Amsterdam   [N 94-2310]

018   From feminist knowledge to data for development : the bureaucratic management of information on women and development
GOETZ, ANNE MARIE - *IDS Bulletin* 25(1994)2 p.27-36 [EN] 60 lit.refs. With English, French and Spanish summary (p.ii, v, ix) ISSN 0265-5012

Information on gender inequalities should be carefully managed. First, information about women's experiences of change has tended to be distilled through the development process in ways which strongly reflect the gender politics and gendered interests of the users of information. Secondly, information about women and their relationship with men has been repeated in the development process, reflecting dominant development paradigms. Third, bureaucratic procedures for information generation and use have had the effect of stripping away the political content. Fourth, information tends to isolate women as the central problem, separating them from their contexts of social and gender relations. Finally, information about women tends to receive policy recognition in proportion to the social and political significance of the informer. It is concluded that feminist research has been politicizing women's experience of development in ways which fundamentally disrupt the interpretive boundaries of the domestic sphere through which women's needs had been supposed to be a matter for private, familial provision, and through which development practice had 'biologized' women to saddle them with reproduction and marginality. More satisfactory translation of feminist knowledge into bureaucratic procedures must involve the pursuit of gender equity in organizational environments and in the ways in which information is collected and knowledge is created.

KIT, Amsterdam   [E 1978-25(1994)2]

019   Violence against women : the hidden health burden
HEISE, LORI L.; PITANGUY, JACQUELINE; GERMAIN, ADRIENNE - *World Bank Discussion Papers* 255. World Bank, Washington, DC ix, 72 p. 1994 [EN] ill., tabs. Bibliogr.: p. 61-72 ISSN 0259-210X ISBN 0-8213-2980-4

Gender-based violence, including rape, domestic violence, female genital mutilation, murder, and sexual abuse, is a profound health problem for women all over the world, but it has received little attention as a public health issue. This paper draws together existing data on the dimensions of violence against women worldwide and reviews available literature on the health consequences of violence. It also explores the relationship between violence and other pressing issues such as maternal mortality, health care utilization, child survival, AIDS prevention, and socio-economic development. Interventions in primary prevention, justice system reform, health care response, programmes to assist victims, and treatment and re-education programmes for perpetrators are explored. It is argued that any strategy to combat violence should attack the root causes of the problem in addition to treating its symptoms. This means challenging the social attitudes and beliefs that undergird men's violence and renegotiating the meaning of gender and sexuality and the balance of power between men and women at all levels of society. Research on gender-based violence and health is needed as a matter of priority. Recommendations for government action to combat violence against women are suggested. Institutions such as the World Bank can urge governments to take violence against women seriously.

KIT, Amsterdam   [K 2481-(1994)255]

020   Questioning synergism : win-win with women in population and environment policies?
JACKSON, CECILE - *Journal of International Development* 5(1993)6 p.651-668 1993 [EN] ill. 58 lit.refs ISSN 0954-1748

This paper takes issue with the convergence of opinion, exhibited in a range of development discourses, which suggests that a synergistic set of policy instruments can be used to achieve population, environment and development objectives in developing countries. Such policies create a powerful synergy that can either enhance or retard the achievement of a more balanced style of development. Having briefly raised some broader concerns about synergism, the justifications for synergism are examined by applying gender analysis to three integrated population-development-environment policies. The fallacy of the idea that systems and synergy can identify policies which can provide common solutions to population, environment and development problems without trade-offs is explored. The gender implications of the following synergistic policies are discussed: clarification of land rights; increased education for girls and women; and empowerment of women. In all of these areas, gender analysis reveals trade-offs and policy conflicts rather than any necessary synergy. The reasons for the attractiveness of the synergy position are seen to lie partially in the legacy of systems thinking and the atmosphere of urgency in Western environmentalism, as well as in the sociology of development agencies. The 'synergy consensus' in population, environment and development policy seems to be a misleading expectation which derives less from the accumulated evidence and arguments of decades of development policy formulation and intervention, and more from the politics of development agencies themselves.

KIT, Amsterdam [E 3118-5(1993)6]

021　Gender bias : roadblock to sustainable development
JACOBSON, JODI L. - *Worldwatch Paper* 110. Worldwatch Institute, Washington, DC 60 p. 1992 [EN] ill., graphs, tabs. Includes lit.refs ISBN 1-878071-10-6

Gender bias is a primary cause of poverty. Conventional development approaches to development do not address any gender biases, ignore the obstacles faced by women and actually formalize and reinforce gender biases in several ways. Women find themselves incapable of transforming their increasingly unstable subsistence economy into a more sustainable one. Until gender bias is confronted, there can be no sustainable development. The dimensions of gender bias are considered, and assumptions in conventional economic thinking that are influenced by gender differences are discussed. Agricultural modernization strategies have limited women's access to land by diminishing the availability of common land and other resources. Women's access to forest land has also been adversely affected, despite their use and management of this resource. As the access of women to resources continues to dwindle in subsistence economies, their responsibilities increase as well as their labour burden. The relation between poverty and population growth within subsistence economies is shown to be a vicious cycle, which can only be broken by designing a new framework for development that establishes an environment in which women and men can prosper together.

KIT, Amsterdam [H 1728-(1992)110]

022　Reversed realities : gender hierarchies in development thought
KABEER, NAILA. Verso, London xix, 346 p. 1994 [EN] ill. Bibliogr.: p. 312-339. Includes index ISBN 0-86091-584-0

This book explores the emergence of women as a specific category in development thinking. Alternative frameworks for analyzing gender hierarchies are examined. Following a brief overview of the emergence of the women-in-development (WID) perspective within the international development arena, the theoretical underpinnings of WID and its contribution to the official policy discourse are assessed, as well as its major limitations. WID is criticized for its inability to challenge gender inequality in any fundamental way. Some of the problems which WID advocates have sought to address are re-examined from a more structuralist perspective, deriving from the Marxist tradition. Economic models of households and household decision-making, and the dominant conceptualization of poverty are argued to be inadequate for clarifying gender dimensions. Social cost-benefit analysis is shown to be unsuitable for addressing women's concerns. The way in which ideas are evolved, clarified or transformed through the experience of development policies and practice is illustrated by population policy, with a focus on the different meanings of control embedded in conflicting interpretations of the unmet need for reproductive technology. The issues of power and empowerment are addressed by comparing attempts to theorize power by social scientists and feminists working in development which are then used to explore the attempts of grassroots NGOs to operationalize these ideas. Principles and guidelines which may help to construct a more feminist population policy which seeks the goal of gender equity and reproductive choice rather than fertility reduction per se are suggested. A comparison is made between different approaches to gender issues in development planning which have been disseminated through gender training efforts over the past decade.

KIT, Amsterdam [N 94-1928]

023　Challenging gender inequalities in Africa
KANJI, NAZNEEN - *Review of African Political Economy* 56. ROAPE, Sheffield 132 p. 1993 [EN] ill., tabs. Includes lit.refs ISSN 0305-6244

Women and gender issues in Africa are addressed focusing on four aspects that have major implications for women: (1) the misguided nature of the attempts to integrate women into development; (2) the straitjacket which global capitalism has placed on African development via the IMF and its structural adjustment policies; (3) the potential but unfulfilled role of the state in

contributing to the transformation of gender relations; and (4) the deepening class and other divisions emergent amongst women themselves. Analyses are presented of men's place in the feminine occupation of domestic service in Tanzania; gender conflict in Kenyan tea-growing households; and male violence against women in Ghana and Tanzania. The impact of structural adjustment on low-income urban women in Zimbabwe and on the student movement in Nigeria, and the response of rice-growing peasant farmers to the economic crisis in Uganda are examined. The way in which gender issues are addressed by the transitional government in Nigeria and the role of the women's lobby in Zambia are explored, as well as legal aspects and women's rights in Namibia. All papers suggest that full appreciation of gender relations is fundamental to the success of policy intervention or to innovation within the productive system.
KIT, Amsterdam   [A 2284-(1993)56]

024   Ours by right : women's rights as human rights
KERR, JOANNA. Zed Books, London xii, 180 p. 1993 [EN] Includes lit.refs, index ISBN 1-85649-228-1
This book is based on presentations at the international conference on 'Linking hands for changing laws: women's rights as human rights around the world'. The conference brought together women who, through their scholarship and activism, are leading the fight in their countries for women's human rights. Some 24 contributions discuss experiences from Africa, Latin America and South Asia, demonstrating the intricacies of the struggles, accomplishments and setbacks in achieving women's human rights. Genuine improvement of the daily lives of women requires substantial reforms on many fronts. These entail attainment and effective monitoring of international laws and conventions; the implementation of national laws and policies which support the rights of women; legal institutions and government systems which recognize women's human rights as legitimate; and, finally, the transformation of cultural or religious societal norms to give priority to the rights of women over oppressive customs. Strategies for action which have emerged in the last few years for linking women's rights to human rights include encouraging institution-building with respect to independent women's centres and groups. Women will be able to build their individual and collective capacity to participate in all national institutions, and to guarantee equality in access to domestic, community, national and international resources. Donors should finance a directory of experienced women professionals to help with constitutional reconstruction; treaty monitoring; juridical and

police training; conflict resolution; international refugee programmes; and direction of funds.
KIT, Amsterdam   [P 94-134]

025   Gender inequality and development strategies : lessons from the past and policy issues for the future
KLASEN, STEPHAN - International Employment Policies Working Paper 41. ILO, Geneva vii, 45 p. 1993 [EN] ill., tabs. Includes lit.refs ISBN 92-2-109177-5
Using theoretical models and recent evidence, the impact on women of policy changes brought about by market reforms in China, by structural adjustment programmes in Africa and Latin America, and by current liberalization policies in Eastern Europe and the former Soviet Union are reviewed. Household models and their predictions of intrahousehold resource allocation, as well as educational choice, fertility and mortality, are discussed. Particular emphasis is placed on the role of female labour participation and women's outside earnings in explaining intrahousehold inequalities in the allocation of food and medical care. Recent policy shifts could account for the increasing deprivation of women in developing economies. In particular, changes in the female labour market and the breakdown or reduction of vital health and social service institutions are stressed in an explanation of recent trends in China and some parts of Africa and Latin America. A policy agenda to meet the strategic needs of women by addressing inequalities in bargaining power over household resources is suggested, including policies aimed at strengthening women's ability to gain outside earnings in the various formal and informal sectors of the economy. Specific policy recommendations are suggested for the different regions and countries. At the policy-making level, problems are identified which have reduced the effectiveness of initiatives attempting to address gender inequality. Recommendations are suggested to improve the gender sensitivity of policy-making and implementation.
KIT, Amsterdam   [U 94-382]

026   La place et le rôle des femmes dans les administrations africaines = The place and role of women in African administrations
LARRIVÉE, ISABELLE; THIAM, MAMADOU - Études et Documents / CAFRAD 7. Centre Africain de Formation et de Recherche Administratives pour le Développement, Tanger 342 p. 1993 [FR, EN] ill., graphs, tabs. Includes lit.refs
The number of women participating in government administrations in Africa is increasing. Although the majority are employed in less satisfying, low status positions, a small number of women are becoming involved in

responsible positions. A number of obstacles still exist with regard to the promotion of women in management, thus hindering women from participating in the development process. A series of research studies was undertaken in Ivory Coast, Ghana, Egypt, Kenya, Mali, Morocco, Nigeria, Senegal, Sudan and Tunisia. One aspect was found to be of overriding importance: the influence of society and cultural traditions on mental images of women in their social life. For each of these countries, the quantitative and qualitative situation of women in government administration, in both the public and private sectors, was analysed. Girls' and women's lack of access to education and traditional perceptions of the role of women are major factors limiting women's access to and participation in senior administrative work. Recommendations are made, including informing women about their legal rights; providing access to education and training; reducing women's dual burden of family life and professional activity by providing nurseries; and deconstructing traditional perceptions underlying the role of women in society and development through awareness-raising campaigns.

KIT, Amsterdam [K 2701-(1993)7]

027   Alternative media : linking global and local
LEWIS, PETER - *Reports and Papers on Mass Communication* 107. UNESCO, Paris 130 p. 1993 [EN] Includes lit.refs ISBN 92-3-102852-9

Local alternative media projects are motivated by a desire to empower marginalized social groups, such as women, whose condition, needs and voices are ignored by the authorities and mainstream media. Case studies of 9 alternative mass media projects from developed and developing countries are presented. The case studies from developing countries are concerned with: the effort of the Sistren Theatre Collective to empower Jamaican women through participatory, popular drama; efforts to empower women through yatra (making a journey), street theatre and video in India; the use of journals supporting an emerging women's movement in Morocco; the contribution to social and political life of radio broadcasting for peasants and miners in Bolivia; the People's Communication Centre project in Peru; the use of alternative video for democratization by workers' television in Brazil; and global computer-mediated communication networks. Finally, the relationship of alternative media to UNESCO policies and international communication debates is discussed. Experiences over two decades indicate that where civil society exists, alternative media are an important feature of the public sphere but that they are not yet sufficiently recognized by politicians and planners of communication policy.

KIT, Amsterdam [K 1200-(1993)107]

028   Gros-plan sur les femmes en Afrique = Afrikanische Frauen im Blick = Focus on women in Africa
LUDWAR-ENE, GUDRUN; REH, MECHTHILD - *Bayreuth African Studies Series* 26. Bayreuth University, Bayreuth 204 p. 1993 [FR, DE, EN] ill., tabs. Includes lit.refs ISSN 0178-0034 ISBN 3-927510-13-0

This collection of articles on various aspects of women's lives and livelihoods in Africa derives from research undertaken in the context of the multidisciplinary research programme on 'Identity in Africa: processes of development and change'. The articles cover a wide range of topics: (1) the concept of 'sleeping pregnancy' (kwantacce) among Hausa women in northern Nigeria. The concept acts as a security valve through which women may reduce a certain kind of social pressure to which they are subjected; (2) the social relationships of female and male migrants in Calabar, Nigeria, focusing on rural versus urban connections; (3) female entrepreneurs in Nigeria, based on re-analysis of previously collected data; (4) problems of primary education of girls in rural northern Cameroon where girls have fewer opportunities than boys to acquire sufficient school education; (5) domestic duties of children in Abidjan, Ivory Coast, illustrating the distribution of tasks according to sex of children in households. This division of labour is also shown to correspond to the informal sector, and it also reflects and is the result of a socialization process which prepares the girls for their later roles as wives, housewives and mothers; (6) the issue of religious pluralism is examined using the example of three cults in Acholi, northern Uganda: a pagan cult; a Christian cult of spirit possession; and a prophetic movement, the Holy Spirit Movement of Alice Lakwena; and (7) the process of administration of estates in Zambia before 1989 which undermined the protection that legislators and courts sought to give to widows.

KIT, Amsterdam [A 2688-(1993)26]

029   Género, clase y raza en América Latina : algunas aportaciones
LUNA, LOLA G.; LEÓN, MAGDALENA. Universitat de Barcelona. Seminario Interdisciplinar Mujeres y Sociedad, Barcelona 204 p. 1991 [ES] ill., tabs. Includes lit.refs ISBN 84-7665-959-8

Some 8 contributions on gender, class and race in Latin America are presented, focusing on women's status. A project which aims to change and transform social and working relations within domestic service in the city of Bogota, Colombia, is discussed. Trends in the female labour force of Latin America in general and Chile in particular over the past three decades are assessed. Using the myth of Malinche, an Aztec princess who received a gift from her lover Cortès in exchange for Mexico, as the starting point, race relations, the legitimacy of male superiority, machismo and patriarchal norms in Central America are examined. The strong impact of audiovisual media on gender, race and class identification is reviewed. The socialization of domestic violence in Chile in the course of democratization is considered. Working women from poor areas of Santa Fé, Argentina, frequently consult female medical counsellors, and this behaviour is examined in the light of gender roles and husband-wife relationships. Finally, difficulties in establishing women's organizations in times of economic crisis in Peru are analysed from a feminist perspective.

KIT, Amsterdam   [N 95-526]

030   Gender and work : past, present and future : the situation of rural Mozambican women at Mazowe River bridge camp in Zimbabwe
MADZOKERE, C. - *Journal of Social Development in Africa* 8(1993)2 p.23-32 [EN] ill., tabs 8 lit.refs ISSN 1012-1080

A study of 200 Mozambican refugee women in the Mazowe River bridge camp, northeastern Zimbabwe, was conducted to determine their roles and status before and during displacement. The roles and status of the refugee women were found to be quite similar to those in Mozambique, with the exception that women's role in food production has decreased as basic food is provided in the camp. Women's status continued to be regarded as subordinate to that of men. Although men's role as family providers is greatly reduced as a result of the lack of employment opportunities, they are still regarded as decision-makers in both their households and camp leadership. The division of labour between women and men, and the gender differences in status are embedded in the traditional culture. Recommendations to improve the roles and status of women include: providing education to women; providing women with the various skills needed to start an enterprise; making efforts to achieve a more balanced gender distribution of camp leadership; and undertaking ongoing research on the effectiveness of programmes offered to refugee women. Men should be sensitized to realize that women can take on decision-making roles.

KIT, Amsterdam   [A 2698-8(1993)2]

031   Major changes and crisis : the impact on women in Latin America and the Caribbean
[PREP. BY THE WOMEN AND DEVELOPMENT UNIT, SOCIAL DEVELOPMENT DIVISION] - *Libros de la CEPAL* 27. UN. ECLAC, Santiago, Chile 279 p. 1992 [EN] ill., tabs. Includes lit.refs ISBN 92-1-121177-8

The integration of women into development in Latin America and the Caribbean is assessed by examining the impact on the female population of crises, major changes, and new uncertainties over a period of some 30 years. The impact of social changes on women's participation in the labour market (1960-1980) is assessed in terms of age, civil status and education, together with the repercussions of the economic crisis (1982-1985) on female employment opportunities. New social demands affecting women in the rural sector, female rural-urban labour migration, and new roles and social scenarios are reviewed. Women's reproductive behaviour, mortality, age structure and migration are examined, as well as the legal status of women under current legislation and actions for legislative reforms at the national level. The role of information and communication in advancing women's status is reviewed. Significant economic and social changes in the region have had major impacts on women's situation, living conditions and social role. In general, women have become increasing participants in economic activity, sharing in general upward social mobility. Many of them have had fewer children and a greater life expectancy. While the predominant pattern of employment is compatible with their traditional role, their autonomy and economic independence has increased. The main obstacles to women's participation lie in: the persistence of cultural stereotypes regarding the role of women; the unfavourable economic conditions affecting large numbers of women; the maintenance of legal restrictions on their role in the family; their still inadequate level of education and training; and the lack of sufficient and suitable employment.

KIT, Amsterdam   [U 93-436]

032   Women in developing economies : making visible the invisible
MASSIAH, JOYCELIN - *Berg/UNESCO Comparative Studies*. UNESCO, Paris 300 p. 1993 [EN] ill., tabs. Includes lit.refs ISBN 92-3-102807-3

Even after 20 years of debate about the invisible work of women, very little has been done to collect information, analyse its contribution to national economies, or to give women adequate financial support or training. Women's productivity remains therefore at a very low level. Information needs to be gathered to make women's work visible and to train planners to become familiar with women's issues and develop measures to include such information in national plans. A study of the socio-economic situation of women in the Commonwealth Caribbean provides basic indicators for equipping planners to take appropriate measures to improve women's quality of life. Case studies from Colombia, Ghana and Tunisia demonstrate the

role of rural and urban women in informal agricultural and industrial activities, and the contribution of their informal work to the survival of households, particularly poor households, and the national economy. Women's role in the informal sector has to be taken into account in national policies and development planning. Quantitative and qualitative data must be collected and analysed to design appropriate measures to incorporate women's concerns and strengthen their role in the informal sector by removing obstacles facing their access to training, credit, inputs, information and other services.
KIT, Amsterdam [U 93-49]

033 Gender in Southern Africa : conceptual and theoretical issues
MEENA, RUTH - *Southern Africa Political Economy Series*. SAPES, Harare xi, 201 p. 1992 [EN] Includes lit.refs, index ISBN 0-7974-1162-3

An overview is provided of methodological and theoretical issues pertaining to gender studies and research in Southern Africa. Liberal and conservative theories underlying explanations of feminism and women's oppression are discussed. Research methodologies to study gender issues, including different feminist theories, women-in-development theory and gender theory, and an agenda for empowerment, are addressed. The concept of feminism is discussed, and three feminist theories of gender are detailed: liberal feminism, radical feminism and Marxist feminism. Botswana is used as a case study to analyse political and socio-economic issues, and to illustrate how feminist theories are applied. A few examples are compared with the case of Botswana, showing how feminism in the region is evolving as a strong perspective in the analysis of gender relations. Bourgeois theories of gender and feminism and their relevance for the Southern African region are illustrated with case studies from Zimbabwe and South Africa. Conventional economic theories are found to have lagged behind in addressing gender issues and thus failed to develop gender theories relevant to the Southern African context. A framework for analysis of sex, sexuality and AIDS is provided, focusing on how each subject specifically applies to women and men in the wider African reality. These three subjects underpin the socio-sexual and health crisis that is affecting all Africans, including children, young people, as well as women and men of all ages and social classes.
KIT, Amsterdam [P 94-130]

034 Modernizing women : gender and social change in the Middle East
MOGHADAM, VALENTINE M. - *Women and Change in the Developing World*. Rienner, Boulder, CO xvi, 311 p. 1993 [EN] ill., tabs. Includes lit.refs,

index ISBN 1-55587-354-5

Social change in the Middle East, North Africa and Afghanistan is examined, particularly focusing on its impact on women's roles and status within the family and society, and women's varied responses to and involvement in change processes. Major social change processes at work are economic development and the expansion of wage employment, political and social revolutions, the demographic transition, changes in family structure, the rise and expansion of Islamic movements, and civil war and political conflict. Two country studies are presented: one examining the contradictions of Islamization and the changing status of women in Iran, while the other deals with the prolonged battle over women's rights in Afghanistan. The sex/gender system in the Middle East is undergoing profound change affecting women's status and position. This change has been met with a politicization of gender and family law, the preoccupation of Islamic movements with women's appearance and behaviour, shifting state policies, and cultural debates about authenticity and Westernization. One important dimension of change in the region has been the weakening of the patriarchal family and traditional kinship systems. Political conflicts and war are an important part of the process of social change in the Middle East. Women have participated in political organizations, social movements and revolutions, and have contributed to economic production and social reproduction, although their contributions are not always acknowledged, valued or remunerated.
KIT, Amsterdam [N 93-5766]

035 Gender and national identity : women and politics in Muslim societies
MOGHADAM, VALENTINE M. Zed Books, London xii, 180 p. 1994 [EN] Includes lit.refs, index, glossary ISBN 1-85649-246-X

Gender politics inevitably exist in all Islamic movements that expect women to assume the burden of a largely male-defined tradition. Even in secular political movements in the Muslim world, notably those anti-colonial national liberation movements where women were actively involved, women have experienced a general reversal of the gains made since independence. The gender dynamics of a variety of political movements, from both theoretical and political angles and with very different trajectories, are explored to demonstrate that nationalism, revolution and Islamization are all gendered processes. Five cases are examined: women's experiences in the Algerian national liberation movement and since independence; women's involvement in the struggle to construct a Bengali national identity and an independent Bangladesh; the events leading to the overthrow of the Shah and subsequent Islamization of Iran; revolution and civil war in Afghanistan; and feminism and nationalism in the context of the Palestinian Intifada (an uprising in 1987), and the role of women and women's organizations within it. It is argued that in periods of rapid political change, women in Muslim societies are central to efforts to construct a national identity.

KIT, Amsterdam   [U 94-205]

036   Different places, different voices : gender and development in Africa, Asia and Latin America
MOMSEN, JANET HENSHALL; KINNAIRD, VIVIAN - *International Studies of Women and Place*. Routledge, London xvii, 322 p. 1993 [EN] ill., graphs, tabs. Bibliogr.: p. 297-316. Includes index ISBN 0-415-07563-7

The book examines women's status in development from the point of view of feminist geographers. It includes some 20 case studies presented at the Commonwealth Geographical Bureau Workshop, held at the University of Newcastle upon Tyne, UK, during April 1989. The case studies comprise regional perspectives on aspects of urban and rural development, household reproduction and production, and community organization. There is a balanced coverage of Asia, Africa, Latin America and Oceania with contextual and theoretical introductions for each region. Many topics covered by the case studies fall within established geographical fields of inquiry:
human-environment relations, demographic analyses, and migration. Others exemplify the broad range of issues covered by 'new geography', embracing new areas of inquiry and methodology. Emphasis on location highlights the differences created by place, challenging much of feminist and post-colonial scholarship of the North.

KIT, Amsterdam   [N 93-4548]

037   Half the world, half a chance : an introduction to gender and development
MOSSE, JULIA CLEVES. Oxfam, Oxford viii, 229 p. 1993 [EN] ill. Includes lit.refs, index ISBN 0-85598-186-5

This book explores the ways in which gender inequalities are constructed and the impact of mainstream development on gender relations. It looks at the position and condition of women throughout the world. Explanations are sought for how discrimination operates within different societies, the reasons why women are disadvantaged in so many ways, and why development initiatives have often failed to help women. It provides an example of the work of Oxfam, an NGO based in the UK, with partners in the South who are committed to addressing

women's immediate and long-term needs for social and cultural change. There are many examples given of women working together to overcome the obstacles they face. If women have the opportunity to be heard, consulted and involved in planning and implementing development projects, the impact and benefit of development on women and the whole community will be greatly enhanced.

KIT, Amsterdam   [P 93-1919]

038   The gender dimension of democratization in Kenya : some international linkages
NZOMO, MARIA Institute of Diplomacy and International Studies, University of Nairobi, Nairobi - *Alternatives* 18(1993)1 p.61-73 [EN] Includes lit.refs ISSN 0304-3754

Democratization processes taking place in Africa and Kenya offer women an opportunity to bring about change in their subordinate status by demanding the inclusion of their gender-based concerns in the new democratic agenda. The demands that pervade the democratization discourse among Kenyan women include: (1) gender-sensitive democratization; (2) equal participation of women in key political and public decision-making positions; (3) gender-based human rights in the democratization process; and (4) defeminization of poverty through domestic and international democratic restructuring. These demands are discussed, stressing the importance of the existence of universal or international linkages and contexts for the struggle of Kenyan women. It is argued that the international community should support these democratization struggles taking place in Kenya and elsewhere in Africa by democratizing the international economic system to facilitate the sustainability of emerging political economies.

KIT, Amsterdam   [H 1869-18(1993)1]

039   Dedicated lives : women organising for a fairer world
O'CONNELL, HELEN. Oxfam, Oxford 60 p. 1993 [EN] ill. ISBN 0-85598-197-0

The lives of 8 women from developing countries are described, based largely on personal interviews. The women are from different social backgrounds and countries: Brazil, Egypt, India, Mexico, Palestine, the Philippines, Senegal and South Africa. The personal histories describe the lives of the women from childhood to the present, placing emphasis on happenings in their environment (apartheid, war, discrimination, protest movements) which led to their awareness of inequality and the importance of education to their personal development. The women are all activists in some way, either in the women's movement or in other movement's confronting prejudice or apartheid. In particular, they question the economic model which has determined development of their countries over the last 40 years and which has exacerbated gender, race and class inequalities. Women and their organizations have adopted different strategies for ending discrimination and transforming their societies. Some are working mainly at local level to encourage women to get together and speak out about their needs and interests. Others have chosen to work with women in mixed organizations to create a space in which they can press for their demands.

KIT, Amsterdam [N 93-6000]

040 Re-creating ourselves : African women & critical transformations
OGUNDIPE-LESLIE, MOLARA. AWP, Trenton, NJ xvii, 262 p. 1994 [EN] Includes index, lit.refs
ISBN 0-86543-411-5

Covering the 1970-1990 period, this collection of papers highlights outstanding issues in Africa: political decolonization, the place of writing and the writer, decolonizing scholarship and research, as well as modes of social activism. It illustrates the long-standing intellectual and activist work which has gone into the development of a feminist practice for black women. The first part comprises theoretical essays on literature, women and society. Forces that shape the condition of the African woman are examined, as well as the representation of women in literature, the commitment of female writers to the African female, and the position of women in Nigeria. With particular reference to Nigeria, the empirical part discusses: experiences gained with women's organizations; the progress achieved in improving women's status and their economic, political, legal and social rights; the relationship between Marxism and feminism; the special role to be played by middle-class women and their organizations; the role of the media in shaping women's image; the social impact of structural adjustment on women; and feminism in an African context. The social transformation being sketched is considered to represent both a challenge to and a means of re-creating feminist practice for black African women.

KIT, Amsterdam [N 94-2469]

041 Changing kinship, family, and gender relations in South Asia : processes, trends, and issues
PALRIWALA, RAJNI - *Women and Autonomy Series*. Leiden University. VENA, Leiden 153 p. 1994 [EN] Bibliogr.: p. 129-153 ISSN 0923-0513 ISBN 90-72631-41-2

Kinship provides organizing principles that govern recruitment to and placement of individuals in social groups in South Asia, as well as obligations and responsibilities of members to each other. Kinship articulates notions of entitlement, whether to membership, inheritance, productive resources, food, health, education, authority or decision-making. Relations between men and women are embedded in kinship systems. An overview is presented of linkages between gender relations and kinship structures in Bangladesh, India, Nepal, Pakistan and Sri Lanka. Changes in family, kinship and gender relations are examined through the arena of law reform, with an emphasis on inheritance, property and marriage. Age at marriage, dowry and ritual dimensions, changing household dynamics, and family and kinship obligations are discussed. Specific attention is paid to the aged and widows in Bangladesh and India. Economic, demographic and political processes have led to patrilineality, patrifocality and the devaluation of women, a trend which permeates gender relations in the region and which is characterized by women's oppression.

KIT, Amsterdam [P 95-320]

042 Who is the 'other'? : a postmodern feminist critique of women and development theory and practice
PARPART, JANE L. History Department, Dalhousie University, Halifax - *Development and Change* 24(1993)3 p.439-464 [EN] Bibliogr. p.459-463 ISSN 0012-155X

In the past decade post-structural and post-modern critiques have increasingly dominated the world of scholarship. Development theories of the past have been called into question; universal principles have been overtaken by particularities and difference. Feminist scholars have reacted to post-modernism in a number of ways. Some reject it, while others call for a synthesis of feminist and post-modern approaches. Many scholars and activists concerned with Third World issues, especially poverty and development, have rejected both feminism and post-modernism, dismissing them as First World preoccupations, if not indulgences. The relevance of post-modern feminism for Third World problems and analysis, particularly its utility for theorists and practitioners concerned with issues of women and development, is explored. A post-modern, feminist perspective should be added to the gender and development analysis which has already enriched the understanding of women and development questions. The addition of a post-modern feminist approach brings into question the uncritical acceptance of modernity, it reminds development specialists that power is not exercised solely at the level of the state, and it urges a closer, more localized and specific examination of women's strategies for survival in developing countries. The recognition of Third World women as persons with their own history, practice and achievements would alter and improve development theory and practice. It would challenge the assumption that development equals modernization. Third World women would become the subject rather than the object of theory and practice relating to women and development.

KIT, Amsterdam   [D 1323-24(1993)3]

043   Socio-economic political status and women and law in Pakistan
PATEL, RASHIDA. Faiza, Karachi iii, 270 p. 1991 [EN] Includes lit.refs

The first part of the book focuses on the laws governing the lives of women in Pakistan. The political rights and the participation of women in democratic institutions are considered in the light of the Islamization of the constitution and laws since 1979. Pseudo-Islamic laws, particulary the adultery and fornication ordinances, have caused suffering to women. Most of the discriminary and detrimental ordinances and their procedures are described in detail, and their impact on women is assessed. Statistics concerning demography, child bearing, literacy, education, employment and income of women are provided. The second part is a critical study of the laws relating to family life (marriage, divorce, polygamy, inheritance), identifying the need for reform to secure more equality in the domain of family and personal relationships.
Recommendations are made in keeping with the spirit of Islam and the Koran. When a man pronounces talaq (declaration of divorce) where the wife is not at fault, it is proposed that the husband should support his ex-wife financially until she re-marries or is able to support herself.

KIT, Amsterdam   [N 92-6559]

044   The intra-household allocation of resources in the Côte d'Ivoire : is there evidence of gender bias?
PATTON, JESSICA - *Development Studies Working Papers* 58. University of Oxford. Queen Elizabeth House. International Development Centre, Oxford 37 p. 1993 [EN] ill., graphs, tabs. Includes lit.refs

National household survey data from the Ivory Coast for 1985/86 and 1986/87 were analysed to establish whether there is male bias in household resource allocation. Following a review of the literature on intrahousehold allocation of resources, the theory underlying household models and the allocation of resources between household members is discussed. The econometric model used to examine household expenditure patterns is described. Analysis of the effects of changes in household composition on household expenditure patterns suggests that an increase in the proportion of children in a

household leads to a reduction in spending on adult goods. However, there is no evidence of discrimination between male and female children in the allocation of household resources. The apparent lack of gender bias may have its origins in the production structure of sub-Saharan Africa which is largely non-mechanized, depending to a large extent of the labour supply of women and girls whose economic value may thus prevent discrimination against them.

KIT, Amsterdam   [E 3136-(1993)58]

045   Sharing commonalities and diversities : forging unity towards indigenous women's empowerment : proceedings
PECUA SANTOS, JOY ANGELICA. Cordillera Women's Education and Resource Center (CWERC), Baguio City x, 242 p. 1993 [EN] ill.

The proceedings of the First Asian Indigenous Women's Conference held in Baguio City, the Philippines, during January 1993 are presented. Out of around 200 million indigenous people, 150 million are found in Asia. Asian indigenous groups are lagging behind in terms of projecting their own issues and having governments or other institutions address their concerns. Women suffer particular disadvantage because most of them are not part of organizations which articulate their issues. This conference was held to let women articulate and project their issues and demands, and to make them visible. The situation of various indigenous women in different Asian countries was discussed. Common factors and differences were identified, including neglect of rights to ancestral lands, customary law, the effects of structural adjustment, domestic violence, discrimination, women's health status and sexuality. Case studies deal with specific issues affecting indigenous women, focusing on customs related to marriage, reproductive health, population transfers, discrimination, the impact of deforestation, the tourist and sex industry, and fundamentalist religious movements. Actions and movements of individual and organized indigenous women that have emerged in response to these issues are reviewed, together with lessons learned. The Asian Indigenous Women's Network was established by the conference participants who also adopted resolutions on land rights, militarization, self-determination struggles, sex trafficking of indigenous women and population control, as well as actions to be undertaken by the Network.

KIT, Amsterdam   [N 94-1931]

046   The gender and poverty nexus : issues and policies
QUIBRIA, M.G. - *Economics Staff Paper* 51. ADB, Manila 28 p. 1993 [EN] ill., graphs, tabs. Includes lit.refs ISSN 0116-273X

Existing theoretical and empirical literature on the gender and poverty nexus are critically reviewed. Empirical data are mainly drawn from developing countries in Asia. Gender disparity is assessed by comparing differential access to land, employment, capital and inputs, including services. Although many women's projects have higher social returns, the returns vary between countries. Likewise, differential investment in women's projects has different social returns even within the same country. Analysis of the causes of greater poverty among women than among men indicates that much gender disparity stems from inequity in the intrahousehold allocation of resources, an area that can not be directly influenced by the government. The rules of intrahousehold allocation are shaped partly by economic forces, and partly by norms and values of the society. While economic forces can be manipulated by government policies, norms and values do not change swiftly in sympathy with government policies. In this sense, some aspects of gender disparity cannot be readily addressed by governments.

KIT, Amsterdam [K 2282-(1993)51]

047   Intergenerational transfers in Philippine rice villages : gender differences in traditional inheritance customs
QUISUMBING, AGNES R. - *Journal of Development Economics* 43(1994)2 p.167-195 [EN] ill., tabs 70 lit.refs ISSN 0304-3878

Traditional inheritance customs govern the transfer of wealth from one generation to the next. Although these practices seem to be enshrined in custom and tradition, they reflect choices made by parents on allocations to individual family members. With a focus on gender differences, education, land and non-land asset transfers from parents to children are examined in five villages in the Philippines. The results suggest that wealth constraints, indicated by differential ability to bestow land, lead to differences in educational investment in children. Poorer families tend to concentrate educational investment in the eldest child, and benefit from the secular expansion of educational opportunities. In a sub-sample with completed inheritance decisions, daughters are weakly disadvantaged in education and receive significantly less land and total inheritance. They may be partially compensated with non-land assets. Daughters of better educated mothers receive more land, non-land assets, and total inheritance, while better educated fathers give land preferentially to sons but favour daughters in education. These inheritance customs in rice farming communities have implications for intrafamily and intergenerational inequality. Women in agricultural communities tend to have lower overall asset positions, unless compensated

by non-land assets or human capital investment. While daughters may not receive more education in older families, the secular expansion of public education implies that later generations will experience a more equitable distribution of educational opportunities between boys and girls. Education may become more desirable relative to land as non-agricultural employment opportunities increase and population pressure on limited land leads to diminishing farm sizes.

KIT, Amsterdam [D 2124-43(1994)2]

048   Report of the world conference to review and appraise the achievements of the United Nations Decade for Women : equality, development and peace, Nairobi, 15-26 July 1985
United Nations, New York, NY iv, 304 p. 1986 [EN] ISBN 92-1-130104-1

The Forward-Looking Strategies for the Advancement of Women for the 1986-2000 period were adopted at an international conference held in Nairobi during 1985. Building on principles of equality, the strategies reaffirm the international concern regarding the status of women and provide a framework for renewed commitment by the international community to the advancement of women and the elimination of gender-based discrimination. The strategies present concrete measures to overcome obstacles to the goals and objectives of the UN Decade for the Advancement of Women (1976-1985) in the field of equality, development and peace. In addition to the complete text of the strategies, the historical background to the conference, attendance and organization of work, the general debate, and reports of the subsidiary committees are included.

KIT, Amsterdam [U 85-1246]

049   Report of the World Conference of the United Nations Decade for Women : equality, development and peace, Copenhagen, 14 to 30 July 1980
United Nations, New York, NY viii, 238 p. 1980 [EN]

The World Conference of the UN Decade for Women: Equality, Development and Peace, held in Copenhagen in 1980, is reported including the programme of action for the second half of the decade, 1980-1985, together with the resolutions and decisions adopted by the conference. Following an historical and conceptual framework, the national, regional and international level programme of action, including policies and programme strategies, objectives and priority areas, are described. Although considerable efforts have been made by the majority of countries in furthering the decade's objectives, the progress achieved has been insufficient to bring about desired quantitative and qualitative improvements in the status of women. The present programme of action focuses on ensuring women's increased participation in the realization of the objectives of the World Plan of Action adopted at the 1975 World Conference of the UN Decade for Women by refining and strengthening the measures for advancing women's status, and by ensuring that women's concerns are taken into account in the formulation and implementation of the international development strategy for the Third UN Development Decade.

KIT, Amsterdam   [U 85-1247]

050   Women, culture and violence : a development, health and human rights issue
RICHTERS, JOHANNA MARIA - *Women and Autonomy Series*. Leiden University. Women and Autonomy Centre (VENA), Leiden xi, 205 p. 1994 [EN] Bibliogr.: p. 177-205 ISSN 0923-0513 ISBN 90-72631-37-4

The fight against gender violence is a priority for women all over the world. The concept of gender violence is examined, sketching the scope of this worldwide problem, and reviewing first hand accounts of women's suffering from gender violence. Aspects of gender violence which are culture specific are identified. Organized activities developed by women at local, regional, national and international levels to combat abuse of their rights are examined. Gender violence is conceptualized as a human rights' problem. A discussion of women and organized violence and gender violence in the family is presented. Intervention strategies for curtailing the practice of gender violence comprise institution-building, consciousness-raising and networking through NGOs or governmental organizations. Only when gender violence is perceived as a political issue, when it is publicly discussed and analysed, will it be possible to achieve a greater insight into its causes and contexts, and to envisage strategies to overcome this situation. Not only gender violence, however, should be brought back to the centre of historical and political discourses, stories, reports and experiences of women's resistance and action in the 'war' between the sexes should also be shared and become part of world history.

KIT, Amsterdam   [P 94-1023]

051   Mujeres y democracia : en busca de una identidad en el sistema político
SALINAS, GLORIA ARDAYA - *Nueva Sociedad* (1994)134 p.70-85 [ES] ill. 8 lit.refs ISSN 0251-3552

Women are not recognized as equal social actors in political or institutional settings. Given that power structures and gender inequalities are institutionalized, it remains difficult for women to be considered equal. Democratization in Latin America should not countenance the piece-meal integration of women into society. Women's status in society and politics need to be redressed. As a result of democratization, women are gaining a new identity in line with their constitutional rights. However, historical research on power structures is necessary to understand the present situation of women. Women's unequal status may explain the previous absence of female solidarity. Prior to the economic crisis, women failed to establish a new gender identity. The integration of women into politics is one way to consolidate the new social and political identity, allowing women to escape from male dominance and the their traditional roles and status. Instead of being marginalized in political planning, women should be able to liberate themselves from social injustice and inequality. This article is derived from the report of a conference on 'Women, politics and communication', organized by UNICEF in Quito, Ecuador, during 1994.

KIT, Amsterdam   [C 2859-(1994)134]

052   Droits des femmes palestiniennes : déclaration de principes
SANBAR, ELIAS - *Revue d'Études Palestiniennes* (1995)2 p.3-5 [FR] ISSN 0252-8290

Based on the Independence Declaration proclaimed during the nineteenth session of the National Palestinian Council in 1988, rights of Palestinian women are formulated in a declaration of principles. The focus is on: safeguarding a coherent Palestinian society; protecting the original Palestinian culture; and sustaining the social and national struggle of Palestinian women. Women should receive equal civil rights, equality with men before the law, and the absence of discrimination in matters relating to marriage and family relations, as well as equal rights in education, employment, health care and other economic and social areas. The efforts of women and other democratic forces in Palestinian society should be united in order to cope with all the obstacles that hamper the equality of women and men, and achieve real national independence, social justice and equity.

KIT, Amsterdam   [B 3256-(1995)2]

053   Women's rights and human rights in Muslim countries : a case study
SARDAR-ALI, SHAHEEN; MULLALLY, SIOBHAN *In: Working out : new directions for women's studies* ed. by Hilary Hinds, Ann Phoenix and Jackie Stacey. - London : Falmer, 1992 p.113-123 [EN] 15 lit.refs

The Convention on the Elimination of All Forms of Discrimination Against Women, adopted by the UN in 1979, represents the first significant challenge to a vision of human rights which has traditionally excluded much of

women's experience. Some of the implications of the convention for Muslim countries are considered, particularly the assertion by a number of Muslim states that the requirements of the convention conflict with Sharia (Islamic law). To date, 10 Muslim countries have ratified the Convention although 7 of these have entered reservations on the basis of conflict with Sharia. The concept of equality is not necessarily in conflict with Sharia, despite the fact that political prejudices have often led to the interpretation of Sharia in a way which discriminates against women. There is considerable scope for differing judgements as to the nature and extent of conflict between Sharia and the requirements of the convention. The struggle for sexual equality in Muslim societies should come from within those societies if it is to be successful. The writings of Taha and others pose a significant challenge which could be taken up by Muslim women to achieve the objectives articulated in the convention. The support and solidarity of the international community is essential.
KIT, Amsterdam   [N 94-2658]

054   Freedom from violence : women's strategies from around the world
SCHULER, MARGARET - *Women, Law and Development*. PACT Communications, New York, NY xv, 354 p. 1992 [EN] ill., tabs. Includes lit.refs, index
   Violence against women is a pervasive and prevalent problem worldwide, touching physical, social, economic, cultural and legal aspects of women's lives. Although violence is increasingly being recognized by governments and international bodies, the work of finding solutions and shaping strategies to address violence in the home, in the street and in the workplace continues to be initiated and implemented primarily by feminist NGOs. In 13 contributions collected in this volume, actions of women organizing to combat violence against women in Bolivia, Brazil, Chile, India, Malaysia, Mexico, Pakistan, Sri Lanka, Sudan, Thailand, USA and Zimbabwe are assessed. Issues covered include: rape and sexual abuse; prostitution; female genital mutilation; and domestic violence. What needs to be done to confront the violence in women's lives is demonstrated from a cross-cultural perspective. Women's responses as well as legal and institutional responses to specific problems in these countries are discussed. Apart from legislation and women's consciousness-raising, police, hospitals, and other institutions need to be sensitized to gender violence. Resources, organizations, facts and statistics are presented in the annexes.
KIT, Amsterdam   [N 94-84]

055   Rethinking men and gender relations : an investigation of men, their changing roles within the household and the implications for gender relations in Kisii District, Kenya
SILBERSCHMIDT, MARGRETHE - *CDR Research Report* 16. Centre for Development Research, Copenhagen 91 p. 1991 [EN] Includes lit.refs ISSN 0108-6596 ISBN 87-88467-19-8
   Traditional male roles and obligations, and the norms and values that encompass and legitimize these roles are examined in Kisii District, Kenya. Data were collected during two periods of field work in 1985-1986 and 1990. Interviews were undertaken with 280 men, aged 19-85 years. Former male activities legitimizing men's roles as heads of household have disappeared. Many men have abandoned their family obligations, and their role as household head seems to be legitimized only by the patriarchal ideology. Unable to fulfil the obligations required of them, men appear to have experienced a loss of identity, often leading to alcoholism, domestic violence and extramarital sexual activity. The undermined traditional hierarchy has not been replaced by new definitions of sexual roles and authority structures, and men seem to be in a particularly insecure position which has led to the increasing prevalence of mental illness. On the other hand, many women have developed a strength in relation to men, despite the limitations that patriarchal structures set for them. Women have been able to retain their original and traditional role within the household and within wider society to a much larger extent than men. These findings challenge the tendency within women's research to see men as winners and women as losers in the process of socio-economic change.
KIT, Amsterdam   [E 2937-(1991)16]

056   Situación juridica de la mujer rural : en diecinueve países de América latina
FAO, Rome xiii, 132 p. 1992 [ES] ill. Bibliogr.: p. 115-132. Includes glossary
   The legal status of rural women in 19 Central and Latin American countries is reviewed in order to identify and design strategies that may improve their subordinate legal position. A brief historical analysis is followed by analyses of the division of labour by gender, the participation of rural women in productive activities, conditions of employment and the work environment. Legal standards with reference to civil rights (marital law, inheritance) are assessed, as well as labour rights, land rights, access to credit, access to technology, and women's participation in organizations. The annexes provide case studies on the constitutional status of women in Colombia, Cuba, El Salvador, Mexico and Venezuela.
KIT, Amsterdam   [U 95-94]

057   Planning and public action for Asian women

SOBHAN, REHMAN. University Press Limited, Dhaka 118 p. 1992 [EN] ill., tabs. Includes lit.refs ISBN 984-05-1198-X

The state's role in improving the conditions of women through planning, policy interventions and public expenditures is explored. Efforts of a number of governments in Asia to integrate women's issues in their planning process are examined. Serious weaknesses in the conceptualization and design of various national plans in addressing the concerns of women, and the inadequacy of resource commitments and weaknesses in the machinery for implementing the respective plan programmes in individual countries are revealed. The weaknesses are attributed to the neglect of women as a social category, and of their particular needs and concerns. The outcomes of public action and interventions are discussed in relation to their impact on the lives of women with special emphasis on their integration into the organized labour market and their human development status. It is argued that the low priority accorded to women's concerns is a major reason for lack of empowerment. Development for women has been viewed as an essentially top-down, bureaucratic exercise to be sustained by public officials. An agenda for public action is proposed, stressing the need for improvements in planning methodology, implementation and supportive action both in the executive and legislative fields to increase women's empowerment.

KIT, Amsterdam   [P 94-235]

058   The family, women's rights and community responsibilities

SOKALSKI, HENRYK J. - *Development* (1993)4. Society for International Development (SID), Rome 88 p. [EN] ill. Includes lit.refs ISSN 1011-6370

The International Year of the Family (1994) is a concerted effort of the international community, and a large number of partners such as governments and NGOs, to support families as the basic social unit. In the process of change in today's world, the family has been both purveyor and recipient; sometimes acting as an agent of change or alternatively being transformed by external forces. In some cases, this process has been adaptive, in others destructive, threatening family survival and needs. This special issue on the family, women's rights and community responsibilities focuses on some of the changing concepts and needs of the family, the consequences for women and implications for their status and rights, and the responses of the community. An historical perspective to the issue of the family is provided, showing how women in the 12th Century faced many of the same dilemmas as women in the poorest sections of society today. The implications of making the family the basic unit of development for development policy- making and programming are reviewed. Changing concepts of the family that have emerged in response to the problem of HIV/AIDS and to the issue of sexuality in determining women's social role within the family are addressed. The impact of displacement as a result of war, violence, persecution or other human rights' abuses on women roles and responsibilities towards the family and community is examined.

KIT, Amsterdam   [H 1000-(1993)4]

059   Breast-feeding and working mothers : laws and policies on maternity and child care

SWAMINATHAN, MINA - *Economic and Political Weekly* 28(1993)18 p.887-891 [EN] 9 lit.refs

In India breast-feeding is being promoted through social policy and legislation. The efforts, however, tend to focus on the health of the children, ignoring the roles and needs of women, working women in particular. It is argued that women's reproductive role should be regarded as a form of 'social production' which needs social support through maternity leave and other benefits to be provided by the state and employers. Present laws and regulations concerning maternity leave and benefits provide only partial support to women working in the formal sector, while leaving out the majority of women who are engaged in informal sector activities. To genuinely promote the health and welfare of both mothers and children, comprehensive legislation and policies which consider maternity and child care services jointly are required. Amendment of the Maternity Benefits Act along these lines is suggested, including the calculation of maternity leave for a period of 4 months from the day of childbirth, and 2-4 weeks leave during the final stage of pregnancy. Legislation and supportive policies should provide an enabling environment for the provision of creches and child care facilities by employers. It is recognized that protective welfare legislation and policies will first become available to women workers in the organized sector, but ways should be found to extend maternity benefits, step by step, to the informal sector through occupation-specific legislation and by developing maternity and child care schemes as part of a social security network for women and children.

KIT, Amsterdam   [B 3057-28(1993)18]

060   Persistent inequalities : women and world development

TINKER, IRENE. Oxford University Press, New York, NY xi, 302 p. 1990 [EN] Bibliogr.: p.

257-291. Includes index ISBN 0-19-506158-6

Despite an improved understanding about women and development, women remain faced with persistent inequalities. Past and current debates in the field of women-in-development that have challenged many earlier assumptions about development and the reality of women's work and lives within and outside the household are highlighted. The politics of the women-in-development approach are addressed from a variety of perspectives, including feminist and gender perspectives. The impact of intrahousehold distribution and control on individual household members, and women in particular, is examined. Empirical data from the Philippines and Sri Lanka indicate that behaviour within the household can be modified by improving women's economic opportunities outside the household. However, such efforts may have little effect on the status assigned to such work because the value of women's work appears to be mediated by patriarchy. Systems of patriarchal control in India, East and West Africa, and the Caribbean are considered, demonstrating that patriarchy has consolidated its traditional dominance and expanded its control as these societies have modernized.

KIT, Amsterdam [N 90-1847]

061 UN Decade for Women : its impact and legacy
TINKER, IRENE; JAQUETTE, JANE - *World Development* 15(1987)3 p.419-427 [EN] 7 lit.refs ISSN 0305-750X

The influence of the UN Decade for Women is assessed at three levels: women and women's groups; national governments; and the international system itself. The impact of the decade is assessed in terms of the progress in creating an international consensus on what women's issues are and the implications of that consensus for changes in policies and in resource allocation. The assessment shows the debates and process by which women's issues have evolved into a woman's international agenda comprising the following issues: legal equality, economic access to resources, sexual exploitation and violence against women, and peace. The role played by specific agencies or offices within agencies, mainstream sympathizers, and women's groups and networks in implementing the international agenda is discussed.

KIT, Amsterdam [E 1271-15(1987)3]

062 Women and human rights
TOMASEVSKI, KATARINA - *Women and World Development Series*. Zed Books, London xiv, 162 p. 1993 [EN] ill., tabs. Includes lit.refs, index ISBN 1-85649-120-X

The book examines the gender gap between the recognition and enjoyment of human rights and fundamental freedoms, arguing that the human rights of women as workers, prisoners and refugees should be equal to those of men. The unequal situation of women, constantly deplored as unsatisfactory, results from gender discrimination. Knowledge of existing human rights' standards which should apply to women but are often unknown to the women themselves, is a weapon with which they can improve their human rights. The gap between women's agenda and the human rights' agenda, ranging from standard setting to policy, practice and action, means that the rights of women are mislaid from the international agenda. The book is particularly intended to stimulate action at the grassroots level. It considers what has been done so far to articulate and define human rights, in particular the Convention on the Elimination of Discrimination Against Women and the continuing lack of adequate response to violations at both national and international levels. It draws attention to those categories of women who are most at risk, including refugees, the disabled, indigenous women and prisoners. Proposals for a plan of action are provided, including educating women as to their rights, community level mobilization, and international networking and litigation.

KIT, Amsterdam [N 94-612]

063 Turkey : women in development
World Bank Country Study. World Bank, Washington, DC xxiii, 205 p. 1993 [EN] ill., graphs, tabs. Includes lit.refs ISSN 0253-2123 ISBN 0-8213-2375-X

This book provides background information about the situation of women in Turkey, including legal and health issues, and examines government strategies to incorporate women into national policies and programmes. While touching on the general situation, the focus is upon women's labour force participation and the constraints they face therein. The position of women was found to vary considerably: from the highly educated, professional urban women in the major cities to the majority of women in the urban and rural areas who are caught between two different worlds, one traditional and one modern. According to socio-economic indicators, the status of women has improved significantly in recent decades. Regional variation and comparison with a group of other countries indicate, however, some areas where further improvement is desirable. The report is intended to serve as the basis of the World Bank's discussions with the Government of Turkey to enhance the participation of women in the economic development process.

KIT, Amsterdam [U 93-355]

064   Women : watched and punished : regional seminar 'Criminal law and women in Latin America and the Caribbean'
VÁSQUEZ, ROXANA; BARTON, MICHELLE.
CLADEM, Lima 316 p. 1993 [EN] ill., tabs.
Includes lit.refs

The regional seminar 'Criminal law and women in Latin America and the Caribbean' was held in 1992 to discuss the position of women in criminal systems. Key papers and conclusions of this seminar are presented. Current conceptions of criminal law and its contribution to the treatment of women's issues are discussed. Case studies come from Bolivia, Brazil, Peru, Puerto Rico and Uruguay, as well as Latin America in general. Violence against women is examined: domestic violence, rape, abortion, prostitution, sterilization and incest. The debate on each form of violence is first reviewed. The strategies for legal reform to meet women's needs are described. The experience of groups acting at the private level which have introduced proposals to confront concrete problems faced by women are analysed. The general recommendations, the conclusions, and the agenda for action agreed upon by the participants are reported. A social and legal inventory of the problems is required in the medium-term. The results of the seminar have been incorporated in a three year working plan (1993-1995) of the Latin American Committee for the Defense of Women's Rights.
KIT, Amsterdam   [N 95-523]

065   Women and emergencies
WALKER, BRIDGET; ANDERSON, MARY B. - *Focus on Gender* 2(1994)1. Oxfam, Oxford 64 p. [EN] ill.
Includes lit.refs ISSN 0968-2864 ISBN 0-85598-266-7

The 14 papers in this special issue explore some of the dilemmas facing those engaged in planning and implementation of emergency relief programmes, drawing on experiences in Bangladesh, India, Kenya, Pakistan, Sudan, Zaire and Zambia. They record the experiences of women in situations of crisis, their particular vulnerabilities and needs, and their capacities and strengths. A prevailing theme is the need to see relief and development as parts of the same whole rather than as different poles. Understanding gender relations is particularly important at times of disaster, not only because women and children are disproportionately affected but also because emergency interventions can seriously compromise the long-term future of women by creating further imbalances in their relations with men at times of stress. Men and women experience different vulnerabilities and have different capacities as a result of their distinct roles. Women continue to be concerned with the provision of the basic necessities of life but the fulfilment of these roles may be constrained by a lack of opportunities and rights, limiting women's capacity to cope and empower themselves. The tool of gender analysis is advocated as a powerful one for accurately diagnosing opportunities and constraints in any refugee programme, and for identifying more effective strategies for delivering emergency assistance so that it supports long-term development for women and men, and girls and boys.
KIT, Amsterdam   [D 3030-2(1994)1]

066   Law, custom, and crimes against women : the problem of dowry death in India
WILLIGEN, JOHN VAN; CHANNA, V.C. - *Human Organization* 50(1991)4 p.369-377 [EN] 42
lit.refs ISSN 0018-7259

The cultural institution of dowry as practised in India engenders substantial violence against women. This takes the form of inter-familial harassment for additional payments of goods and money which can culminate in the murder or suicide of the bride. Reduction of this abuse of women is attempted through law and education. The primary means of controlling these abuses, the amended Dowry Prohibition Act of 1961, is widely regarded as not having been effective in reducing so-called 'dowry deaths' and 'bride-burning'. Some 1319 dowry deaths were reported nationally in 1986 although far more violence may occur than official figures indicate. The causes of dowry problems are a product of the low economic value of women, loss of effective social control of abuse as a result of urbanization, and pressures caused by economic transformation. The traditional family, caste and community controls have been reduced in effectiveness and should be replaced by state functions. The foundation of state control is universal marriage registration and licensure. A broad programme to increase the economic value of women would be the most useful means of eradicating problems associated with dowry.
KIT, Amsterdam   [H 1957-50(1991)4]

067   Changing roles and statuses of women in Thailand : a documentary assessment
YODDUMNERN-ATTIG, BENCHA - *IPSR Publication* 161. Mahidol University. Institute for Population and Social Research, Salaya, Thailand vi, 128 p. 1992 [EN] ill., tabs. Includes index. Bibliogr.: p. 105-116 ISBN 974-5874-35-3

A review is provided of the changing roles and status of women in Thailand. Seven major roles are looked at: parental, occupational, conjugal, domestic, kin, community and individual. The traditional Thai family system is described with special attention to the differential roles for males and females in terms of residence pattern, decision-making and familial roles. The life history of a rural woman illustrates how socio-economic change and family demands have affected women's roles and status over time. Role strain, deprivation and conflict are shown to have occurred as a result of women's failure to fulfil the expectations of a given role because of financial, resource or time constraints. The integration of women into Thai development plans over the past 30 years demonstrates that women's status and roles have not been fully recognized in terms of law and policy. It is recommended that women should be integrated into future development plans by expanding non-formal and formal education for women who lack opportunities to develop their skills, rural women in particular; by continuing to improve laws concerning women's employment and wages; and by allowing women to participate in policy-making by appointing women to the National Development Board.

KIT, Amsterdam   [N 94-2657]

068   Planning development with women : making a world of difference
YOUNG, KATE. St. Martin's Press, New York, NY vii, 187 p. 1993 [EN] Bibliogr.: p. 166-181. Includes index ISBN 0-312-09090-0

The way perceptions of women have been affected by development thinking over the past three decades is examined. A gender perspective in development planning is required in order to support and enhance women's participation and empowerment. Women's contribution to African agriculture, industrial development in Asia, and the informal sector in Latin America is analysed. Contrasting the two main perspectives, women-in-development and gender and development, conceptual problems involved in gathering statistical gender-sensitive data are identified in relation to women's economic activity and the household, and the balance of power between the sexes. It is concluded that sustainable change in women's material conditions will never come about unless collective empowerment enables them to dismantle the underlying structures that produce the imbalance between the genders. If women's organizations are to play a key role in participatory planning, certain prerequisites should be met: (1) these organizations should look very stringently at their own mechanisms of participation, democratic decision-making and accountability; (2) they must get financial resources, training and access to information; and (3) they should play a prominent part in wider social movements so as to prevent gender issues from becoming marginalized.

KIT, Amsterdam   [N 93-5002]

2 Education and training

A critical review of education and training

Maaike Jongepier and Marguérite Appel

Five years ago, governments around the world committed themselves to reach the goal of Education for All by the year 2000. Nevertheless, in 1995 there are approximately 948 million people who are still illiterate and a growing number of children are excluded from any type of education. Indeed, 60% of all people over 15 years of age have no access to basic schooling. It is however remarkable that two-thirds of all illiterates are women.

The International Conference on Education for All, held in Jomtien, Thailand, during 1990 reconfirmed education as a basic human right. 'Basic education' to meet basic learning needs was recognized as being the main priority. It encompasses early childhood and primary education for children, as well as education in literacy, general knowledge and life skills for youth and adults. In this definition, basic education refers to the hierarchical, structured and organized system for primary schooling upwards, as well as types of education that take place outside the established system, including pre-school and adult education which are non-formal in character. In addition to highlighting basic education as the main issue, the conference reached general agreement that women should receive special attention because they have been marginalized in education. The intention to eliminate disparities in access to basic education arising from gender, age, income, family, cultural, ethnic and linguistic differences and geographical remoteness was asserted.

The worsening of the international economic crisis, rising indebtedness, political instability, ethnic conflicts and natural disasters in the 1980s coincided with the decline of education systems in many developing countries. Educational expenditures in sub-Saharan Africa have severely declined and the situation is expected to deteriorate further. As a consequence of structural adjustment programmes, social spending on health and education has been cut and governments have shifted responsibilities for schooling to families. Direct costs, such as school fees, uniforms, books and transport, previously paid for by the government, now must be covered by parents. These developments have had a negative impact on educational opportunities for girls. Shortfalls in household income are forcing more women to enter the paid labour market. When this happens, daughters often have to take over family responsibilities at the expense of their education. If choices have to be made about which child can go to school, preference is given to boys because they are still considered a main source of economic security for parents in their old age. However, boys too may have to stay at home when the expenses of their education cannot be met. As a result, groups of children who have not been able to enter school are becoming the next generation of disadvantaged adults. Recent studies on the gender dimensions of structural adjustment reaffirm the negative impact on women in terms of increasing workloads, deteriorating health and deficits in food consumption as a result of poverty (Kurian 1994). Earlier gains in the quality of education, specifically women's access to education, have been destroyed by the implementation of these policies. Growing concern about the 'feminization' of poverty has frequently been expressed.

Public discussion has moved education into a central position in the debate on human resource development. However, this attention has not led to educational programmes which confront gender and contribute to the process of empowerment. In addition, the fact that education is intrinsically linked to cultural, economic, social and political factors, which not only strongly differ among countries but even within small communities, makes Education for All by the year 2000 a difficult objective to achieve. Nevertheless, important positive developments with regard to education for women have taken place in recent years.

This paper covers policy options on education for women which are currently favoured, reviewing both their advantages and disadvantages. Development of policies on education for women should be regarded as an ongoing debate, formulated at world conferences and, potentially, adopted by governments, communities and NGOs. Experience shows that implementation does not always coincide with policies that have been advocated. First, some comments are made on the selective use of certain educational concepts in the debate on human resource development. Literacy is one of the main statistical indicators for estimating the level of education in a country. Whether education is simply a matter of literacy alone is examined. The role of statistics in demonstrating gender disparities in access to and participation in education for women is considered. The obstacles impeding women's enrolment and retention in the education system are then discussed. Whether educational policy approaches have taken women's concerns sufficiently into account is also considered. One of the latest approaches to integrating women's needs has been the empowerment approach. Apart from some local initiatives, only a small number of donor organizations have concentrated on issues of women's empowerment by providing gender training. The approach followed during gender training is described. Finally, case studies are used to illustrate different approaches to empowerment.

Literacy as the main statistical indicator for education

Statistical handbooks, based on census data, appear to be efficient instruments for gaining an overview of literacy and education in individual countries. In reality, census data can be rudimentary and frequently unreliable. In discussions on human resource development, literacy is often used as the main indicator for the general standard of education in a country with the inherent risk that education will be reduced to literacy alone. This basis is further undermined by the fact that there is no standard, generally accepted definition of literacy. The UNESCO definition is the most widely accepted but is not easy to translate into measurable indicators: 'a person is functionally literate who can engage in all those activities in which literacy is required for effective functioning of his group and community and also for enabling him to continue to use reading, writing and calculating for his own and the community's development.' It is important to know what is actually meant by literacy in a specific context to be able to evaluate the statistics. For example, the meaning of literacy varies from country to country. Literates' definition of their own literacy is also important. Is literacy based on the ability to memorize school texts, read and understand newspapers, or to recite Koran texts without being able to interpret them?

Although literacy is often considered to be the most relevant indicator of human resource development, other indicators are available in most handbooks and statistical reports, including enrolment rates at primary, secondary and tertiary level for males and females and differences in repetition and drop-out rates. By distinguishing between male and female enrolment figures, statistics show the discrepancy between men and women in terms of their access to education. Nonetheless, these indicators reveal virtually nothing about elements which are difficult to quantify but which are no less important to the discussion on gender disparities in education: the curriculum, geographical distances to schools, the number of female teachers in a school, types of teaching materials, educational attainments of men and women, differences in school performance, opportunities after school, age of marriage, and frequency of early pregnancies among adolescent girls. All of these indicators need to be taken into account when building a more detailed picture of the actual situation. Even then, equal access does not imply equal outcome. In Latin America, for example, initial enrolment rates for women are almost equal to men's but high drop-out and repetition rates for women result in unequal attainment. Thus, equal initial enrolment rates for boys and girls are not a measure of equity.

Despite the limitations of statistics, they do play an important role in clarifying the fact that many people still lack access to any type of education, and that this group mainly consists of girls and women. Moreover, the educational opportunities for women are even poorer in rural areas than in urban areas and are expected to worsen. If present gender disparities continue, basic education for all will never become a reality.

Factors affecting girls' participation in education

The reasons girls are excluded from school in developing countries are complex and differ from country to country and from community to community. The factors affecting the access to and participation in the school system appear to be strongly related to historical, cultural, political, social and gender issues. Relevant literature reveals that various efforts have been undertaken to arrange these factors into frameworks. Colclough (1994) has attempted to synthesize the main lessons from the literature on gender and education in Africa, distinguishing between factors that influence the demand for and the supply of schooling. She has, together with other authors, argued that the factors determining school access for girls and boys are different in degree but not in kind. A distinction is made between those factors that play a role in the family or household group, factors at school level and those which are influenced by the community (Helleman 1992). The division of labour by gender is strongly related to ideas about the role of women as mothers, wives and family caretakers. Although these categories are intrinsically linked, all three are influenced by prevailing gender-related ideas about male-female relationships and sex roles.

Gender-related factors do not function in isolation. They are influenced by cultural, religious, socio-economic and political motives. For example, women have different statuses and roles in a matriarchy than in a patriarchy. *Purdah* imposes restrictions on women's physical mobility, influencing community expectations with regard to women's behaviour. These expectations, in turn, contribute to the character of current role models for women. Countries with the highest illiteracy rates among women are usually those where the social system, under the influence of religion, imposes heavy restrictions on women's behaviour. Further, poverty and politics also affect education. Ethnic conflicts and migration can change role models, which might have either a negative or positive impact on access to education for women.

Cammish (1994) has assessed these gender-related factors in Vanuatu, arguing that the traditional role of women and their traditional low status ('they come third it is said after man and pigs') have militated against equal opportunities for females in education. The situation in Vanuatu is one of numerous examples where the low status of women has resulted in limited access to and participation of women in the educational system. Parents, teachers and the girls themselves often have low aspirations regarding academic achievement and occupation. Early marriage also gives rise to a low demand for the education of girls. Personal observation in Uganda showed that parents were unwilling to pay for the education of daughters who would belong to another family after marriage. The limited decision-making power of women with respect to access to knowledge and training, and their low degree of mental and physical autonomy are seen in these example.

Household and family considerations

Gender differentiation permeates the family and household group, the school and the community. At household level, the lack of financial resources plays an important role. Cost-sharing, where parents share the cost of a child's education with the government, has become a common component of educational and health programmes supported by governments and donors. Parents must now pay for uniforms and other school costs, a further constraint on their decision to send daughters to school. Moreover, labour requirements force girls to stay at home to take care of siblings and do domestic work. Even if a girl is allowed to attend school, a heavy workload awaits her at home, resulting in lower academic performance.

Another important consideration in sending a girl to school relates to security. If schools are relatively remote from the parental home, sending a girl to school might endanger her safety and honour and thus that of the whole family. On her way to school, a girl might not be sufficiently protected from exposure to public view.

Schools

The absence of schools or school-type facilities within a reasonable distance may encourage parents to keep daughters at home. Culturally appropriate school facilities, in terms of sanitation or boundary walls, will encourage parents to send daughters to school. The sex composition of teaching staff is also relevant. The presence of female teachers appears to be an important stimulus for parents, particularly in countries in which sex segregation permeates all social life and where it is not acceptable for girls to be taught by male teachers. In Pakistan, this constraint has resulted in the establishment of special community schools for girls which meet the educational needs of children who had no access to the regular school system. Many of these community schools were originally started in the house of a female teacher. By making use of the home of a known and respected person and by ensuring that no men are involved in the teaching process, girls are expected to be sufficiently protected from sexual harassment. Female teachers also provide role models for girls, another positive side-effect of their presence. On the other hand, teachers' attitudes towards girls in the formal education system often reflect low expectations about their learning aspirations. The male-biased character of teaching material enforces the idea that education is irrelevant for girls.

School regulations regarding teenage pregnancies further disadvantage girls. As Maimbolwa-Sinyangwe (1994) explains, drop-out rates among adolescent girls in Zambia are high because of early pregnancies. Pregnant pupils are generally not tolerated at school because of their perceived immorality. In many countries, early pregnancies are a common phenomenon and are not tolerated by the school system. According to the regulations, a girl is obliged to leave school while the boy involved in the pregnancy is allowed to continue his education. Parents in Soroti, a rural area of Uganda, complained about the lack of proper sex education at school. They argued that sex education, taught by a female teacher and at the right age, could prevent many unwanted pregnancies (Van 't Rood and Jongepier 1994).

Community leadership and norms

The role of the community should not be underestimated in discussion of factors affecting girls' participation in schooling. The support or lack of support of an influential community leader for education of girls is important (Helleman 1994). Community leaders' lack of awareness about the significance of education for girls has a multiplier effect on and impedes overall awareness among community members with regard to girls' education. It can hinder resource mobilization, while competitive demands for resources and lack of appropriate job opportunities make the education of girls a low community priority. A number of studies have identified obstacles facing women's access to and participation in education. Most of them emphasize that social disparities in access to education and educational attainments between men and women are strongly related to community-bounded socio-economic, political and cultural conditions.

The role of education in the current development debate

Educational problems, such as low literacy levels and limited access to education for girls, have been reflected in the international development debate. During the 1950s and 1960s, underdevelopment was usually regarded as a socio-economic condition in which a society simply lacked industry, capital, technology and an educated labour force. Developing countries merely had to acquire the missing elements to become developed (Bray 1986). This assumption reflected the general ideology of that period: development was mainly perceived in economic terms and education was regarded as an instrument that would facilitate economic growth. Cookson (1992) found little evidence to support the argument that educational reform revitalizes the economy and society. The educational crisis of the 1980s occurred not just because education failed to produce desired outcomes but because education was not able to formulate answers to social problems. Over the last decade, governments and observers have postulated that economic growth is just one instrument in the process of development. Nevertheless, an analysis of recent development policies shows that a strong link between education, economic growth and expected development is still assumed.

Current arguments for investment in women

At the same time, the approach to women has also changed in accordance with the current development debate. Buvinic (1983) has analysed the shift in policies in terms of the welfare approach, the equity approach, and the anti-poverty approach. These frameworks use women's reproductive or productive roles to legitimize investment in the development of women, who are generally regarded as an isolated group. Some elements of these various approaches are still popular among donors and governments. Moser (1993) has argued that there have been two additional approaches to women: the efficiency approach and the empowerment approach. The efficiency approach is currently popular with governments and multilateral agencies. The deterioration in the world economy and policy measures, such as adjustment programmes, have given rise to a new appreciation of the important role of women in the development process. Accordingly, within the efficiency approach, women are regarded entirely in terms of delivery capacity, as instruments of development. Apart from their participation in the economic process, their role as providers of social services is emphasized. In a speech for the World Bank, Summers (1992) argued that educating women is an investment that will yield a higher rate of return than any other investment available in the developing world. He stressed that educating girls yields benefits by reducing child mortality, fertility, maternal mortality and the spread of HIV/AIDS, as well as having important environmental benefits. Summers pointed out that even after discounting the time lag between the period when girls are educated and when they grow up and have children, the social benefits of educating girls more than cover the costs.

This ideology of efficiency has become common; it is no longer limited just to multilateral agencies and governments. King (1993) illustrates the strong link between women's education and their role in the production process. She points out that educating girls and women promotes both individual and national wellbeing and prosperity. It has also been stressed that priority should be given to literacy programmes for women and girls because educated mothers will positively affect the health and nutritional status of all household members, especially children, and consequently contribute to socio-economic development and poverty alleviation (*Alphabétisation: clé du développement* 1992).

Apart from a few comments, no collective criticism has been expressed of instrumental approaches in which women are seen as tools to stimulate social development. On the contrary, the Plan of Action on Population and Development, approved during the UN International Conference on Population and Development, held in Cairo during 1994, argues that education for women positively influences family health, the environment and sustainable development. Here too, women are considered instruments for passing on the benefits of education to their families. Such an instrumental approach ignores the impact on the personal lives of women of the nature, causes and effects of demographic processes (Jongepier 1994). Access to education for women is legitimized by its social and economic benefits rather than the recognition that education is a basic human right for both men and women.

Education for empowerment

Little has been written about the role of education in facilitating information dissemination, knowledge and skills, to strengthen women's self-esteem and personal fulfilment. Education should be considered an important condition for attaining autonomy. Equipping people with socio-cultural, economic and political knowledge enables them to analyse their own identity and situations. The empowerment approach to education considers aspects of self-esteem and personal fulfilment to be important objectives in the educational process. In contrast to the approaches mentioned above, this framework has largely been articulated by women from developing countries.

The starting point is women's subordination, which is seen not only as a problem stemming from men but also as a consequence of the oppressive social system. Empowerment approaches acknowledge the causes, dynamics and structures of women's oppression. By considering practical and strategic gender needs, this approach attempts to transform the situation of oppression. Empowerment also acknowledges how important it is for women to increase their power, not in terms of domination but rather in terms of self-reliance and internal strength. Thus, power is identified as the right to determine one's own choices in life and to influence the direction of change through the ability to gain control over crucial material and non-material resources (Moser 1993).

Unfortunately, empowerment approaches are unpopular with governments and agencies. The concepts of power and transformation, intrinsically linked to empowerment approaches, may be considered threatening to the status quo. Empowerment approaches may also remain unsupported because they openly recognize the limited ability of government legislation to meet strategic gender needs. Instead, key roles are reserved for women's movements and NGOs. Moser (1993) identifies political mobilization, consciousness-raising and popular education as the main facilitators for the process of empowerment. For her and others, the work of Paulo Freire, one of the key figures in popular education, has been instrumental in providing concepts related to consciousness-raising and transformation by political action.

The concept of empowerment is slowly taking root in different cultures. Various models have been developed. Stromquist (1990) has explained empowerment as a process in which consciousness-raising and action have been combined so that individuals not only understand their society and their current place in it but are also encouraged to undertake efforts to modify social relations which affect gender. Education is identified as the most powerful facilitator of change. Stromquist particularly stresses the role of literacy as a crucial force in individual and social change. Kan Feng Ming (1994) emphasizes the importance of formal education for women in Hong Kong and China. She argues that formal education has traditionally been used as a powerful instrument to maintain women's subordination in terms of gender disparities in access to education, teachers' attitudes towards pupils, and educational materials which reflect traditional stereotypes. Socialization through traditional education within a patriarchal society strengthens patriarchal attitudes and values that subjugate women. Nevertheless, knowledge equips educated women with the power and confidence to look critically at women's subordination. The strength of formal education therefore lies in its ultimate effect. Educated women are able to challenge gender-imposed inequality if they want to.

Many different definitions of empowerment exist, reflected in various theories. Although Western writers tend to focus on empowerment as a women's issue, an Asian workshop on women and education held in 1993 argued that empowerment is a process which should target both women and men (Garnier forthcoming). Workshop participants argued that empowerment of women involves social change that both women and men should initiate. It is not practical to expect structural changes in the social conditions of women if men have not been involved in the process from the start. Policies aimed at improving access to education for women should focus on both women and men.

Gender and popular education

The term popular education describes the education for social change approach which emerged in Brazil in the 1960s. Its ideas and methods have been used at the grassroots level in other countries throughout the world. It challenges the way people are taught in schools, which silences them and makes them conform, and questions schooling that is part of an oppressive political, social and economic system. Popular education aims to empower and raise consciousness, and change the oppressive social structures. In a participatory process, people look critically at power relations and are supported in organizing to change their situation. The women's movement worldwide has used popular education practices to understand and challenge unequal gender relations.

The role of gender training

Gender training is an important strategy for changing the approach to gender of organizations and institutions; it has become increasingly popular since the mid-1980s. Such training is either organized around the broad issue of gender and development or around particular issues, like reproductive health, violence or the environment. Experiences with gender training exhibit a wide variety of approaches, objectives, underlying assumptions and differences in the extent to which the professional, political or personal dimension is addressed. Different approaches reflect ways of thinking about gender and development, ranging from concern about the efficiency of development efforts to analysis of institutions from the perspective of feminist theories and analysis, or creating a package of planning tools for integrating a gender perspective. Women's empowerment as a strategy for change is often located at the centre of feminist gender training programmes, formulating goals of empowerment 'to challenge subordination and oppression and to transform the structures, systems and institutions which support inequality' (Batliwala 1993). This diversity of means and ends has clear implications for the extent to which gender training can influence and support transformations required in the educational system to improve women's access, enrolment and performance, alleviate basic societal constraints and change oppressive gender relations.

Lack of transformative education

The factors affecting girl's participation in education mentioned above are also reflected in a study undertaken in Tanzania (Mbilinyi 1991). This critically reviewed and assessed the available knowledge on women in the educational system, specifically primary, secondary, adult, vocational and technical education, and indicated implications for policy support. The educational system is seen to have failed to bring about transformative education. Gender discrimination and differentiation persist at all levels, despite government efforts to promote equity in its social policies. A 'macho' school environment, authoritarian learning and teaching methods, and lack of progressive content in educational materials and programmes reinforce gender stereotyping. Recommendations include a range of measures to promote transformation of gender relations and strategic implementation, both within and outside the schooling system. Teacher rehabilitation is mentioned as a priority area, particularly the motivation and support of transformative teachers, with the adoption of new pedagogical and management skills and in-service training, including gender sensitization and the creation of teacher associations.

Examples of the use of gender training to motivate the efforts of key, transformative teachers are not widely documented. Gender and popular education workshops at the Centre for Adult Education (CACE), University of the Western Cape, South Africa, have however aimed to support the work of community, adult and popular educators who are developing ideas that challenge women's oppression (Mackenzie 1993). Educators have worked in different contexts with different groups, challenging violence against women, developing literacy materials and examining racism.

The methodology followed during CACE's gender training is described below, based on the experiences of three workshops for adult educators in health, church, community, service and trade union organizations. Two workshops for five and three days, respectively, were for women only; a one-day event was designed to include men but very few attended.

Workshop approach to challenge women's oppression

The workshops are based on learners' concerns, examining unequal power relations in society, encouraging everyone to learn and to teach, involving high levels of participation, and including people's emotions, actions, intellects and creativity. Structured exercises help a group focus on an issue by including these different aspects. The workshops follow a 'learning spiral', starting with people's own experiences and moving from experience to analysis. The analysis is designed to encourage collective action to change oppressive systems and reflects and evaluates its own process. Using this approach, the unequal power relations of gender and the relationships between gender and race, class, and culture are examined. Creating and maintaining an atmosphere of learning is built in by giving information beforehand, introducing people, setting group rules to help create a safe space where people can trust each other, and using varied activities that encourage everyone to participate. Small group sessions are used to share personal experiences. Group and local cultural activities, such as songs and dances, are included.

Shared leadership is another important aspect of the approach, in which all participants take responsibility for what happens in the group, respecting everyone's experience. The coordination of this process must be sensitively handled as group dynamics are complex and affect people's feelings and ability to participate. Facilitators work as a team and have developed common understandings and approaches. Their main task is to ensure that the group achieves its aims and to encourage active participation. Active involvement of the group is encouraged by asking volunteers to take on different roles (observers, summarizer, time-keepers).

The incorporation of gender in popular educational methodologies, the experimental nature, targeting both the personal and the organizational, and drawing from participants' own experiences of gender oppression, lead to a deeper understanding and ongoing action: participants organize themselves after the workshop to take further action. The experiences with this training approach provide valuable strategies to challenge and change practice in the educational system.

Case studies of educational projects

Three different education projects are described below which have been initiated with the purpose of contributing to the process of empowerment. Although different approaches are followed, all three consider participation and consciousness-raising as their main objectives. All three projects are examples of non-formal education projects. The first two focus on adult women, while the third is meant for girls but has responded to the learning needs of the parents as well. In addition, the projects illustrate why education must be viewed as a primary means of empowerment of people and not merely a tool to promote increases in literacy or economic growth.

Case one: training as a medium in the process of social change in India
ASHTA, a voluntary organization in southern Rajasthan, India, aims to raise awareness among women's groups. Training programmes are used to make women aware of their resources and develop organizational skills through training programmes, which are seen as an important instrument of change and development. Most of the participants are illiterate. They are actively involved in the planning of the programme, while demonstrations, exercises and role-play are used as training methods to develop communication, problem solving and planning skills. The training is based on an analysis of the society and the role of women in that particular society. This type of training has been successful because the women are eager to learn and like the methods used. The following incident illustrates the empowering effect of training: women were informed about the existence of a minimum wage and became aware that less than half the minimum wage was paid for daily work in their local area. Women participants organized other women and initiated a demonstration. They showed the workplace to local officials. Through this, women were able to force their employers to pay higher wages. Men were also beneficiaries of this process and from then on they started encouraging their wives, mothers and sisters to attend meetings (Society for Participatory Research in Asia 1989).

Case two: empowering community techniques
ActionAid, a UK-based NGO, has recently introduced the Participatory Rural Appraisal methodology into adult literacy programmes in Bangladesh, El Salvador and Uganda. Facilitators of this methodology develop a wide range of techniques for structuring and focusing discussions whereby communities are encouraged to use local materials to construct maps, calendars, matrices and diagrams based on their reality. The introduction of the written word can then take place in a way that will facilitate recognition. As learners become more confident using their symbol-cards to construct maps and charts, they are able to explore local issues more systematically and thus collectively generate their own curriculum materials. These self-made teaching materials help them analyse and systematize their knowledge and effectively communicate their needs to development workers from outside the community. Each community uses these techniques to develop their own analyses and set their own agenda. Learning skills are meant to help in the process of securing and sustaining change. Literacy and other elements of the local development process are more closely linked than in conventional literacy programmes.

Case three: community schools for girls
Local NGOs, supported by donors, have introduced community schools for girls in rural areas of North West Frontier Province (NWFP), Pakistan. These types of schools were originally successful in Baluchistan and were introduced to NWFP as the next pilot area. Although the political, socio-economic and cultural conditions were not

the same, the concept remained unchanged. Lack of appropriate school buildings within safe walking distance and the absence of female teachers at formal schools were the main reasons that parents kept their daughters at home. Community educators of local NGOs argued that the active participation of the parents was required because parents can play a significant role in reducing the drop-out rate, improving educational quality and efficiency, and maintaining school facilities. For this, they need to be informed and actively assisted by the educational system. Parents and NGOs were involved in the appointment of female teachers. Parents were also held responsible for providing land for the original school building. Several project visits to community schools found that the schools were mainly situated in the female teachers' compound (Yates and Jongepier 1994). This had the advantage that schools were located within the community boundaries. The local teacher was a trusted member of the community, contributing to parents' willingness to send their daughters to school. Parents were held responsible for the establishment of village education committees to monitor the school. Some of the female teachers have also started adult education classes for mothers, teaching them basic skills. The government has been requested to participate in the community schools by supporting training for the teachers, paying their salaries and supplying instructional materials. However, in contrast to Baluchistan, donors have taken over for this responsibility in NWFP. Nevertheless, the government has recently announced its commitment towards this programme.

Meanwhile, community schools are gaining in popularity. A number of schools have been established, enrolment rates among girls in these areas have increased, and the drop-out rate among girls has been reduced. The positive achievements of community schools have been observed by formal schools, which are learning from their experience.

These three projects show that increasing participation and contributing to awareness-raising, simultaneously remove obstacles that impede women's education. To achieve this, the following concrete measures have been taken: education has been brought closer to the communities, both literally and figuratively; female teachers have been attracted, thus reducing parents' concerns about their daughters' morality and safety; curricula have been developed in accordance with community needs with local materials being used for constructing educational materials; elements of social mobilization and advocacy have also been integrated to raise awareness and generate action; and the active participation of the community has been stimulated in all the projects.

Participation has many faces

The three examples show how participation in education can be approached in different ways. Levels of participation differ, reflecting the situation in the field. White et al. (1994) use figurative language to explain the concept of 'participation'. They explain that participation is kaleidoscopic: it changes shape easily. Numerous definitions of participation can be found and participation differs in context, type, level of intensity, extent and frequency. Deshler and Sock (1985) distinguish two levels of participation: 'pseudo participation' in which participants are viewed as subjects who only have to listen to what has been planned for them and 'genuine participation', which refers to partnership and delegation of power.

Lessons from experience

Since McNamara introduced people's participation as the new strategy of the World Bank in 1973, this concept has attained a central place in the jargon of development planners and policy planners. Community participation has had a limited impact on development assistance because there has been only limited delegation of power and responsibilities. Donors' interpretations of the concept of participation has meant that community participation has often been restricted to pseudo participation. In education, for example, this has involved donors reminding parents of their duties in educating their children. The increasing requirement for parental contributions towards education either in labour or in cash is now legitimized by the idea of 'community participation'.

Recently, the importance of involvement in decision-making at the grassroots level seems to be permeating other areas. Under the guise of participation, NGOs and women's groups were explicitly invited to the International Conference on Population and Development, held in Cairo during 1994. However, NGOs and women's groups were situated in a different building than the government officials. Only a few accredited NGOs had access to the official part of the conference. The NGOs and women's groups had limited opportunities for public comment or for influencing the decision-making. The involvement of NGOs and women's groups at international conferences is extremely important, even if they are only permitted such pseudo participation. In Cairo, media attention and mutual discussions between NGOs from all over the world have contributed to the exchange of useful information.

Education for All, especially for those groups of people previously left out, was an important social issue at the Cairo Conference. Government officials considered that education deserves more attention in the future. Participants agreed that education is invaluable for the propagation of information and awareness on the major issues and concerns affecting women. Nevertheless, no serious efforts or plans were made to implement educational policies. The same situation occurred at the Social Summit in Copenhagen. Education for the empowerment of women and girls as an intrinsic component of social policy was regarded as an essential feature of the action plan of the Copenhagen Summit but these promises were not followed by commitment to action. It remains to be seen whether the Fourth World Conference on Women, held in September 1995, will be able to transform its commitment to education into concrete actions and policies.

Bibliography

'Alphabétisation: clé du développement'. *Famille et Développement*, no. 62 (1992), pp. 5-20.

Bray, M., P.B. Clarke and D. Stephens, *Education and society in Africa*. London, Edward Arnold, 1986.

Batliwala, S., 'Women's empowerment: towards a conceptual framework'. In: S. Batliwala (ed.), *Empowerment of women in South Asia: concepts and practices*. 1993, pp. 7-13.

Buvinic, M., 'Women's issues in Third World poverty; a policy analysis'. In: M. Buvinic, M. Lycette and W. McReevey (ed.), *Women and poverty in the Third World*. Baltimore, Johns Hopkins University Press, 1983, pp. 14-31.

Cammish, N. K., 'Island daughters; factors affecting the education of girls in Vanuatu'. *Journal of Comparative Education*, vol. 24, no. 2 (1994), pp. 139-156.

Colclough, C., 'Under enrolment and low quality in African primary schooling; towards a gender sensitive solution'. Unpublished paper, 1994.

Cookson, P.W. Jr., A.R. Sadovnik and S.F. Semel, *International handbook of educational reform*. New York, Greenwood Press, 1992.

Deshler, D. and D. Sock, 'Community development participation: a concept review of the International Literature'. An unpublished paper presented at the International League for Social Commitment in Adult Education, Ljungskile, Sweden.

Garnier, B., Empower women through education. Report of World University Service Asia Workshop, May 1993. Bangkok, World University Service, (Forthcoming).

Helleman, C., 'Education for women's development?' *Vena Journal*, vol. 4, no. 1 (1992), pp. 2-5.

Jongepier, M., 'Population education: a key for conscious choice.' Paper presented at the Cairo International Conference on Population and Development, 1994. Unpublished.

Kan Feng Ming, *Empowering women through formal education*. The Hague, Centre for the Study of Education in Developing Countries, 1994.

King, E. M. and M.A. Hill (ed.), *Women's education in developing countries: barriers, benefits and policies*. Baltimore, Johns Hopkins University Press, 1993.

Kurian, R., 'International economic changes and their effect on women'. Note written as a contribution to the Dutch Working Group for the Fourth World Conference on Women. Unpublished paper, 1994.

Mackenzie, L., *On our foot: taking steps to challenge women's oppression: a handbook on gender and popular education workshops*. Bellville, Centre for Adult Continuing Education, University of the Western Cape, 1993.

Maimbolwa-Sinyangwe, I. M., 'Factors influencing the education of girls in Zambia'. Paper presented at the conference on Quality of Education in the context of Culture in Developing Countries, 13-15 January 1994, Lapinniemi Conference Centre, Tampere Finland, Zambia Educational Research Network School of Education, University of Zambia. Unpublished paper, 1994.

Mbilinyi, M., *Education in Tanzania with a gender perspective: summary report.* Stockholm, Swedish International Development Agency, 1991.

Moser, C.O.N., *Gender planning and development.* London, Routledge, 1993.

Naik, C., *Education for All summit of nine high population countries.* New Delhi, UNESCO, 1993.

Rood, R. van 't and M.E. Jongepier, 'A school is not just a building: research on the rehabilitation of education in Soroti Catholic Diocese'. Research report for CEBEMO/SOCADIDO. Unpublished paper, 1994.

Society for Participatory Research in Asia, *Participatory training for women.* New Delhi, 1989.

Stromquist, N. 'Women's education in development: from welfare to empowerment'. *INNOTECH Journal*, vol. 14, no. 1 (1990), pp. 78-84.

Summers, L.H., 'Investing in all the people: educating women in developing countries'. Paper prepared for a Development Economic Seminar at the 1992 World Bank annual meetings. Washington, World Bank, 1992.

White, S., K. Nair and J. Ashcroft, *Participatory communication: working for change and development.* New Delhi, Sage Publications, 1994.

Yates, R. and M.E. Jongepier, 'Report on an ODA/DGIS appraisal mission on community participation within the North West Frontier Province Primary Education Programme'. Unpublished paper, 1994.

Annotated bibliography

Education and training

069   Major constraints to women's access to higher education in Africa
ALELE WILLIAMS, GRACE *In: Higher education in Africa : trends and challenges for the 21st century* Dakar Regional Office. - Dakar : UNESCO, 1992 p.71-76 [EN]

Factors militating against the participation of girls and women in higher education in Africa can be divided into cultural, religious, sociological, economic and educational factors, and government policy. These factors are discussed, including the productive role of girls and women in households, the attitudes of parents towards the education of girls, and the relevance of the curriculum. It is argued that some of the factors may be offset by clear and positive government statements. Other suggestions to increase the number of females in pre-tertiary educational institutions are the creation of well-defined guidance and counselling units in schools, and the introduction of adult and job training for young mothers. The role of the government in providing an environment that positively affects the participation of girls and women in both pre-tertiary and tertiary education is also considered.

KIT, Amsterdam   [U 94-155]

070   Women, literacy and development : challenges for the 21st century
BHASIN, KAMLA - *Convergence* 27(1994)4. ICAE, Toronto 82 p. [EN] ill., tabs. Includes lit.refs ISSN 0010-8146

Some of the papers presented at the fifth assembly of the International Council for Adult Education on 'Women, literacy and development: challenges for the 21st Century', held in Egypt during September 1994, are contained in this special issue. A list of papers and workshops is also included, together with declarations, statements and proposals. Following a general introduction to the relationship between women, education and development, explanations for the high levels of illiteracy among women and girls are provided from the perspective of literacy workers. Literacy initiatives should go beyond

mere improvement of women's literacy status towards a structural transformation of women's position and condition in society. A case study of female literacy in Pakistan illustrates the impediments to participation in adult education. A further study addresses issues facing adult educators and trainers in dealing with the delivery of adult basic education and training in South Africa. The role of NGOs in Egypt, Caritas Egypt in particular, in the provision of literacy and education services is explored. Some 12 actions are proposed to achieve the global objective of literacy for all by providing, developing and improving basic education among children, youth and adults.

KIT, Amsterdam   [H 1967-27(1994)4]

071   State, status and the status quo : factors affecting the education of girls in Cameroon
CAMMISH, NADINE K.; BROCK, COLIN - *International Journal of Educational Development* 14(1994)3 p.233-240 [EN] ill., tabs 15 lit.refs ISSN 0738-0593

The underlying causes of low participation of girls in education in Cameroon is examined, based partly on a survey of 320 primary pupils in schools throughout the country. Although only slightly more boys than girls are enroled at 6-14 years of age, at 15-19 years there are twice as many boys as girls, and at 20-24 years there are six times as many boys. Girls' educational opportunities appear to be affected by regional indigenous cultural differences, disparity between urban and rural areas, and the colonial legacy. Socio-cultural attitudes and traditions determining the status of women and girls preserve the status quo as far as girls' education is concerned. The economic factor, in terms of the opportunity cost of sending girls to school, was reported as the most important factor affecting female participation in education. Factors within the actual education system and the schools themselves, including school fees, are also identified. At the national level, girls' participation in education is being supported through laws, planning and policies. Committed leadership from district education officers, local

politicians and religious leaders is required if the traditional status of women and girls and the status quo in girls' education are to be changed.
KIT, Amsterdam [E 3273-14(1994)3]

072   Reading the word and the world : literacy and education from a gender perspective
CLAESSEN, JEANNETTE; WESEMAEL-SMIT, LILIAN VAN. Vrouwenberaad Ontwikkelingssamenwerking, Oegstgeest 173 p. 1992 [EN] ill., graphs, maps, tabs. Includes lit.refs ISBN 90-800281-6-9
This book comprises proceedings of the seminar 'Reading the word and the world: literacy and education from a gender perspective', held in Ede, the Netherlands, in 1991. The relationship between women, literacy and empowerment was addressed. Empowerment of women can be seen as a process by which women acquire the knowledge, tools and techniques to be able to transform their lives and the wider society. Within this process, transformation of the existing power relations is considered crucial. The importance of working on literacy from a gender perspective, and the scope and restrictions in practice were discussed. Methods were recommended to stimulate women's empowerment through literacy programmes or programmes with a literacy component. The papers address approaches and strategies for empowering women through literacy and education in Bangladesh, India, Peru, South Africa; discuss the relationship between income generation and literacy; and examine post-literacy programmes in Latin America. The report concludes with practical information, including guidelines for development programmes and women's non-formal education which emerged from a conference on non-formal education for women, and a checklist on women, education and development which was developed by the Dutch Ministry of Foreign Affairs. A major lesson is that the involvement of women in the preparation and execution of the programmes is a prerequisite.
KIT, Amsterdam [P 92-4518]

073   The politics of women's education : perspectives from Asia, Africa, and Latin America
CONWAY, JILL KER; BOURQUE, SUSAN C. University of Michigan Press, Ann Arbor, MI viii, 261 p. 1993 [EN] ill., graphs, tabs. Includes lit.refs ISBN 0-472-10446-2
This book comprises 16 papers concerned with education as a means to improve women's social and economic status in selected countries of Africa, Asia and Latin America. The cultural and historical differences between countries are reflected in varying levels of economic growth, literacy, and educational access. Furthermore, class, ethnic, religious and regional differences

make the experiences of women in any single country unique. All the chapters share an appreciation of the importance of educational institutions. Tension between formal and non-formal educational systems is also addressed. On the positive side, access to university has led to the mobilization of elite women and their commitment to reform. Similarly, for women of limited resources, access to both formal and non-formal education has been linked to an increased sense of self-esteem and empowerment. There is a need to come to terms with the relationship between the educational system and the development model developed by the national political elites. Some papers stress the failure of economic development models adopted in the past and the need for a new concept of development which is not tied to economic growth.
KIT, Amsterdam [N 94-607]

074   Tools for the field : methodologies handbook for gender analysis in agriculture
FELDSTEIN, HILARY SIMS; JIGGINS, JANICE - *Kumarian Press Library of Management for Development*. Kumarian, Westport, CT xvi, 270 p. 1994 [EN] ill., graphs, tabs. Includes lit.refs, index ISBN 1-56549-028-2
This book offers a practical set of research tools and methodologies for gender analysis in agriculture. It provides examples of how to use such methodologies for collecting gender-sensitive data. Under the influence of farming systems research and extension, these methodologies have been designed to examine small farm dynamics and identify gender differences to be taken into account during interventions in small farm households. They consider small farm dynamics in the light of the understanding that small farms are not cohesive decision-making units but rather demonstrate complex interaction between the individual interests of male and female household members. Some 39 case studies from Africa, Asia and Latin America illustrate a range of techniques from making gender-sensitive interview guides to ensuring that participatory rural appraisal methodologies include a gender-perspective. Topics covered include: learning about the farming system and initial diagnosis; research planning, on-farm experimentation and assessment of trials; continuous diagnosis and special studies; and extension, training and institutionalization. Understanding gender differences is important in helping science shape improved technologies to meet the needs and fit the circumstances of small farm households.
KIT, Amsterdam [N 94-1282]

075   Functional literacy and civic education among rural women

Asia-Pacific Programme of Education for All (APPEAL). UNESCO. Principal Regional Office for Asia and the Pacific, Bangkok 42 p. 1990 [EN] ill., tabs. Includes lit.refs

Based on experiences exchanged and strategies suggested at a workshop on functional literacy and civic education for women in Asia, the situation of women, functional literacy programmes and civic education efforts are reviewed. The following sets of problems were found to impede women's empowerment: individual and family-related problems; community-level problems; socio-political and cultural problems; and economic problems. Rural women generally have little or no formal schooling which deprives them of the usual channel for civic education which is an inherent part of formal schooling. An overview of adult literacy and civic education programmes in the region reveals that planning of education programmes is mostly centralized and therefore area-specific; need-specific programmes for women are rarely implemented. The curriculum seems irrelevant to the needs of women and there is very little flexibility at the grassroots to change or modify the programme according to the needs of the learners. Activities to tackle the problems related to functional literacy and civic education for women are proposed, such as innovative educational materials and delivery methods. Overall strategies, policies and plans that will enhance women's access to and participation in education are suggested, including mobilizing the community to promote the education of girls and women, and making elementary education for girls universal.

KIT, Amsterdam   [U 91-225]

076   Girl's and women's education, women's empowerment and population issues

UNESCO - *Population Education in Asia and the Pacific Newsletter and Forum* (1994)40 p.22-23 [EN]

Women's right to education is a basic human right. It is perhaps the most important means of empowering women to exercise their rights in society and at home. The UNFPA advocates more and better basic education, particularly for women, and has identified benefits and constraints in educational development. The social and economic benefits of educating girls and women comprise: a smaller family size and reduced child mortality (educating girls is three times more likely to lower family size than educating boys); improvement of the quality of life and family health (educated women are more likely to pursue sound hygienic and nutritional practices); and a greater economic productivity

and improved earning capacity. The most important barriers to female education include cultures and traditions that perpetuate gender stereotypes, the opportunity costs of educating girls, the location of schools, and the poor quality of education. Consequently, six recommendations are made: schools should be located closer to the community, and community and parent involvement with the school should be increased; costs of educating girls should be lowered as an incentive to parents; advocacy and social mobilization must be promoted; schools and programmes should be designed to meet the needs of girl students; relevant curricula should be developed; and efforts should be undertaken to meet the needs of illiterate adult women and girls and of women who have dropped out of formal schooling.

KIT, Amsterdam   [K 1506-(1994)40]

077   By and for women : involving women in the development of reproductive health care materials

IBRAHIM, BARBARA; HULL, VALERIE - *Quality/Calidad/Qualité* 4. Population Council, New York, NY 28 p. 1992 [EN] ill. With French and Spanish summary ISBN 0-87834-057-2

Women's participation in the development of reproductive health care information materials is discussed. Three case studies describe different approaches: (1) a women's health collective produced a comprehensive reference book for women in Cairo, Egypt; (2) a women's group in Peru, with the extensive involvement of their illiterate audience, developed a series of illustrated teaching materials; and (3) an all-women production crew in the South Pacific produced three motivation and teaching videos, developed in response to the expressed needs of Pacific Island women. The projects demonstrate that there is no standard pattern for success in developing appropriate material and that only general recommendations can be made.

KIT, Amsterdam   [D 2924-(1992)4]

078   Triple roles, gender roles, social relations : the political sub-text of gender training

KABEER, NAILA - *Discussion Paper / IDS, University of Sussex* 313. IDS, Brighton BN1 9RE. 45 p. 1992 [EN] Includes lit.refs ISSN 0308-5864 ISBN 0-903715-94-5

The inability of past policies to take women's needs and interests into account has generated a body of knowledge from which to shape better practice in the future. One means by which these lessons are disseminated is gender training and there is a proliferation of methodologies with which this is being carried out. Most gender training initiatives share a common objective in challenging biases in the planning process by alerting planners to gender divisions in resources and responsibilities, but vary in terms of their world view and their visions of gender equity. Three different training frameworks are examined to show how differences in their implicit world views affect their treatment of efficiency and equity issues: the triple roles framework (TRF), the gender roles framework (GRF) and the social relations analysis (SRA). All three frameworks consider the household division of labour. The TRF offers a gender planning methodology which addresses women's needs, while the GRF aims at merely 'grafting' gender onto existing planning methods. The SRA seeks to explore the planning process itself as a site of gender politics. The TRF and SRA have a common understanding of gender as a product of social-structural, rather than individually determined,inequalities and offer similar guidelines for transformatory strategies. Where they differ is in the importance given to men and women outside the planning institutions as agents in the planning process. Women and men in households, markets and communities manage their lives and the development process in ways which reflect their felt needs and perceived interests. However, these needs and interests may not necessarily be shared by bureaucracies which are organized around different goals and reflect different institutional imperatives. SRA sees the issue of strategic gender interests as an issue of politics rather than of better information (GRF) or more enlightened planning (TRF).

KIT, Amsterdam   [E 2206-(1992)313]

079   Gender, development, and training : raising awareness in the planning process
KABEER, NAILA IDS, Brighton BN1 9RE - *Development in Practice* 1(1991)3 p.185-195 [EN] 10 lit.refs ISSN 0961-4524

Several decades of development experience have yielded a wealth of findings about the key assumptions, procedures, and practices by which women have been marginalized in development planning. Ways in which women have been kept out of development are discussed, including the use of abstract and aggregative concepts of the poor, the household, and women, which neglect to differentiate internal categories of people and thereby have helped to render women invisible; and shortcomings in data collection which are responsible for underestimating women's productive activities. An alternative approach to development, development with a gender perspective, is proposed which will: (1) distinguish between 'biological' sex and socially-constructed gender; (2) examine and analyse the different relations and processes which construct gender in different cultures; (3) focus on the gender division of labour; (4) rethink the meaning of production in the light of analysis of the gender

division of labour; and (5) focus on strategies for empowerment. It is concluded that the aim of gender planning should be to move away from the abstract and aggregated concepts of development that planners have worked with in the past, and to work towards a more holistic understanding of development. This requires an awareness of the human and gender implications of all forms of policy intervention which is informed by the multiple linkages between production and reproduction, and between the creation of material resources and human resources; gives as much weight to process (how things get done) as to outcome (what gets done); and, finally, recognizes that gender equity in social transformation requires the empowerment of women and alliances with men if it is to be a sustainable achievement.

KIT, Amsterdam   [D 2672-1(1991)3]

080   Gender in development
KAMARA, SIAPHA; DENKABE, ALOYSIUS - *Handbook on Participatory Approach to Training* 2. Freedom, Accra, Ghana xiii, 35 p. 1993 [EN] ill., graphs, tabs. Includes lit.refs ISBN 9964-91-594-2

A participatory training approach to gender in development is presented, based on the participatory experiences of the joint Canadian University Services Overseas and Committee on Churches Participation in Development training programme for NGOs in northern Ghana. This programme, initiated in 1988, was intended to improve the skills of NGO personnel (managers, technical officers and technical assistants) in project planning and management, agricultural extension and gender in development. Following an introduction to the principles of participation in training and development, the steps taken to involve the trainees in the training process, to organize a participatory training programme, and to include basic concepts on gender in development are discussed. Analysis of gender roles and responsibilities of farm family members is detailed, together with ways of designing gender-sensitive agricultural extension.

KIT, Amsterdam   [Br N 94-320]

081   Women in development : training experiences in sub-Saharan Africa
KERENGE, APOLLONIA - *Cahiers de l'IPD/PAID Reports* 14. PAID-GS, Douala, Cameroon 98 p. 1992 [EN] ill., graphs, maps, tabs. Includes lit.refs ISSN 0256-4912

Experiences of the Pan African Institute for Development, West Africa (PAID-WA) with in-service training for male and female development staff on the subject of 'women and development' are evaluated. The focus is on the way in which the institute has introduced a women and development module into the training curriculum for its 9-month diploma course on

Integrated Rural Development and into a series of shorter courses on selected issues. The experiences from field studies carried out as part of the institute's training courses are also evaluated. The evaluation suggests that PAID-WA has made progress with the integration of women and development in its training courses. The course module is appreciated and relevant for African women and men who participate in the courses. It is concluded that more research on women and gender issues is needed to obtain an understanding of the barriers to women's advancement. There is a need to conduct in-house seminars and workshops to sensitize PAID staff, whose perception of women and gender has been shaped by stereotyped culture and traditions. Furthermore, the number of female faculty members needs to be increased, not only in predominantly female professions but in all other disciplines where possible. Another major concern of PAID, as well as of other development agencies, is the challenge to change the current system of values, beliefs and attitudes which is a major constraint to an effective integration of women in the development process.

KIT, Amsterdam   [A 2621-(1992)14]

082   Gender awareness and planning manual for training of trainers, project planners and implementors in the cooperative sector
KERSTAN, BIRGIT; AGUSNI, SULIKANTI; PARIS, YULIANI; ADELSTAL, BERNT. ILO. Cooperative Project, Jakarta xi, 144 p. 1993 [EN] ill., tabs ISBN 92-2-109144-9

This manual on gender awareness for training of trainers, project planners and project staff in the cooperative sector was tested in West Sumatra, West Java and South Sulawesi, Indonesia. The workshop should enable participants to formulate strategies to enhance women's participation in the cooperative sector in accordance with national policy. The course consists of 6 sessions: (1) introduction to the workshop; (2) gender awareness in the cooperative sector; (3) gender analysis; (4) planning for action; (5) adapting gender awareness training materials for further training; and (6) the workshop evaluation. The sessions provide information about learning objectives, duration and proposed methods and materials. The worksheets contain strategic definitions, tools and media related to the gender analysis method, and describe the tasks of working groups during the workshop. The manual should be regarded as a source of ideas rather than a definite lesson plan.

KIT, Amsterdam   [U 94-274]

083   Women's education in developing countries : barriers, benefits, and policies
KING, ELIZABETH M.; HILL, M. ANNE. Johns Hopkins University Press : publ. for World Bank, Baltimore, MD xiii, 337 p. 1993 [EN] ill., graphs, tabs. Includes index, lit.refs ISBN 0-8018-4534-3

Despite the great expansion of educational opportunities worldwide during the past 30 years, women still receive less schooling than men. Based on extensive data for 152 developing countries, a review is provided of the level of female education and the gender gap in education. Analysis of the economic and social rates of return to women's education reveals that greater investments in the primary and secondary education of women are warranted on economic grounds. The current status of women's education and factors influencing the schooling of girls and women in sub-Saharan Africa, the Middle East and North Africa, Latin America and the Caribbean, and South and East Asia are addressed. The regional overviews illustrate the diversity of cultures, institutions and economic conditions that result in distinct barriers to the education of women. Despite clear regional differences in cultures and institutions, striking commonalities in the factors influencing women's educational attainment are also indicated at the level of the family and home, the school and the community, including parents' education and the perceptions of teachers. Various policy interventions intended to raise women's educational attainment are analysed. Examples of past and current education programmes are reviewed to demonstrate what types of schemes have been effective. It is suggested that educating girls can help break the cycle of female deprivation. Increased schooling has similar impacts on the incomes of women and men, but educating girls generates much larger social benefits. Interventions that have been effectively used to stimulate the participation of girls in education include the provision of monetary incentives to parents and the availability of female teachers.

KIT, Amsterdam   [U 93-373]

084   Getting down to business : a manual for training businesswomen
KRAUS-HARPER, USCHI; HARPER, MALCOLM. Intermediate Technology, London vii, 166 p. 1992 [EN] ill., tabs. Includes lit.refs ISBN 1-85339-113-1

Many women in developing countries are generating income for the family and society through self-employment and businesses of various kinds. Such women are not full-time entrepreneurs because of the many other demands on their time and energy, but experiences everywhere show that they repay loans more reliably and spend their earnings more responsibly than most businessmen. The contribution of these enterprising women is increasingly being recognized and many institutions are organizing training programmes which address the special problems and opportunities which face women in business. This manual is designed to assist trainers to organize and conduct more effective training courses for women in business. It provides detailed guidelines for a full course of 29 sessions, which can also be used on their own or as components of the programme, together with suggestions as to how the hand-outs, case studies and other exercises can be adapted to local circumstances. Material is also included on the special training of businesswomen, on recruitment and selection of participants, and on how to evaluate the training. The course includes preparation and design of both business plans and business records. The examples primarily refer to the tailor and garment business, addressing all the special problems and opportunities encountered by women in business.

KIT, Amsterdam [N 94-264]

085   Promoting women's participation in teaching research and management in African universities

LAMPTEY, ALICE SENA In: Higher education in Africa : trends and challenges for the 21st century Dakar Regional Office. - Dakar : UNESCO, 1992 p.77-92 [EN] ill., graphs 10 lit.refs

During 1975-1982 female tertiary student enrolment grew at an average annual rate of more than 10% but women still only accounted for 27.3% of total student enrolment. Despite this recent improvement, female participation rates in higher education in Africa continue to be the lowest in the world. Factors contributing to this situation are identified, including high drop-out rates, sex role differentiation, and family and domestic responsibilities. Many women express a feeling of ambivalence towards advancing themselves professionally because this may have negative consequences, such as unpopularity and loss of femininity, and lead to unsuccessful relationships with less chance of finding a life partner. Stereotypes about the unsuitability of women as managers also constrain female participation in university management. Promotion of women's participation in higher education should include awareness creation among women, re-orienting attitudes of male counterparts, changing the attitudes of parents, and the design of government policies that provide an enabling environment. Studies should be conducted on the gender distribution of professional positions in African tertiary educational institutions, and recommendations should be formulated for the individual countries of the region.

KIT, Amsterdam [U 94-155]

086   Femmes, alphabétisation et développement : défis pour le 21e siècle = Mujeres, alfabetización y desarrollo : desafíos para el siglo XXI = Women, literacy and development : challenges for the 21st century

LIMAGE, LESLIE - Convergence 27 (1994)2-3. International Council for Adult Education, Toronto 208 p. 1994 [EN, FR, ES, AR] Includes lit.refs ISSN 0010-8146

Case studies from Bangladesh, Iran, Nepal, Poland and South Africa illustrate different literacy and post-literacy programmes, Islamic education, women's access to education and employment, and social development. They discuss the situation of women in these societies and the gender-related inequalities and political, social, cultural and religious practices obstructing women's access to education, employment and equal opportunities. Challenges and strategies for the 21st Century are identified.

KIT, Amsterdam [H 1967-27(1994)2/3]

087   On our foot : taking steps to challenge women's oppression : a handbook on gender and popular education workshops

MACKENZIE, LIZ - Adult Education and Development (1993)41-Supplement. University of the Western Cape. Centre for Adult Continuing Education, Bellville 171 p. [EN] ill., maps. Includes lit.refs, glossary ISSN 0342-7633 ISBN 1-86808-108-7

This handbook constitutes the outcome of experiences gained by the Centre for Adult and Continuing Education (CACE), University of the Western Cape, South Africa, in running workshops on women's oppression and popular education in 1990 and 1991. The workshops were part of an ongoing project on gender and popular education at CACE. The project aims to develop methods of education which help people to challenge the gender bias in organizations and educational programmes. This handbook can be used as a guide for organizing and running a workshop on gender and women's oppression. In addition to introducing popular education and its main principles, the handbook provides: examples of where and how women's oppression happens around the world; introduces popular education and its main principles; suggests practical ideas and worksheets to plan for and design a workshop; suggests ideas and guidelines to facilitate the workshop; provides background information on group building and exercises that can be used in a workshop; and gives instructions for activities to use in a workshop, including exercises that will help the group examine gender and its relationship with other oppressive social systems.

KIT, Amsterdam [E 3125-(1993)41 suppl.]

088   Women leading from strength : a forum organized by the AAAS sub-Saharan Africa Program, Washington, DC, May 18, 1993
MAKHUBU, LYDIA P. - *Science in Africa*. American Association for the Advancement of Science, Washington, DC vi, 175 p. 1993 [EN] ill., graphs, tabs. Includes lit.refs

This book comprises the proceeding of the meeting on 'Science in Africa: women leading from strength' which was held in Washington DC, USA, during 1993. The potential contribution of women in building Africa's science and technology capacity was discussed. The significant under-representation of women in science and technology at the leadership and research levels deprives the continent of a substantial input. Although relevant aspects of girls' and women's primary and secondary education are considered, the emphasis is on women's participation in tertiary education, drawing on case studies from Ghana, Ivory Coast, Uganda and Zimbabwe. In spite of heavy investment in higher education, the number of students enroled in tertiary institutions in Africa is lower than that in other regions. Women are generally under-represented in higher education although a steady increase in female enrolment is observed. Further, the number of students graduating in science and science-based disciplines is much lower than in other disciplines, and is amongst the lowest of the world. The number of women graduating in these fields is much lower than that of men. These findings suggest a need to revitalize science and technology education in African higher education institutions, both at the undergraduate and the post-graduate level. Special attention should be paid to the development of post-graduate training in the sciences as a way of strengthening the institutions' production of science and technology manpower, and also as a means of providing greater opportunities for women to pursue advanced studies in science without jeopardizing their family commitments.
KIT, Amsterdam   [N 94-947]

089   Gender planning and development : theory, practice and training
MOSER, CAROLINE O.N. Routledge, London xii, 285 p. 1993 [EN] ill., tabs. Bibliogr.: p. 261-275. Includes index ISBN 0-415-05621-7

Gender planning is a new tradition whose goal is to ensure that women, by empowering themselves, achieve equality and equity with men in developing societies. Attaining this goal will vary widely in different contexts, depending on the extent to which women as a category are subordinated in status to men as a category. The relationship between gender and development is explored, and a comprehensive introduction to gender policy and planning practice in developing countries is provided. The conceptual rationale for a new planning tradition, based on gender roles and needs, is explored by examining feminist theories and the women-in-development and gender and development debates in terms of their relevance for gender planning. Fundamental misconceptions and assumptions which have caused development planners, even if inadvertently, to discriminate against or ignore women are identified. The different components of the planning process and the implementation of a gender planning process are described, including methodological and operational procedures. The role of training in creating gender awareness and sensitivity, providing practitioners with appropriate tools and techniques, is also addressed. The mixed experience of women's organizations and movements in developing countries in raising consciousness to confront women's subordination, and in creating alliances and linkages to ensure the success of planning processes is examined. Entry points for these organizations to negotiate for women's needs at household, civil society, state and global levels are highlighted. Practical gender planning exercises for trainers are included.
KIT, Amsterdam   [P 93-3364]

090   Training microentrepreneurs : does it pay?
NÜBLER, IRMGARD Institute for World Economics, Free University of Berlin, Altensteinstrasse 40, 1000 Berlin 33 - *Small Enterprise Development* 3(1992)4 p.34-44 [EN] ill., mainly tabs 2 lit.refs
ISSN 0957-1329

Women entrepreneurs have, among other constraints, very little access to management training. Mainstream training programmes tend to neglect women's specific needs whereas those programmes targeting only women mostly fail to offer business training. The Grassroot Management Training methodology has been developed to meet the entrepreneurship training needs of businesswomen in the informal sector. The training methodology involves a course of seminars covering a period of 5 days. The seminars last 4-5 hours per day so that the women can meet their multiple commitments. The effectiveness of training courses undertaken by the ILO during 1989-1990 in Ivory Coast, Kenya and Tanzania was evaluated. In each country, 40 businesswomen were selected from the programme's target group. Effectiveness was measured by a newly developed set of relevant, sensitive and practical indicators: reaction criteria, learning criteria, behavioural criteria and result criteria, while efficiency was determined by a modified cost-benefit approach. The results demonstrate that it is possible to measure the effects of even light interventions in the informal sector. Furthermore, there is evidence that basic management training seminars are effective and provide substantial benefits to the participants. In all countries, the benefits accrued to the participants exceed the costs. The ratios become even more favourable if benefits from additional employment are taken into account. Based on the findings, management seminars are found to be an effective as well as efficient type of assistance to promote businesswomen and small enterprises in the informal sector.

KIT, Amsterdam   [E 3166-3(1992)4]

091   Gender and development : a practical guide
ÖSTERGAARD, LISE. Routledge, London xiv, 220 p. 1992 [EN] Bibliogr.: p. 198-213. Includes index ISBN 0-415-07132-1

Gender relations, namely the social, economic, political and legal roles of men and women within a society, vary greatly from culture to culture and have a marked effect on how individuals behave and react to new ideas. It is argued that any project should be preceded and accompanied by a gender analysis which takes into account the needs and roles of females and males in the area where the project will be implemented. Gender relations and issues constraining women's advancement are assessed in various sectors. Constraints to agricultural production in sub-Saharan Africa include sexual stereotyping in development planning and policy at local, regional, national and international levels. The importance of gender in understanding patterns of employment is demonstrated by presenting sectoral trends and examining the nature of women's employment in India. Women workers earn consistently less than male workers and are found predominantly in manual, low-skilled and casual work, mostly employed in the informal sector which is beyond the reach of legislation. A case study of the roles of men and women in a Tiv farm household, Nigeria, illustrates problems that can arise when gender relations in intrahousehold resource management are not taken into account. To be adequately informed, planners need gender-disaggregated data, backed by microlevel studies with a gender perspective, to incorporate gender awareness into the administration and activities of donor agencies.

KIT, Amsterdam   [P 92-4493]

092   Another point of view : a manual on gender analysis training for grassroots workers
PARKER, A. RANI. United Nations Development Fund for Women (UNIFEM), New York, NY viii, 106 p. 1993 [EN] ill., tabs. Includes lit.refs

This manual on gender analysis training for grassroots workers has been developed in response to a stated need by a group of Middle Eastern development practitioners working in NGOs. It is intended to help practitioners learn about and use a new tool, the gender analysis matrix, developed specifically to fit the needs of community-based development work. The matrix serves two purposes: it provides a community-based technique for the identification and analysis of gender differences to assess the different impact of development interventions on each gender; and it initiates a process of analysis that identifies and challenges, in a constructive manner, assumptions about gender roles within the community. The training methodology and approach are described. The first section involves participants in practical applications that will help them learn to identify the matrix's uses and limitations. The second and last section emphasizes the facilitation skills necessary to use the gender analysis matrix with a community group. Within each section, basic instructions are provided to the facilitator for conducting the session, together with supplementary materials that include hand-outs, examples of what can be written on a flip chart, and notes for alternative ideas.

KIT, Amsterdam   [U 94-30]

093   Gender analysis in development planning : a case book
RAO, ARUNA; ANDERSON, MARY B.; OVERHOLT, CATHERINE A. - *Kumarian Press Library of Management for Development*. Kumarian, West Hartford, CT viii, 103 p. 1991 [EN] ill., tabs. Includes lit.refs ISBN 0-931816-62-9

This manual comprises a set of conceptual perspectives and analytical techniques to deal explicitly with gender issues in a range of development projects. Descriptions of actual projects from Asia are used to demonstrate the effectiveness of the gender analysis framework. The framework aims to improve the definition of project objectives, assess how to relate these to women's involvement, and anticipate the effect of the project on women. This framework is also applicable to projects where women's roles and responsibilities have only been implicitly noted in project design and implementation. The case study projects are concerned with: irrigation in Bangladesh and the Philippines; access to schooling in India; employment generation in Maharashtra, India; batik production in Indonesia; and dairy farming in Thailand.

KIT, Amsterdam   [N 92-5918]

094   Reflections and learnings : gender trainers workshop report, Royal Tropical Institute, Amsterdam, June 1993
RAO, ARUNA. Royal Tropical Institute, Amsterdam 119 p. 1994 [EN] ill., tabs. Includes lit.refs ISBN 90-6832-706-2

Presentations and discussions from the 'Tools for gender trainers' workshop, held in Amsterdam, the Netherlands, during 1993, are reported. Gender concepts are discussed including three gender training frameworks and their shortcomings: the gender roles framework developed by Overholt et al.; the triple roles framework developed by Moser; and the gender analysis matrix of Parker. Various planning models, approaches and techniques, including participatory rural appraisal, are introduced. A series of institutional diagnosis and organizational development models and interventions, in which gender issues constituted the driving force for change, are reviewed. An exercise conducted for a management training institution in West Africa and a project which aimed to help Canadian NGOs integrate gender issues into their own organizational systems and programming procedures are described. The need for gender training frameworks dealing with attitudes, values and behaviour towards gender issues is emphasized. A model of gender training for men which aims to develop allies among men or to neutralize potential obstacles in family, organization or community settings is discussed. The participants designed regional follow-up plans for Asia and the Pacific, Africa, and the English-speaking Caribbean. Suggestions for a gender training manual are put forward.

KIT, Amsterdam [N 94-1923]

095 Legal literacy : a tool for women's empowerment
SCHULER, MARGARET; KADIRGAMAR-RAJASINGHAM, SAKUNTALA - *Women, Law and Development*. PACT Communications, New York, NY xiv, 346 p. 1992 [EN] ill. Includes lit.refs, index

Legal literacy promotes women's capacities to understand and criticize the law and the scope of rights, to assert rights as a political resource, and to take action to change limiting definitions of gender roles, status and rights in the law and daily practice. Experiences with and strategic approaches to legal literacy from Africa, Asia and Latin America and the Caribbean are presented in this book, demonstrating a mix of resources, agents, methods and strategies by which legal literacy and its long-term political goals are pursued. A conceptual overview of the use of legal literacy as a tool for women's empowerment is provided, addressing how women develop awareness of their rights and the cognitive, social and political skills needed to take action on them. Case studies from Bangladesh, India, Peru, the Philippines, Sri Lanka and Uganda highlight the role of lawyers and non-professional community-based organizers as agents of legal literacy in making the law accessible to women. Studies from Africa and Mexico deal with legal

literacy as an essential part of developing the political capacities of women. The problem of legal literacy and law enforcement issues in Ghana are examined, together with experience from Zimbabwe that offers some useful methodological insights into how to foster awareness of rights. The case studies highlight gender-based inequities in the legal and political systems, as well as pervasive social oppression. They provide evidence of unequal outcomes for women in the distribution of economic resources and in the delivery of justice, even where the laws themselves are neutral and non-discriminatory.

KIT, Amsterdam [N 94-86]

096 Tools for community participation : a manual for training trainers in participatory techniques
SRINIVASAN, LYRA - *PROWWESS/UNDP Technical Series involving Women in Water and Sanitation*. UNDP, New York, NY 179 p. 1990 [EN] ill. Includes lit.refs ISBN 0-912917-20-2

This manual focuses on the field experience of PROWWESS (Promotion of the Role of Women in Water and Environmental Sanitation Services) in adapting and building on a participatory training methodology in the water supply and sanitation sector. PROWWESS is a UNDP programme, initiated in 1983, which aims to demonstrate how women can be effectively involved in water and environmental sanitation projects. Participatory training using the SARAR approach, based on self-esteem, associative strengths, resourcefulness, action planning and responsibility, is elaborated. Many of the techniques and activities are described in a step by step fashion. An overview is presented of training and evaluation techniques, tools, workshop activities, and training methodologies. Women form the target group as they are the main collectors and users of water as well as the guardians of household hygiene and family health.

KIT, Amsterdam [U 92-210]

097 Women and education in Latin America : knowledge, power, and change
STROMQUIST, NELLY P. - *Women and Change in the Developing World*. Rienner, Boulder, CO x, 310 p. 1992 [EN] ill., tabs. Includes index, lit.refs ISBN 1-55587-286-7

A collection of research studies on women's education in Latin America is presented. The relations between education, the state and the economy are assessed, and women's status in the formal education system and literacy programmes is reviewed. Furthermore, participation in emancipatory forms of popular education and educational efforts to change the status quo are discussed. Case studies from Argentina, Brazil, Chile, Costa Rica, Mexico and Peru illustrate gender inequalities in education and in job opportunities.

KIT, Amsterdam [N 92-2229]

098   Social gains from female education : a cross-national study
SUBBARAO, K.; RANEY, LAURA - *World Bank Discussion Papers* 194. World Bank, Washington, DC ix, 49 p. 1993 [EN] ill., graphs, tabs. Includes lit.refs ISSN 0259-210X ISBN 0-8213-2387-3

An examination is presented of the social gains from female education at the secondary level. The impact of female education (measured by gross enrolment rates at the secondary level) and improved health and family planning services on fertility and infant mortality is analysed. Data on 72 developing countries from various secondary sources are examined. Simulations show that doubling of the female enrolment rate during the 1975-1985 period reduces infant mortality rates by 64%, while halving the ratio of population per physician reduces infant deaths by only 2.5%. Another simulation for the same period shows that doubling female secondary enrolment, keeping all other variables constant at their mean levels, lowered births by 29%, while doubling the family planning service score would have reduced births by 3.5%. Generally, female secondary education, family planning and health programmes all affect fertility and mortality, and the effect of female secondary education appears to be very strong. The results suggest that family planning will reduce fertility more when combined with female education, especially in countries that now have low female secondary enrolment levels.

KIT, Amsterdam [K 2481-194]

099   Education for women's development
VEENHOFF, ANN - *VENA Journal* 4(1992)1. Leiden University. Women and Autonomy Centre, Leiden 72 p. 1992 [EN] ill. Includes lit.refs ISSN 0925-9333

This special issue discusses various experiences with regard to women's education and literacy in different situations and in different parts of the world, placing emphasis on the potential role of education/literacy as a catalyst for building critical attitudes, for strengthening analytical capacities, for constructing new knowledge, and for challenging and changing existing values, attitudes and inequities between and among genders. The factors that may influence women's access to and participation in education and literacy efforts are explored and the potential contribution of education to women's development is examined. Literacy programmes, popular education, technical training and educational aspects of women-in-development

programmes are discussed, together with case studies from Bangladesh, India, Indonesia, Mali, Nicaragua and Thailand. A list of relevant organizations for adult education and literacy is included.

KIT, Amsterdam [D 2412-4(1992)1]

100   Participatory development and gender : articulating concepts and cases
WEEKES-VAGLIANI, WINIFRED - *Technical Papers / OECD Development Centre* 95. OECD. Development Centre, Paris 66 p. 1994 [EN] Includes lit.refs

The need for a gender perspective in the participatory development field is explained, and the goals of participatory development, namely efficiency, empowerment and sustainability, are outlined. Having considered the rationale for a focus on participatory development and gender, obstacles to achieving participatory development are discussed, including cultural perceptions, opposition of men, and the social organization of work. The role of outsiders in overcoming some of these obstacles are explored, as well as the roles of focusing efforts, adapting the incentive structure, and enhancing gender sensitivity. In addition, advocacy and evidence that participation works are required. The ways in which gender relations are being dealt with in major participatory development debates are discussed, together with examples from the literature and interviews which illustrate how practical progress can be made towards strengthening local institutions and social actors. Issues related to women's organizations and ideas for linking the local, national and international donor levels are also addressed. Prerequisites to achieving the objectives of gender-sensitive participatory development include institutional reforms, a change in the language, and refining the concepts of participatory development.

KIT, Amsterdam [K 2542-(1994)95]

101   Women's interests and empowerment : gender planning reconsidered
WIERINGA, SASKIA - *Development and Change* 25(1994)4 p.829-848 1994 [EN] 56 lit.refs ISSN 0012-155X

The concept of gender planning is of recent origin and reflects the growing realization in development circles that women's issues cannot be dealt with in isolation but should be seen in the context of power relations between women and men. Efforts to address women's concerns in development processes date back to at least the International Women's Year in 1975. Various approaches have been distinguished, including the welfare, equity and anti-poverty approaches, and the efficiency and empowerment approaches. Of these, the latter approach seems the most useful for study and analysis in the field of women and development. It is argued that gender planning should be carried out in the context of women's empowerment. Two distinct though overlapping problems of gender planning in relation to the empowerment approach are addressed: the conceptualization of women's gender interests; and the fear engendered by and the limitations of the transformative potential of gender planning. It is argued that the distinction between women's practical and strategic gender interests, which was introduced by Molyneux and popularized by Moser, is theoretically unfounded and empirically untenable because it is another attempt to control rather than explain reality. Gender planning in all cases should be based on a careful and sensitive process of analysis, which involves not only the planners or their consultants, but also the women of the target group. Gender planning, empowerment and transformation should be intricately linked, welded by a feminist-informed analysis. Gender planning should go beyond the gender needs of poor women, paying attention to issues such as sexual violence and its impact on women's lives.

KIT, Amsterdam   [D 1323-25(1994)4]

102   The Oxfam gender training manual

WILLIAMS, SUZANNE; SEED, JANET; MWAU, ADELINA. Oxfam, Oxford xiv, 634 p. 1994 [EN] ill., tabs. Includes index. Bibliogr.: p. 613-631 ISBN 0-85598-267-5

This training manual draws on experience and is designed for the use of staff of NGOs who have some experience in running workshops or training courses, and for experienced gender trainers. Gender training is a key strategy to sensitize NGO staff and partners to gender issues. Practical tools are offered for the training of development workers who are in a position to influence the planning and implementation of development and relief programmes at different levels. The manual combines self-awareness work, through activities which address women's and men's self-awareness and gender awareness, with training in gender

analysis methods and techniques. Key concepts related to gender and to gender and development are summarized, together with the principles behind gender training. Steps to follow when planning and carrying out a workshop are presented. Methods and case studies of gender-sensitive appraisal and planning are discussed. Some of the analytical frameworks learned are used to examine the following global issues from a gender perspective: conflict, the environment, economic crisis and culture. Suggestions are made on how to work with women and men in NGOs, in villages and in communities. Ways of making and using images and text to communicate gender-sensitive messages are presented. Activities are described which aim to help workshop participants use their acquired awareness and analytical skills to plan practical action. The final section lists publications on gender and development, materials and manuals on gender training, and organizations and networks.

KIT, Amsterdam   [G 94-528]

103   Group learning by mothers about primary health care

YOOSUF, ABDUL-SATTAR - *World Health Forum* 14(1993)1 p.20-22 [EN] 1 lit.ref ISSN 0251-2432

A group teaching approach to health education was adopted in the Maldives during 1988-1989 in order to improve the knowledge of mothers about various aspects of primary health care. An experimental and a control group, each comprising 200 mothers with children of less than 3 years of age, in Thaa and Laamu atolls were tested for their knowledge of antenatal care, control of diarrhoeal diseases, immunization, family planning, nutrition and endemic communicable diseases, before and after the training intervention. The group learning approach proved to be an effective instrument for enhancing mothers' knowledge and awareness of primary care and services.

KIT, Amsterdam   [K 1884-14(1993)1]

3 Economic participation

A critical review of structural adjustment and increasing women's economic participation[1]

Wilma Wentholt, Annelies Zoomers and Loes Jansen

There is an ever growing awareness that women's economic participation is important. Women play a key role in the development of national economies and in improving the living standard of individual households. They constitute an essential part of the labour force and form the core of the agricultural system, providing labour for export and domestic crop production. Women's participation in gainful employment in the formal and informal sectors of the economy has been substantial and is increasing in most countries.

Structural change in the international and national economies has had an important bearing on employment opportunities and conditions for both men and women in various sectors of the economy. One major international phenomenon has been the worldwide economic crisis of the early 1980s and the ensuing economic reform measures in the form of stabilization programmes and structural adjustment programmes. Regions hardest hit by the economic crisis have been Latin America, Africa and some countries in South Asia and the Middle East. Although men have been adversely affected by international recession, women are especially vulnerable because they are frequently poorer than men and have primary responsibility for the household, particularly children.

This article will concentrate on the effect of structural adjustment on women's economic participation and illuminate the barriers which gender relations create to the operation of adjustment measures aimed at achieving economic development. Women's role in economic development will be highlighted. It is argued that the best way to counterbalance the negative effects of adjustment is to maximize the primary income-generating activities of the poorer segments of the population by improving access to employment opportunities and assets and by raising the productivity of these assets. Subsequently, the results of projects promoting women's economic participation are reviewed and evaluated. The discussion will be restricted to projects in the agricultural sector and small enterprises in the informal sector, both of which are characterized by high levels of female labour participation.

Assessing the impact of structural adjustment

Since the late 1970s, increasing numbers of developing countries have experienced growing financial imbalances and a deterioration in the growth performance of their productive sectors. These difficulties originated from external shocks, such as oil crises and world recession, as well as internal and external policies. In their attempts to restore an equilibrium in their balance of payments and to create conditions for resumed growth, several countries in the Middle East, Africa and Latin America adopted structural adjustment policies. These adjustment programmes differed from country to country. In general, they entailed a package of the following measures: devaluation of overvalued currencies; a closer alignment of domestic prices with world prices through the removal of food, import and input subsidies; an emphasis on tradeable goods and the gradual withdrawal of restrictions on competition from abroad; privatization of government undertakings; and a decrease in government spending in the public sector with wage freezes and restrictions on taking on new employees (Gladwin 1991). These packages were financed by the World Bank, the International Monetary Fund and bilateral donors.

The outcome of these adjustment policies appears to have been rather mixed (World Bank 1988). A detailed review of the effects of structural adjustment packages indicates that positive impacts have generally been observed on the price and fiscal fronts: devaluations have usually led to more realistic and flexible exchange rates; price deregulations have brought about an improvement in the domestic price structure; and budget deficits have generally declined. At the same time, however, a rather negative picture has tended to emerge: investment rates have regularly declined; growth targets have not been reached; and unemployment has drastically increased. The short-term costs of structural adjustment have not yet been balanced by benefits in many cases. In addition, many indicators of human welfare (standards of health, nutrition and education) have shown marked deterioration in many countries, thereby hurting the poorest segments of the population.

Most countries had to endure slow economic growth during adjustment. Change in relative prices has left some groups worse off than before, even in the medium-term. A number of old assumptions have been called into doubt. These assumptions argued that the benefits of structural adjustment would trickle down automatically to the poorest segments of the population, that adjustment would make the distribution of income fairer in the end, and that the poor as a group would probably have suffered considerably more if adjustment programmes had not been introduced. Mounting unemployment, the inflationary effects of devaluation and reduced public spending have nevertheless increasingly resulted in new poverty.

The impact of adjustment on women

In the late 1980s, numerous studies were undertaken to assess the gender differentiated impact of structural adjustment (Altomore 1991, Elson 1991, Gladwin 1991, Palmer 1991, Rocha 1989, Sparr 1994). It is difficult to generalize about the net effects of adjustment programmes because their specific characteristics vary from country to country, and because the various policy instruments which constitute the adjustment package have often had conflicting results. For example, the positive impact of higher producer prices for farmers may be counteracted by rising production costs as a result of higher inflation and the elimination of subsidies on fuel, seeds and fertilizers. Assessment of the impact of adjustment on a specific population category is also hindered by the lack or inadequacy of statistical sources, as well as by uncertainty as to whether positive or negative trends in particular sets of macro-economic indicators can be ascribed to adjustment. Increased poverty at the household level, for example, is not necessarily a direct result of adjustment but can also be the result of economic recession. It is also difficult to determine how the economy would have developed in the absence of the adjustment efforts. Further, the effects of poverty vary from region to region. For example, cuts in government expenditure on marketing and the infrastructure of input delivery will particularly hurt farmers in the most remote areas. Such farmers will often not respond to price incentives because middlemen will simply raise their profit margin as soon as the increased producer prices are announced, and extra inputs are generally difficult to acquire (Zoomers 1994).

It is difficult to assess the effects of structural adjustment on women because the impact varies from social group to social group (small farmers, landless workers, unskilled labourers, informal sector workers) more obviously than between the genders. Despite these constraints, several studies have been able to show evidence of the negative effects of structural adjustment on women. Case studies undertaken by Altomore in Ghana, Ivory Coast, Jamaica and Pakistan found that women and members of female-headed households tend to suffer relatively more during economic recession because they are frequently poorer at the outset. Women were also found to act as shock absorbers during adjustment, curtailing their own consumption and increasing their workload in order to compensate for household income losses, such as those caused by the unemployment of their spouses. Women suffered more from reductions in social spending because they are often more dependent on social and health services as a result of their childbearing and child rearing roles. Further, the shrinkage of government services 'off-loads' responsibilities to women. Where there is a relatively higher representation of women in the public sector, public expenditure restraint may have a greater impact on women than men. In the agricultural sector, the emphasis on export production put pressure on women to reallocate their time and, in some cases, increase their workload for the production of male control-led cash crops. Sometimes this emphasis resulted in a reduction of the land available to women for producing food crops for their own consumption and local sale, making it more difficult to look after family needs (Altomore 1991).

The same USAID study concluded that the gender differentiated impact of structural adjustment follows three different response scenarios. Theoretically, in countries where mobility, education and access to resources are uniform across gender, the impact on men and women will be more or less equal. In those countries with practically no economic participation of women, such as Pakistan, adjustment does not result in increased differentiation along gender lines. However, in most African and Asian countries, the relative position of women slides despite their significant economic involvement because this involvement is based on unequal terms. Women are not sufficiently mobile or educated to participate in the new growth and they lack access to resources (Altomore 1991). The results of these studies in the late 1980s led to an international debate on the gender differentiated impact of structural adjustment policies.

Women's economic participation and adjustment

Much of the literature discussing gender issues in the context of structural adjustment has concentrated on the impact of measures on vulnerable groups as summarized above. More recently, other authors have tried to intervene in the debate about the effectiveness of adjustment policies in achieving balanced economic growth by illuminating the barriers which gender relations create to the operation of adjustment measures (Elson 1992). The barriers which gender relations place in the way of effective operation of adjustment measures have been analysed in different ways (Lockwood 1992). These approaches commonly no longer regard households as indivisible units as in the case of macroeconomic analysis but, rather, as a collection of individual stakeholders.

Collier et al. (1994) has pointed out that the sexual division of labour may act as a constraint to the economic success of adjustment programmes by treating male and female labour as different production factors. He argues that the theoretical basis of adjustment, the free trade model, is in fact a trade model with imperfect mobility of factors. Male and female labour are separate resources; their distribution is skewed differentially in various sectors of the economy. In Africa, women are over-represented in the production of non-tradeable crops (food production) and in informal, low technology activities, while men tend to dominate the tradeable sector, producing export crops or working as wage labourers in the cities, mines and estate agriculture. Structural adjustment policies are designed to encourage resources to flow into the production of tradeable goods. Hence, this sector will need to attract female labour away from food production.

Women's labour is, however, less mobile than men's. According to Collier et al. (1994), four distinct processes account for why women face differential constraints upon their economic activities. The first process is discrimination in labour and credit markets. The second concerns the replication of gender role models: economic opportunities initially taken up by men are diffused over a male population by a mechanism that does not transmit them to the female population. The third process is the result of asymmetric rights and obligations of men and women in the household. The fourth is reproduction, which makes extra demands on the time and health of women, adding to their inflexibility. As a consequence, women are usually active in those sectors which are less subject to these constraints.

Other authors also stress women's comparative disadvantage in the labour market. They argue that labour allocation within a household can be explained in terms of opportunity cost of the time of each person. This, in turn, is determined by the comparative advantage of each household member in different kinds of production. Women's participation in the market economy is hindered by higher opportunity cost because of their reproductive tasks. In this respect, Elson (1992) speaks about 'the reproduction tax on women's work – women's work which is not valued by the market economy – which needs to be removed to allow markets to operate efficiently.' According to Lockwood (1992), these gender specific constraints are not the result of socio-cultural traditions but are a product of the economic and colonial history. Discrimination against women in the labour market started with the establishment of the plantation and mining sectors, whereby predominantly male labour was drawn off to these work sites as in Kenya and Southern Africa. Another process involved male adoption of cash crops which made women more responsible for food supply.

Another group of authors concentrate their debate more on the contribution of women producers to the economy by considering the increased feminization of agriculture (the process in which women cultivators become more and more responsible for agriculture as labourers and farm operators). They argue that the economic concept of the free competitive market underlying structural adjustment policies is not the most effective instrument for resource allocation by demonstrating that this market does not work at microlevel in sub-Saharan Africa (Gladwin 1991). Theoretically, women farmers should have benefitted from adjustment because these packages were especially designed to renew agricultural production and to align local prices with world market prices. However, the reality of social stratification and differentiation at the village and household levels, and imbalances in power relations which determine who gets access to the means of production and who controls that production, have hampered female producers from responding to greater producer incentives. Women lack access to land, know-how, agricultural inputs, credit and, in many societies, they do not have the right to grow cash crops (Lele 1992, Gladwin 1991 and Goheen 1991). Adjustment packages must be redesigned to stimulate food production if a future African food crisis is to be prevented.

Palmer (1991) argues that population growth is an important constraint to the economic and social development sought by adjustment programmes. The positive correlation between high female education and economic participation rates and birth control in Kerala, India, has demonstrated that fertility rates are influenced by women's socio-economic status (see also Eapen 1992). Palmer confirms the negative impact of adjustment, arguing that economic development can only be achieved if alternative economic policies are included to enhance women's status. Any attempt at economic development for women, however, must take into account the factors discussed in the following sections.

Policy and project interventions to improve women's economic participation

Since the early 1970s, all kinds of development organizations have invested in projects aimed at improving the socio-economic situation of women. There have been two main strategies: separate small projects focusing on a particular aspect of women's lives, or the addition of a women's component to general mainstream projects (Young 1993). Project interventions directed towards women can be divided into the following areas:
- agriculture: agricultural extension, horticulture, kitchen gardening, animal husbandry (particularly dairy, poultry and pig farming);
- processing of agricultural products: introduction of improved, labour-saving technologies for cereal husking and milling, coconut, palm oil and groundnut oil processing, fish processing, processing of seasonal fruits, local cassava proces-

sing, and production of local weaning foods;
- handicrafts and home-based industries: projects related to a large variety of manufacturing and/or semi-industrial activities, including weaving, carpet making,
  pottery and ceramics, cane and bamboo production;
- natural resource management: interventions aimed at preventing environmental
  degradation, including reforestation and agroforestry; introduction of renewable
  energy technologies, such as micro-hydro power, wind, solar and biogas technologies; and energy saving devices, particularly introduction of improved stoves;
- credit: introduction of formal and/or informal credit systems;
- health, water and sanitation, and education: drinking water, environmental health
  and literacy programmes.

Interventions in the field of small enterprises and agricultural development have a
number of typical characteristics. Projects aiming to improve women's employment
opportunities in the small enterprise sector have preferred to support the production
of simple consumer goods such as food and textiles. Priority is usually given to
micro and small-scale activities which are adapted to local conditions, make use of
familiar labour patterns and equipment, pose few demands on local management and
technical skills, and are based on locally available raw materials. Technology used is
usually small-scale, low cost and labour intensive.

In the agricultural sector, activities in the 1980s focused initially on improving
women's access to agricultural extension by creating a network of female extension
workers and increasing the productivity of typical on-farm women's activities, such
as vegetable gardening, poultry raising and post-harvest technology. Women's
access to means of production such as irrigation water, land and credit received
attention from the late 1980s onwards. Project interventions then began to involve
women in less traditional activities such as water management and agroforestry.
Compared to the bulk of interventions targeted at women, these efforts are still very
limited.

Interventions in both sectors have also been expected to achieve more ideological
goals such as empowerment. Projects in the field of vegetable gardening and grain
milling, for example, aimed to improve the quality of life (drudgery alleviation) and
strengthen the power of rural women. It was assumed that the installation of grain
mills in villages would function as an instrument for increasing women's autonomy
and strengthening their potential for collective action. Another characteristic of
women's projects and women's components of larger projects was the emphasis on
the participatory approach. Interventions and technology have been devised in
collaboration with the women who would benefit from them. Joint responsibility and
collective ownership were often considered sufficient conditions for the successful
operation of technology-based income generation projects. For agricultural activities,
the focus shifted from collective fields to individual plots at an early stage. Training
in functional literacy, book keeping, administration or management was seen to be a
crucial component of all projects. These project interventions contributed to the
recognition of women's roles as producers, as generators of income and as repro-
ducers of human resources. Most projects started from the prevailing sexual division

of labour within the household and tried to enhance the position of women by creating women's groups and by improving the productivity of exclusively female activities. The contribution of these projects to improving women's access and control of resources, creating employment opportunities and encouraging mobility in the labour market, particularly from the non-tradeable towards the tradeable sector, will be assessed next.

Assessing the results

In the 1990s, projects promoting women's economic participation have been criticized from a gender perspective which drew attention to women's practical and strategic needs and the intrahousehold distribution of responsibilities and rewards (Moser 1989). The main criticisms of such an approach and such projects are summarized below, based in part on the authors' personal experience in Africa and India.

Small enterprise development

Many women's projects in this field have not achieved their objective of increased levels of economic participation. This is because activities supported by project interventions are in sectors with limited economic potential. Results of small enterprise development have been disappointing due to a variety of factors (Zoomers 1994, 1995). First, marketing considerations have not been taken sufficiently into account. Second, women's projects usually pursue various goals such as empowerment, production increases, employment generation, food security and income redistribution. Favourable business results and profit maximization have not generally been the primary goals and women have not been encouraged to join the more profitable tradeable goods sector. Third, most women's projects are implemented at the microlevel, making it difficult to achieve economies of scale. Their small-scale character means that it is not possible to obtain lower prices for inputs, nor is it feasible to conduct large publicity campaigns. Fourth, management capacity is often low due to poor delegation of tasks and responsibilities among group members, and a lack of training and/or market information. Finally, women's groups are often not able to influence forward and backward linkages (marketing, input supply) because of prevailing power relations and role models within the market.

Agricultural development

Support to income-generating activities in agriculture either through women only or integrated projects has not substantially increased incomes because their resource base was too marginal (e.g., poor soil conditions, small plot size). Women have not controlled marketing and have not had sufficient access to inputs. Strategies followed rarely touched upon the implications of women's unequal access to productive resources. Instead, support was given within the framework of prevailing gender relations, focusing on women's ability to earn an income through independent activities while disregarding the importance of women's roles in other agricultural production activities.

At the household level, women have different rights and obligations than men. The obligations of women in rural societies have changed over time as a result of historical economic processes, including colonial rule. Women perform the majority of agricultural tasks in both cash and food crop production in many African countries. The number of female-headed households has increased because men have taken permanent or seasonal off-farm employment. Women's new obligations have not been matched by new rights of access to and control of agricultural production, hindering improvements in agricultural productivity. In migrant labour households, for example, decisions concerning the use of casual labour and other investments often cannot be taken by the resident female farm operator.

With the introduction of the market economy in both Africa and India, the importance of food crops, such as millet, traditionally in women's domain is declining compared to modern cash crops controlled by men. In Africa, official land legislation practices have favoured male household heads, undermining the traditional land use rights of women. Men are able to obtain bank loans because the title deeds to land are in their name. They are also able to buy seeds, pesticides and fertilizers. Women must depend on men if they want to apply these inputs to food crops. New tasks in cash crop cultivation have accrued to women, often conflicting with traditional obligations related to food supply and reproduction, and resulting in a competing demand for women's labour. For example, availability of female labour has become a significant constraint in the cultivation of cotton in Mali. Further, agricultural extension services focus on men and not on women; information does not automatically trickle down to women. Women then feel ignorant because they are not well informed about agricultural technology. This reduces their willingness to express their views at household and community level, contributing to the tendency to regard women merely as unpaid family labour. Women are also increasingly excluded from decisions which they used to take about production. In India, women complained that they lost control over production in the transition from a subsistence economy towards a market economy. The focus on marginal women's activities in many project interventions has contributed to women's exclusion from economic decisions that directly affect them (Gianotten et al. 1994).

Constraints facing project planning

In the case of official bilateral/multilateral development cooperation, project planners often either neglect these problems or do not know how to incorporate gender issues successfully. Attempts to integrate gender issues have been restricted by inappropriate planning mechanisms, weak institutional settings, limited budget allocations and constrained human resources. Women have not been sufficiently consulted from the beginning of the planning process. Women's projects have often resulted in the creation of an isolated women-in-development wing within a development institution without direct linkages to mainstream activities. Thus, implementation has not been integrated into the institution's general policies and work approach. These small projects have been used by development institutions as a justification that they are doing something for women (Young 1993).

In the integrated projects, special women-in-development units have been established. Most of these focus on specific women's activities; when they do not, their ability to ensure the involvement of women in mainstream activities is hampered by the weak institutional linkages between the women-in-development section and the core of project decision-making. Besides, these so-called women's activities have often been implemented by an external agency or specially appointed additional staff. There has also been a lack of expertise in the field of gender and development issues in agriculture; most expertise is in the area of women and empowerment.

When development projects in these sectors have been successful, their impact has been restricted because of their limited, microlevel scope. Results have often not been communicated in a language understood by policymakers operating at a more macrolevel who are susceptible to macroeconomic and efficiency arguments. According to Elson (1992), projects have only had an impact on the spending ministries such as rural development, health and education, and not the more influential ministries of planning and economic affairs. In small enterprise development, for example, little attention has been paid to the extent to which women-focused projects are appropriate from the macroeconomic and business points of view. Many projects do not take into account the need for economic activities to fit into the broader macroeconomic environment and they are, therefore, unable to tackle the real issues facing women's participation in economic development.

Recommendations for policies and projects

Remedial policy measures to counterbalance the social costs of adjustment have focused on the need to maximize the primary income-generating activities of the population. According to the World Bank (1989), the most effective way to tackle poverty without watering down macroeconomic goals is to help vulnerable groups, such as women, by: (1) improving access to employment opportunities and income-generating assets; (2) raising the productivity of these assets; and (3) restructuring social expenditures towards basic, low cost services for the poor. Incorporating gender analysis into economic planning would enhance the effectiveness of new policies.

Recognizing the need to introduce a more market-oriented approach, it is necessary to give priority to those sectors that offer the best opportunities and which are crucial for sustained economic growth. This is not restricted to the production of tradeable goods for the export sector. Collier et al. (1994) argues that in many countries the food sector should be expanded as much as the export sector, particularly where food is an unprotected import substitute or export product. 'For this to happen, either male labour must shift into this activity, or female labour supply must increase (a diversion of time from other activities), or females must be able to increase their labour productivity by investment.' Food can be both a non-tradeable product for home consumption and an unprotected import substitute for urban consumption. In the latter case, a redistribution of food crops from rural areas to urban areas should take place. Thus, the food marketing sector should be expanded.

In Africa, food marketing is commonly carried out by women and will require further resources (Collier et al. 1994). This implies, on the one hand, that when prices of food crops are falling, the reallocation of women's labour will be a condition for successful structural adjustment. Since women's access to the official labour market is restricted, this relocation is likely to involve women entering new activities as entrepreneurs. On the other hand, development of the food sector would require a reallocation of land and capital, which could benefit women. Recommendations are made below for small enterprise development and the agricultural sector which aim to translate this macroeconomic view on improving the effectiveness of structural adjustment programmes into concrete project interventions.

Small enterprises

Small enterprise development efforts should aim at mobilizing women in the *winning sectors* of economic life (tradeable goods, export production). This could be achieved, first, by paying more attention to product diversification and the development of new production lines with favourable sales potential instead of starting from the existing situation. Second, the prevailing gender role models with regard to economic participation should be modified through education and training and appropriate organizational forms. Third, the level of operation needs to be scaled up to achieve economies of scale. Fourth, appropriate support networks should be established. If women are to benefit from adjustment, it is important to build up appropriate and sustainable systems for the delivery of advice and information. Women entrepreneurs in agriculture, manufacturing and processing should be helped to identify new market niches and to streamline marketing efforts. Support programmes should be aimed, among other things, at quality control, marketing and adequate handling, resulting in more stable product delivery in terms of quantity, quality and timing.

Agricultural sector

In the agricultural sector, attention should shift from developing employment opportunities or alternative income-generating activities for women to bringing more resources under the control of women to augment agricultural productivity. Interventions should focus on improving women's access to information on mainstream agriculture through agricultural extension; improving women's access to resources (land, credit, water); increasing productivity and marketing; and introducing improved water and fuelwood supply and child care provision in circumstances where women's labour is constrained.

Concluding comments

Many of these ideas are not new. What should change is the scope of these interventions, the use of a market-oriented perspective, and the real incorporation of gender relations in a participatory planning phase. Mainstream institutions should be made accountable for strengthening the entitlement of women who have prime responsibility for the care of other family members. The shift from women-in-development, focusing more on women's activities, to a gender and development approach that strives for 'mainstreaming' is part of a step-wise learning process. The approach for the forthcoming decade should focus upon creating an enabling environment within mainstream institutions capable of implementing gender-specific policies; better communication of success stories to policy level; and providing new scope for women beyond their traditional gender roles so that they are able to meet their new responsibilities.

Notes

1   Women's economic participation can be defined either in terms of women's proportion of the economically active population (aged 15 years or over) or on the basis of female labour force participation rates as a proportion of the total female population aged 15 years and over.

Bibliography

Altomore, M., *Gender and adjustment*. Washington DC, Agency for International Development, 1991.

Collier, P., A.C. Edwards, J. Roberts and K. Bardhan, 'Gender aspects of labor allocation during structural adjustment'. In: S. Horton, R. Kanbur and D. Mazumdar (ed.), *Labour markets in an era of adjustment. Volume 1*. Washington DC, Economic Development Institute, World Bank, 1994, pp. 277-307.

Eapen, M., 'Fertility and female labour force participation in Kerala'. *Economic and Political Weekly*, vol. 27, no. 40 (1992), pp. 2179-2188.

Elson D., 'Male bias in macro-economics: the case of structural adjustment'. In: D. Elson (ed.), *Male bias in the development process*. Manchester, Manchester University Press, 1991.

Elson D., 'Gender issues in development strategies'. *Women 2000*, no. 1 (1992), pp. 7-12.

Gianotten V., V. Groverman, E. van Walsum and L. Zuidberg, *Assessing the gender impact of development projects: case studies from Bolivia, Burkina Faso and India*. Amsterdam, Royal Tropical Institute, 1994.

Gladwin, C.H., 'Fertilizer subsidy removal programs and their potential impacts on women farmers in Malawi and Cameroon'. In: C.H. Gladwin (ed.), *Structural adjustment and African women farmers*. Gainesville, University of Florida Press, 1991, pp. 191-216.

Goheen, M., 'The ideology and political economy of gender: women and land in Nso, Cameroon'. In: C.H. Gladwin (ed.), *Structural adjustment and African women farmers*. Gainesville, University of Florida Press, 1991, pp. 239-256.

Lele, U., 'Women, structural adjustment, and transformation: some lessons and questions of the African experience'. In: C.H. Gladwin (ed.), *Structural adjustment and African women farmers*. Gainesville, University of Florida Press, 1991, pp. 46-80.

Lockwood, M., *Engendering adjustment or adjusting gender? Some new approaches to women and development in Africa.* (Discussion Paper no. 315) Brighton, Institute of Development Studies, 1992.

Moser, C.O.N, 'Gender planning in the Third World: meeting practical and strategic gender needs.' *World Development*, vol. 17, no. 11 (1989), pp. 1799-1825.

Palmer, I., *Gender and population in the adjustment of African economies: planning for change.* (Women, Work and Development no. 19) Geneva, International Labour Office, 1991.

Rocha, L., *The invisible adjustment: poor women and the economic crisis.* Santiago, Regional Programme for Women in Development, Americas and the Caribbean Regional Office, UNICEF, 1989 (Second edition).

Sparr, P. (ed.), *Mortgaging women's lives: feminist critiques of structural adjustment.* London, Zed Books, 1994.

World Bank, *Social dimensions of adjustment in Sub-Saharan Africa. Project summary.* Africa Regional Office, Social Dimensions of Adjustment Project Unit, 1988.

World Bank and UNDP Regional Programme for Africa, *Assessment of the social dimensions of adjustment in Sub-Saharan Africa.* Washington DC, World Bank, 1989.

Young, K., *Planning development with women: making a world of difference.* New York, St. Martin's Press, 1993.

Zoomers, E.B., 'State of the art in the social dimensions of adjustment discussion: are 'social dimensions' the red herring across the path to a more substantive discussion about poverty alleviation?' In: A. Harts-Broekhuis and O. Verhoven (ed.), 'No easy way out. Essays on Third World development in honour of Jan Hinderink.' *Nederlandse Geografische Studies*, no. 186 (1994), pp. 127-136.

Zoomers, E.B., 'From service delivery to business development: experiences of a rice milling project for women in Mali'. In: E.B. Zoomers et al., *Supporting small-scale enterprise: case studies in SME interventions*, Amsterdam, Royal Tropical Institute, 1995 (Forthcoming).

Annotated bibliography

Economic participation

104   Abuja Declaration on participatory development : the role of women in Africa in the 1990s
UN. ECA, Addis Ababa iii, 39 p. 1990 [EN]
    The Abuja Declaration is the outcome of the fourth Regional Conference on the Integration of Women-in-Development and on the Implementation of the Arusha Strategies for the Advancement of Women in Africa, held in Abuja, Nigeria, during 6-10 November 1989. The conference was attended by representatives of over 41 African governments, UN observers, international organizations and NGOs. The general framework and basic obstacles described in the Arusha Strategies for the Advancement of African Women beyond the UN Decade for Women were found to still be as valid as when they were set in 1984. Areas of substantial progress, areas of slow progress and areas where implementation is being initiated are identified. In the light of an assessment of the situation of women in Africa, the Abuja Declaration was designed and adopted by a consensus of the 1187 participants. The Declaration sets goals for equal access to education, science and technology, food, and employment. NGOs and national, regional and international organizations should promote establishment of data banks and information networks, support institution-building and cooperation, and provide technical assistance in order to achieve the objectives.
KIT, Amsterdam   [Br U 92-90]

105   Gender, work & population in sub-Saharan Africa
ADEPOJU, ADERANTI; OPPONG, CHRISTINE. Currey : publ. for ILO, London x, 245 p. 1994 [EN] ill., graphs, tabs. Bibliogr.: p. 226-240. Includes index
ISBN 0-85255-407-9
    Sub-Saharan Africa has the highest rates of female economic participation, fertility and maternal and child mortality in the world. In spite of marked advances made in the past two decades, these economic and demographic facts and their linkages are neither accurately recorded and analysed in the majority of the countries of the region, nor adequately addressed in population and development discourse and planning. Various aspects of the culturally prescribed roles of women and men in sub-Saharan Africa are examined, as well as their relevance to a set of economic and population concerns, especially the recording of the economic and demographic facts upon which policies and plans are supposed to be based. A demographic profile of mortality, fertility and migration in sub-Saharan Africa is provided. The following themes are addressed: the gender bias in women's work and women's active roles as family labourers and independent farmers; the culturally distinct African forms of domestic organization and systems of marriage, parenthood and kinship that need to be taken into account when collecting and analyzing economic and demographic data for policy-related purposes; how women balance their productive and reproductive roles; and family welfare and family planning issues, including the role of grandmothers in household maintenance. Case studies from Botswana, Ghana, Kenya and Zimbabwe are presented, together with regional analyses.
KIT, Amsterdam   [U 94-137]

106   Female labour force reporting in South Asia : some issues
AFZAL, MOHAMMAD *In: Population transition in South Asia* ed. by Ashish Bose and M.K. Premi. - Delhi : BR Publishing Corporation, 1992 p.41-61 [EN] ill., tabs 20 lit.refs
    The crucial need for reliable and accurate data on female labour force participation is being increasingly recognized in South Asia and other developing regions. Such data are needed to assess women's contribution to the national economy and to formulate measures in the field of human resource development for the advancement of women. A comparative review of urban and rural estimates of female participation rates in economic activity as provided by population censuses and labour force surveys in Bangladesh, India and Pakistan is presented. The validity of these estimates is assessed by comparing them

with estimates provided by other sources such as fertility surveys and agricultural censuses. Despite some improvements in census and survey design and data collection, the statistical data relating to female labour force participation are still unsatisfactory in these countries. There is a need to initiate institutionalized research efforts to improve census and survey data collection. Such efforts should be based on continuous analysis of the critical components of the data collection systems under different cultural and socio-economic situations to get the best possible assessment of national patterns of female labour participation in rural and urban areas.

KIT, Amsterdam   [P 94-808]

107   Gender and adjustment

ALTOMORE, MARY. US Agency for International Development. Bureau for Program and Policy Coordination. Office of Women in Development, Washington, DC 194 p. 1991 [EN] ill., tabs. Includes lit.refs

Gender dimensions of adjustment policies in developing countries are assessed, based on case studies from Ghana, Ivory Coast, Jamaica and Pakistan. After a review of concepts, methodology and theories, the case studies address the social, political and historical backgrounds, review policies regarding gender issues, and focus on women's participation and employment. Women's participation is not an adjustment issue but a developmental one. Prior to and during adjustment processes, a balanced set of gender indicators of social and economic conditions and development potential should be identified in order to provide donor countries with an extended development perspective on gender and adjustment issues. The evidence suggests that gender-related constraints frustrate the objectives of structural adjustment. Two alternative approaches are possible: either devoting more resources to reducing female barriers to resource acquisition and transfer; or adopting a gender-blind approach to poverty alleviation while surgically removing specific obstacles to female integration into the supply-side of economic adjustment. Either way, it is clear that female illiteracy has a high opportunity cost. Educational reform, in terms of relaxing the constraints that exclude women from all levels of schooling, should be at the heart of any attempt to invigorate the supply-side response of the economies in Ghana and the Ivory Coast.

KIT, Amsterdam   [N 92-5229]

108   Technical innovation by women : implications for small enterprises

APPLETON, HELEN - *Small Enterprise Development* 5(1994)1 p.4-13 [EN] 14 lit.refs ISSN 0957-1329

Technology development, where it is understood to mean introducing machinery from abroad, may have the effect of weakening the skills and capacity to innovate of local small-scale entrepreneurs. Technology includes both the hardware and the software aspects of production, both machinery and skills; to neglect the latter is to ignore the capacity to innovate which is essential when entrepreneurs face changes in their environment. Women's technical skills and innovations are often ignored because they may relate to their domestic responsibilities, or because they do not have obvious income-generating potential. Those working with women need to be aware of these skills, partly to help women derive the maximum benefit from them, and partly because a recognition of their own technical capabilities is a considerable boost to women's self-confidence. Case studies from Peru, Sri Lanka and Zimbabwe illustrate the value of a gender analysis of technology to agencies working with small enterprises, women's enterprises in particular. Lessons for small enterprise programmes are drawn, including that women and men may have quite different priorities for technical decisions, and that external agents must be aware of their own assumptions about technical hardware and software and about men's and women's existing technical capacities. It is concluded that technical capacity is an important indicator of enterprise strength and potential which is demonstrated in different ways and in different areas by men and women. Small enterprise programmes need to recognize explicitly the gender differences in capacity and to provide appropriate support.

KIT, Amsterdam   [E 3166-5(1994)1]

109   The dynamics of women participation in workers' struggles in Uganda : a case study of the National Union of Clerical, Commercial, Professional and Technical Employees (NUCCPTE)

ASOWA-OKWE, C. - *Working Paper / Centre for Basic Research* 40. Centre for Basic Research, Kampala 47 p. 1994 [EN] Includes lit.refs

The participation of women in the labour movement in Uganda since colonialism is traced with special reference to the National Union of Clerical, Commercial, Professional, and Technical Employees (NUCCPTE), located in Kampala. Both primary and secondary data sources were used, including interviews conducted with a sample of 200 respondents. The history of working class formation and the trade union movement in colonial and post-colonial Uganda is reviewed, paying particular attention to the factors that shaped the formation of the working class and its organs of articulation. An historical account is given of the formation of NUCCPTE, its organizational structure, the type of leadership, and the role and position of women in the Union. Finally, an attempt is made to arrive at a conceptualization of gender and gender-related issues on the basis of the concrete experience of NUCCPTE. NUCCPTE launched a women's wing in 1976 and many women joined. Participation of women in NUCCPTE is particularly subject to the attitudes of husbands and relatives. Women's roles in four specific militant labour struggles in the 1980-1991 period demonstrate that women can play leading and decisive roles in the resolution of labour disputes. However, the majority of women still have a marginal status, even in labour organizations. The debate on this issue and the struggle for its resolution must continue within the unions and the wider social environment.

KIT, Amsterdam   [D 2985-(1994)40]

110   Women's time, labour-saving devices and rural development in Africa

BARRETT, HAZEL R.; BROWNE, ANGELA W. - *Community Development Journal* 29(1994)3 p.203-214 [EN] ill., tabs 27 lit.refs ISSN 0010-3802

All approaches to rural development in Africa implicitly require more responsibility and input from women. As a result, women's workloads in rural areas have increased dramatically. One of the most time- and energy-consuming tasks performed by women in Africa is the preparation of grain. Using the Gambia as an example, the impact of the introduction of mechanical cereal mills on the lives of women and their communities is assessed. More than 20 villages with mechanical mills were visited, representing all types of mills in use. One village, Basori, was studied in detail and 95 women were interviewed. The research shows that labour-saving devices make a significant positive impact on women's welfare by alleviating their workloads. This is achieved more by the saving of energy than the gaining of time, although both are important in enhancing women's health and wellbeing. In terms of equity, the mills are an essential first step to raising women's labour productivity. The time saved could potentially be used for income generation, although this is not yet evident in the villages surveyed. It is found that the energy saved is of great significance to rural women, enabling them to contribute more effectively to village life. Owing to constraints of illiteracy and poverty, the mills have not yet resulted in greater autonomy and power for women in their communities.

KIT, Amsterdam   [E 1073-29(1994)3]

111   Gender, small-scale industry and development policy

BAUD, ISABELLE SUZANNE ANTOINETTE; BRUIJNE, G.A. DE. Intermediate Technology, London ix, 214 p. 1993 [EN] ill., graphs, maps, tabs. Includes lit.refs ISBN 1-85339-156-5

The contribution of small industries to the development process has received increased attention in recent years. Research has also been focused on the part played by women's employment in these industries within the framework of gender and development research, and indicated that women are often a major part of the workforce in small-scale production and the associated domestic outwork. The role of small industrial units in the development process, the sexual division of labour in such industries, and the way in which women combine employment and their reproductive tasks and community roles are analysed. A gender perspective on small industry which explicitly concentrates on social groups is linked to a perspective commonly used by economists which stresses the economic questions of higher employment and wider distribution of production. Recommendations are made and examined in the light of case studies in the footwear industry. It is concluded that existing models do not adequately consider the gender perspective in approaching the role of small industries in development, nor the different approaches to employment which women utilize. Intervention programmes for women which differentiate between these groups, and further systematic research in these areas are both needed to encourage evolution of a more balanced perspective on development.

KIT, Amsterdam   [N 93-846]

112   Accounting for women's work : the progress of two decades

BENERÍA, LOURDES - *World Development* 20(1992) 11 p.1547-1560 [EN] 52 lit.refs ISSN 0305-750X

The progress made towards a more accurate statistical recording of women's economic activities is reviewed. Beginning with an assessment of the main areas in which the underestimation of women's work has been prevalent, the conceptual, theoretical and methodological progress made during the last two decades is examined. This progress has contributed to the improvement of statistics regarding women in subsistence production and has set the basis for the inclusion of domestic work in national accounts. Despite this progress, much remains to be done on a practical level, particularly in the informal and voluntary sectors and at national level.

KIT, Amsterdam   [E 1271-20(1992)11]

113 Providing enterprise development and financial services to women : a decade of Bank experience in Asia

BENNETT, LYNN; GOLDBERG, MIKE - *World Bank Technical Paper* 236. World Bank, Washington, DC vii, 59 p. 1993 [EN] ill., graphs, tabs. Includes lit.refs ISSN 0253-7494 ISBN 0-8213-2682-1

Increasing women's productivity and earning potential is recognized as an important element of the World Bank's efforts to promote sustainable growth and poverty reduction in borrower countries. The number of World Bank projects providing enterprise development and financial services to women (EDFS/W) has grown markedly in Asia over the past decade. Based on 27 projects, a review is presented of the EDFS/W project portfolio in the region. The major types of assistance offered to improve the productivity of women entrepreneurs are analysed: financial services, enterprise development services and social intermediation services. The rapid growth of EDFS/W projects has been hampered by the absence of practical guidelines which would help managers translate World Bank policy regarding financial sector operations into specific project activities. Three design characteristics were found to contribute to overall project success: (1) training which recognizes the economic constraints and cultural barriers faced by women clients; (2) the incorporation of women staff members in both promotion and delivery of project services; and (3) the use of community networks and self-help groups. Project design can be improved by facilitating access of women clients and by initiating a business-oriented approach in the provision of enterprise development and financial services.

KIT, Amsterdam   [K 2526-(1993)236]

114 Rural household transport in Africa : reducing the burden on women?

BRYCESON, DEBORAY FAHY; HOWE, JOHN - *Working Paper / African Studies Centre* 15. African Studies Centre, Leiden 38 p. 1993 [EN] ill., graphs. Includes lit.refs ISSN 0924-3534 ISBN 90-5448-004-1

The significance of African women's role in rural transport has been highlighted in the development literature over the past 10 years. A brief review of salient findings on rural household transport demand, emanating from surveys and literature reviews covering East and West Africa, is given. Household transport requirements, the allocation of intrahousehold transport tasks, women's participation in rural transport, and attitudes towards women's transport role are discussed. External agency involvement should be amended in line with the perspective of women as transport suppliers. Preliminary evidence suggests that policies and measures advanced to alleviate

women's transport burden have benefited men rather than women as a result of underlying assumptions regarding rural households, female labour and women's transport needs and objectives. Certain vital dimensions of female transport work are not incorporated in current survey methods. Suggestions are made for devising effective assistance to alleviate the transport burden of women.

KIT, Amsterdam   [A 2523-(1993)15]

115 Muchacha, cachifa, criada, empleada, empregadinha, sirvienta, y... más nada : trabajadoras domésticas en América latina y el Caribe

CHANEY, ELSA M.; CASTRO, MARY GARCIA; GUAYARA SÁNCHEZ, CONSUELO. Nueva Sociedad, Caracas 425 p. 1993 [ES] ill., graphs, tabs. Bibliogr.: p. 393-421 ISBN 980-317-039-2

This book comprises 24 contributions on the status of female domestic servants in Latin America, offering a synthesis on the situation of domestic workers in the Americas. In many Latin American countries, domestic workers constitute 20%-30% of the female labour force. The first part deals with the history of domestic service in Latin America. The second part confronts the ideal and real status of maids, illustrated with case studies of different Latin American cities, domestic servants in New York, and the impact of popular magazines on perceptions regarding domestics and their relationship with their employers. The following parts investigate the possibilities of organizing domestic workers into labour unions; the impact of feminism on their status, social relations and class struggle; and the improvement of labour conditions and educational possibilities. Part V offers the history of two labour unions of domestics in Chile and Colombia, together with examples of experiences, perceptions and opinions of domestic servants themselves. The final part consists of a resource and reference list.

KIT, Amsterdam   [N 93-5954]

116 The role of women in rural production systems

CLEAVER, KEVIN M.; SCHREIBER, GÖTZ A. *In: Reversing the spiral : the population, agriculture, and environment nexus in sub-Saharan Africa* Kevin M. Cleaver, Götz A. Schreiber. - Washington, DC : World Bank, 1994 p.73-96 [EN] lit.refs in notes

Analysis of the sexual division of labour in agricultural production and farming systems in sub-Saharan Africa reveals that the organization of farm labour and production responsibilities varies widely. In much of the region, men and women produce different crops on separate plots, reflecting two distinct gender-specific farming

systems operating side by side but with large differences between the two systems. In contrast to men, women have little or no access to land, capital, labour and extension services. These constraints, combined with intensifying pressures on women's time to meet their household and community obligations, severely impede women's productivity. Efforts to intensify agriculture, conserve natural resources, and reduce population growth will therefore have to be focused to a significant extent on women, and should be aimed primarily at reducing women's time constraints; lowering the barriers impeding women's access to land, credit and extension; introducing technologies usable by and beneficial to women; and upgrading women's educational standards and skills. The severe and increasing pressure on women's time and the significant constraints faced by women in their pursuit of both traditional and non-traditional farming activities may be preventing the emergence of women's demands for fewer children and thereby contribute to the persistence of high fertility rates.
KIT, Amsterdam   [U 94-509]

117   Gender aspects of labor allocation during structural adjustment
COLLIER, PAUL; EDWARDS, A.C.; ROBERTS, J.; BARDHAN, KALPANA In: Labor markets in an era of adjustment ed. by Susan Horton, Ravi Kanbur, Dipak Mazumdar. - Washington, DC : World Bank. Economic Development Institute, 1994. - Vol. 1: Issues papers p.277-307 [EN] ill., tabs 40 lit.refs

At the economic level, structural adjustment is essentially about resource mobility: the labour market being one of the central processes for this mobility. Given that women in Africa are less likely to work for wages than men, the reallocation of their labour as a response to structural adjustment could be more difficult. Women face particularly severe constraints upon reallocating both their labour and other resources under their control outside the context of the labour market. The focus is upon women as participants rather than victims of adjustment. The price changes that constitute structural adjustment are designed to achieve reallocation of factors. Hence, factor mobility is a direct, central constraint. Price and wage rigidities increase the magnitude of required resource mobility. They also convert resource mobility from a voluntary to an involuntary process with potentially high short-term social costs borne by those households whose members lose their jobs. The macroeconomics of structural adjustment can be understood only by a more disaggregated model than that which has been used for most macroeconomic analysis: output must be disaggregated at least into three sectors.

Analogously, the microeconomics of structural adjustment can benefit considerably from disaggregation of agents by gender. The capacity to be mobile, the requirement to be mobile, and the capacity to provide a household income security strategy are all likely to differ by gender.
KIT, Amsterdam   [U 94-375]

118   African trade unions and the challenge of organizing women workers in the unorganized sectors
DATE-BAH, EUGENIA - Labour Education (1993)92 p.42-50 [EN] 15 lit.refs ISSN 0378-5467

Trade unions in Africa have recently been called upon to broaden their scope to include workers in the informal and rural sectors (constituting the majority of workers in the region) and other categories of unorganized workers. The major disadvantages faced by women workers in the unorganized sectors are outlined. Factors which have contributed to the women's unfavourable position are discussed. Trade unions may have to adapt their strategies and approaches, and need additional financial and human resources in their effort to mobilize the unorganized. Case studies of unions' attempts to organize unorganized workers, particularly women, are discussed. It is concluded that the trade unions' coverage of informal and rural sector workers is an important means of empowering these vulnerable groups of workers and giving them the protection and avenues for development that they need. It is also an essential means of empowering the trade unions themselves through expansion of their membership and diversification of their approaches.
KIT, Amsterdam   [K 1969-(1993)92]

119   The growth and dynamics of women entrepreneurs in Southern Africa
DOWNING, JEANNE; DANIELS, LISA - GEMINI Technical Report 47. GEMINI, Bethesda, MD iii, 28 p. 1992 [EN] ill., tabs. Includes lit.refs

The results of surveys on the development and growth pattern of small enterprises run by women in Lesotho, South Africa, Swaziland and Zimbabwe are presented. Data were gathered from both male and female entrepreneurs by means of household surveys and street-by-street enumeration of enterprises along roads, in commercial and industrial districts, and in traditional market areas. The findings reveal a relative lack of growth of women's enterprises compared to men's. It is contended that research on gender issues within the small enterprise sector is required to design appropriate interventions for female entrepreneurs and to measure their impact. Directions for future research are suggested.
KIT, Amsterdam   [Br N 93-82]

120   Politiques et moyens d'intervention pour
améliorer l'accès des petits paysans au crédit : le
cas de la femme dans les mécanismes de crédit en
zone rural
EHUI, MAMOU K. - *Food and Agriculture in Africa*
(1994)5 p.1-25 [FR] 18 lit.refs
    Credit is the most important means of
increasing female productivity and, to a large
extent, of developing the rural sector. The
existing credit market in rural Africa is examined
and factors constraining women's access to credit
are identified. Policy measures should be
designed to improve women's access to credit and
remove the social, legal and financial constraints
encountered by women. Several programmes
which have successfully provided credit to
women in different African countries are
reviewed. Among the lessons learned are the need
to minimize formalities for loans applicants, to
eliminate difficulties borrowers face in meeting
collateral requirements, and to encourage the
positive results of group lending.
KIT, Amsterdam   [K 2637-(1994)5]

121   Assistance to women's businesses :
evaluating the options
EIGEN, JOHANNA - *Small Enterprise Development*
3(1992)4 p.4-14 [EN] ill., tabs 4 lit.refs ISSN
0957-1329
    The women-in-development movement and
women's income generation programmes have
traditionally taken a broad-based welfare approach
which has emphasized improving women's
general living standards rather than enhancing
their independence and active participation in the
mainstream of the economy. Over the past several
years, there has been increasing awareness of the
need to focus on entrepreneurship development as
a more specific objective in the support of women
in developing countries. The effectiveness of
development programmes focusing on women's
entrepreneurship, however, has been hampered by
the fact that there is still too much emphasis on
gender and not enough emphasis on
entrepreneurship as such. A strategy for more
effective development of women's
entrepreneurship through a gender-neutral
approach, based on the experience of the Kenya
Women's Finance Trust, is outlined.
KIT, Amsterdam   [E 3166-3(1992)4]

122   Economic interest groups and their
relevance for women's development
EL-BUSHRA, JUDYACORD - *Yearbook of
Co-operative Enterprise* (1993) p.185-194 [EN]
ISSN 0952-5556
    ACORD, an operational development agency
based in the UK, aims to strengthen local
structures and enhance the ability of the poor to
cope with and promote change. Such objectives

are carried out through women's groups,
generally those with a production, small business
or credit focus. Programmes in Uganda began
with a specific, imported concept of promoting
self-sufficiency through group structures and
sought out existing economic interest groups to
graft onto. In Benin, no such structure existed and
it was difficult to establish women's groups. The
development of the programmes in Uganda and
Benin was shaped by key staff who were
committed to a specific approach aiming to
strengthen and, if necessary, to create groups.
Both programmes attempted to combine the
advantages of individual benefit and mutual
support. Support from men in the community has
been critical in both cases. Groups can overcome
constraints of the undervaluation of women's
rights and their contribution to the community
because they encourage women to pool their
resources, channel resources to them, raise their
political profile in the community, and divert
women's resources away from control by men.
However, the group strategy seems to be better at
meeting women's practical needs than at
transforming the underlying gender relations
which keep women in a subordinate position.
Therefore, issues of gender, poverty and
vulnerability must be kept in mind throughout the
design and implementation of projects.
KIT, Amsterdam   [E 2097-(1993)]

123   Gender-aware analysis and development
economics
ELSON, DIANE Department of Economics,
University of Manchester, Manchester M13 9PL -
Journal of International Development 5(1993)2
p.237-247 [EN] 34 lit.refs ISSN 0954-1748
    Economic analysis that is gender-aware, in the
sense of recognizing that all economic activity
works through and within gender relations, has
the potential to generate both a better understanding
of the development process and of the policies
required to reduce gender inequality. The extent
to which neoclassical and structuralist approaches
to the economics of development are gender-
aware is explored, and both paradigms are found
to be seriously deficient. Two recent examples of
gender-aware development economics are discussed:
a feminist adaptation of the neoclassical framework
which is used to consider the impact of gender
relations on structural adjustment in sub-Saharan
Africa (Palmer); a feminist political economy
which draws on structuralist and Marxist
approaches to an analysis of agribusiness and the
food crisis in Senegal (Mackintosh). Suggestions
are made about how to improve gender-awareness
in development economics. The potential
contribution of a critical institutionalist approach
is highlighted.
KIT, Amsterdam   [E 3118-5(1993)2]

124   Enhancing women's participation in economic development

WORLD BANK - *World Bank Policy Paper*. World Bank, Washington, DC 76 p. 1994 [EN] ill., graphs, tabs. Includes lit.refs ISSN 1014-8124 ISBN 0-8213-2963-4

International experience has proved that support for a stronger role for women in society contributes to economic growth through improved child survival rates, better family health, and reduced fertility rates. Nevertheless, women still face many barriers in contributing to and benefiting from development. These include low investment in female education and health and restricted access to services and assets. This study highlights five areas that could help change this inequitable situation: education, health, wage labour, agriculture and natural resource management, and financial services. A gender and development strategy is suggested that would take into account the relative roles and responsibilities of women and men, implying that the actions and attitudes of men must change.

KIT, Amsterdam   [U 94-372]

125   Survival strategy or business training ground? : the significance of urban agriculture for the advancement of women in African cities

FREEMAN, DONALD B. - *African Studies Review* 36(1993)3 p.1-22 [EN] ill., tabs 46 lit.refs ISSN 0002-0206

Analysis of interview data collected in a 1987 sample survey of active cultivators in Nairobi, Kenya, explains why urban agriculture is not merely a survival strategy. Male urban farmers tend to combine cultivation with small enterprises directly related to crop production. However, urban farming is mostly performed by women, the majority of whom have no assistance in cultivation. The principal motives for urban farming are to minimize cash purchases and to supplement bought food for family consumption. As cultivation is practised on both private and public open spaces, urban farming remains a risky business and the status of female farmers is particularly vulnerable. Three case studies of women farmers illustrate the main categories of motivation for urban farming. The most important motivation was found to be the need for extra cash income to invest either in the education of children or in small businesses. Successful female entrepreneurs can act as business role models for others and demonstration effects are already visible in this city. Subsistence cultivation constitutes an integral part of urban life for most women. The assumption that urban farming is a strategy of recently arrived immigrants, coping with a hostile environment until they acquire wage employment, can be rejected. Although city planners in the Third World generally prefer

orderly development of urban land use, urban farming cannot be ignored. Hence, cultivation and related informal practices should be integrated into urban planning.

KIT, Amsterdam   [A 1381-36(1993)3]

126   Assessing the gender impact of development projects : case studies from Bolivia, Burkina Faso and India

GIANOTTEN, VERA. Royal Tropical Institute, Amsterdam 103 p. 1994 [EN] ill., tabs. Includes lit.refs ISBN 90-6832-707-0

Gender analysis can help improve the efficiency and effectiveness of development projects by examining the possible consequences of projects for women as compared to men, and by using the information obtained to improve the design and planning of projects. Three pilot studies are reported which have been undertaken to test a preliminary gender assessment framework which was established to assess expected impacts of development interventions on women and the extent to which women's interests and needs are addressed. The studies comprise: an environmental management project in Bolivia; an integrated development programme in Burkina Faso; and two irrigation projects in Andhra Pradesh, India. Gender assessment provides hypotheses about a project's expected impact on the beneficiary group, making it a useful planning instrument which can help remedy problems prior to project implementation. The strength of a gender assessment is considered, focusing on the analytical structure of context analysis, project analysis, institutional analysis and gender analysis at local level. Gender assessment also has limitations; it is relatively time-consuming and costly, and it may unduly raise expectations of the population involved in the gender analysis at local level. A gender-oriented approach is needed to gain realistic insights into the way in which the relations between women and men are shaped in society, and how women are affected by project interventions.

KIT, Amsterdam   [N 94-2653]

127   Structural adjustment and African women farmers

GLADWIN, CHRISTINA H. University of Florida. Center for African Studies, Gainesville, FL viii, 413 p. 1991 [EN] ill., tabs. Includes lit.refs, index ISBN 0-8130-1063-2

In the 1980s, development experts and donor agencies agreed on the importance of macroeconomic policies to the development of sub-Saharan Africa. These structural adjustment policies comprised: devaluation; increases in artificially low food prices and interest rates; emphasis on exportable goods; decrease in government spending; wage freezes; and removal of subsidies. Some 16 papers consider the effect of these policies on women and whether they have stimulated or hindered socio-economic development. Some authors argue that adjustment policies were a way to exhilarate stagnating economies, while others argue that a structural transformation of the economy (i.e. substantial shifts in the structure of demand and production) is needed in the development process rather than monetarist polices. Others claim that adjustment policies are ignoring the reality of life at microlevel, where up to 80% of the food consumed is produced by women farmers. Although African income distribution might have been improved, the effects appear to have been negative at the household level: (1) the costs for schooling and medical care have been augmented; (2) remittances of sons and husbands have stagnated due to wage freezes; (3) agricultural inputs have become too expensive since (fertilizer) subsidies no longer exist; (4) subsistence crops have been neglected in favour of commercial crops; and (5) food prices have risen. The rise in food prices has endangered food security and is held responsible for the African food crises of the 1990s. It is concluded that women's access to land, credit, inputs and key services, including employment, must be enhanced in order to increase their economic opportunities. Given women's substantial role in agriculture, particularly in Africa, economic growth and change cannot be realized without their participation.

KIT, Amsterdam [N 92-8613]

128   Working (with) women : theory, vision, policy and practice of income generating projects in Zimbabwe
HELLINGS, ELLY; MARTENS, HELMA. Catholic University Tilburg, Tilburg 127 p. 1992 [EN] Thesis

Theoretical and empirical evidence is presented on the theory, policy and practice of income-generating activities in Zimbabwe. Development approaches to improve the position of women are described, paying particular attention to income generation as an aspect of the women-in-development (WID) approach. A review of relevant literature for Zimbabwe is presented, addressing the various factors influencing women's lives, theoretical approaches to women and income generation, and the role of NGOs in income-generating projects. Based on visits to three NGOs (a training centre, a church organization and a women's organization) and some of their projects, the NGOs' objectives, policy and practice for WID and income generation are reported. Four bottlenecks are discussed: Western WID theories appear not to be suitable for the situation in Zimbabwe; sex roles

and labour division are culturally specific; the unequal balance of power between the sexes; and women cannot be seen as a single target group. The development of a vision which will provide the basis for guidelines for WID and income generation policy is recommended. All three NGOs argue that a business approach might be a solution for failing projects. In order to make these projects succeed, feasibility studies are indispensable. These studies should provide overviews of all possibilities and constraints on economic, socio-cultural, legal, political and environmental areas. Subsequent projects should be based on thorough examination of the target group (comprising both women and men), aims and objectives.

KIT, Amsterdam [N 93-3487]

129   Financing women's enterprise : beyond barriers and bias
HILHORST, THEA; OPPENOORTH, HARRY. Royal Tropical Institute, Amsterdam 104 p. 1992 [EN] Includes lit.refs ISBN 90-6832-705-4

Constraints faced by poor, self-employed rural women in gaining access to financial services, particularly credit and savings, are analysed. Other forms of financing, such as risk and profit sharing, are also considered. The access of most poor women to formal credit is very limited because of their lack of collateral, the small amounts needed and inappropriate delivery systems. Poor women frequently have to rely on informal sources which have a number of disadvantages (such as high rates of interest) but which are relatively accessible (less paperwork). In designing any new institutional arrangement, it is necessary to take enough time and to aim for structural change. The level of funds for loan must be maintained and even expanded, while costs should be covered by the interest margin. Institutions will require subsidies in the short run but these should not be used to subsidize interest rates for users directly. Given that programmes often fail because of false assumptions and lack of information and confidence, it is advisable to involve both informal lenders and beneficiaries with local knowledge. Flexibility, creativity and experimentation are important for designing, developing and delivering financial services to poor rural women. The book is based on the symposium on 'Women's access to financial services', held at the Royal Tropical Institute, the Netherlands, during January 1991.

KIT, Amsterdam [N 92-6763]

130   Increasing the access of African women to credit : an integrated approach
AFRICAN TRAINING AND RESEARCH CENTRE FOR WOMEN. UN. ECA, Addis Ababa x, 52 p. 1990 [EN] ill. Includes lit.refs

Women's access to credit is considered essential for improving their effective participation in productive activities. Guidelines for an integrated approach to increasing women's access to credit in Africa are presented, based on the experience of the UN African Training and Research Centre for Women. The integrated approach aims to address the various needs, requirements and risk factors which constrain women's access to credit through packages of assistance. The focus is on rural and urban poor women who have great economic potential which is impeded by their fragile financial base. Enhanced participation can only be possible if the enabling financial resources are made available to women through favourable credit programmes with less rigid terms and conditions. Macro- and micro-level policy measures should be undertaken before implementing the integrated packages in order to mobilize resources, guarantee efficient utilization of resources acquired through credit, and establish an environment within which women's access to credit can be improved.

KIT, Amsterdam   [Br U 92-100]

131   Political economy and gender in Latin America : the emerging dilemmas

KELLY, MARÍA PATRICIA FERNÁNDEZ - *Working Paper Series / Latin American Program, Woodrow Wilson International Center for Scholars* 207. WWICS, Washington, DC 22 p. 1994 [EN]

The issue of gender is addressed from the perspective of political economy and with special reference to Latin America. Following a summary of perspectives on development, the concept of gender and its relationship to development is discussed. Gender is used to assign men and women to different areas of production and thus contributes to the distribution of power in both public and private spheres. Analyses of migration along the USA-Mexico border and the expansion of Mexico's maquiladora (export-oriented light industry) programme are presented to demonstrate how economic internationalization has challenged gender definitions. Internationalization is altering the conditions under which Latin American countries seek to develop. The growth of export-processing zones and maquiladora programmes, as well as the North American Free Trade Agreement, are some of the symptoms of the economic integration. Among other consequences, internationalization has resulted in an unprecedented incorporation of women into the labour force in conjunction with their continued involvement in the informal sector. In addition, changes in production, investment in capital goods, and the integration of advanced technology have resulted in a recomposition of tasks and labour. These shifts, combined with the

demands generated by increased poverty, have changed the kind of work undertaken by men and women, exemplifying that gender is a dynamic and continually evolving concept.

KIT, Amsterdam   [H 2032-(1994)207]

132   Beyond profit : ASEAN women managers in government and not-for-profit organizations

LICUANAN, VICTORIA S.. Asian Institute of Management, Metro Manila xii, 331 p. 1992 [EN] ill., tabs. Includes lit.refs

The path to success for female executives in South East Asia is fraught with difficulties imposed by traditional value systems. Some 18 case studies of women managers both in government service and non-profit organizations in Indonesia, Malaysia, Philippines, Singapore and Thailand illustrate the complex role and status of these women. Every woman interviewed stated that combining work with the role of mother and wife is most arduous and that they could not manage without the support and encouragement of their husband. Apart from the personal views of the respondents, the case studies include the organizational structure of their office, work relations, time management, practical, educational and family backgrounds, and perceptions and viewpoints of outsiders. Social transformation, especially in the field of education, is needed to increase the number of senior women managers and erase traditional role models.

KIT, Amsterdam   [N 94-282]

133   Engendering adjustment or adjusting gender? : some new approaches to women and development in Africa

LOCKWOOD, MATTHEW - *Discussion Paper / IDS, University of Sussex* 315. IDS, Brighton BN1 9RE45. 20 p. 1992 [EN] ill. Includes lit.refs ISSN 0308-5864 ISBN 0-903715-96-1

Gender aspects of macroeconomic adjustment have been analysed to address how men and women might be affected differently by certain policies. Having reviewed two ways in which economists have analysed gender and applied these analyses to the position of women under structural adjustment, a new approach to the economics of gender is presented and its assumptions and implications are assessed. The new approach implies that gender factors will hinder the adjustment process in Africa because it leads to the misallocation of labour between sectors (especially the concentration of women in the production of non-tradeables), and to the immobility of labour between sectors (women are hindered from moving into the production of tradeables). Gender inequalities can thus partly account for the failure of structural adjustment policies to bring about the expected or desired response, especially in labour markets.

KIT, Amsterdam [E 2206-315]

134   Women in trade unions : organizing the unorganized

MARTENS, MARGARET HOSMER; MITTER, SWASTI.
ILO, Geneva xiv, 204 p. 1994 [EN] Includes
lit.refs ISBN 92-2-108759-X

In many developing countries, women are generally employed in small-scale enterprises, the rural and urban informal sectors, home-based units or domestic service. In the current climate of deregulation and high unemployment, this situation is also by no means uncommon in developed countries. In newly industrializing countries, women are often employed in export processing zones which are not usually subject to labour regulations. It is difficult to persuade women in the unorganized sectors to join workers' organizations because such women are often found in dispersed workplaces and because they often lack the means for collective action. Case studies on organizing female domestic workers, homeworkers, rural workers, the self-employed and women working in the informal sector and in export processing zones in Brazil, Burkina Faso, India, Ivory Coast, Mauritius, Mexico and Namibia are provided. Education for women members of rural workers' organizations in Asia and Africa is also addressed. Four case studies are from industrialized countries. The case studies illustrate approaches to organizing women in the unorganized sectors. Experimenting with institutional structures and linking cooperative economic activities with trade unionism have proved effective means of mobilizing women, especially around income-generating projects for the poor self-employed.

KIT, Amsterdam [U 95-83]

135   Women and fishing in traditional Pacific Island cultures

MATTHEWS, E. - Inshore Fisheries Research Project Technical Document (1993)5 p.29-33 [EN] 15 lit.refs ISSN 1018-3116

Women are involved in many types of fishing in the traditional cultures of the Pacific Islands. The extent to which women fish varies greatly from island to island. Most women, however, tend to fish in shallow waters close to shore, without the use of canoes and with no implements apart from baskets and sticks. Fishing studies tend to concentrate on the often highly ritualized, dangerous pursuit of ocean fish which is primarily a male-dominated activity. Studies have often overlooked women's roles in fish collection as a result of the use of general terms such as 'fishermen' and because early researchers were men. Further, men in the Pacific Islands also

minimize the importance of women's contribution to fish collection. As women fish on a daily basis, they supply a great deal of the protein obtained in many subsistence diets.

KIT, Amsterdam [K 2745-(1993)5]

136   Women and the pursuit of local initiatives in Eastern and Southern Africa

MBILINYI, MAJORIE In: Reviving local self-reliance : people's responses to the economic crisis in Eastern and Southern Africa ed. by W. Gooneratne and M. Mbilinyi. - Nagoya : UNCRD, 1992 p.51-98 [EN] Bibliogr.

During the last two decades an enormous increase in the number of women's groups has taken place in Africa, far outnumbering other organized local initiatives in the region. Women organized themselves to survive the economic crisis and to resist oppressive and exploitative social relations on an individual and collective basis. Organizational initiatives of women in Eastern and Southern Africa are explored. Conceptual issues related to women's organizational initiatives, including the women-in-development approach and government and donor development strategies pursued during and after the colonial period, are discussed. Particular attention is paid to government policy towards peasant agriculture, its impact in terms of the intensification of women's agricultural labour and changing patterns of labour participation, and women's individual responses. Case studies of different types of women's groups in Tanzania demonstrate that women organize themselves to increase income and employment and to acquire functional and vocational skills. The growth of women's organizations at grassroots and national level has been both a cause and an effect of growing gender consciousness among women in different classes and ethnic groups. Heightened consciousness is associated with the expansion of women's education, women's increased participation in market-oriented activities, and the increased dependence of households and families. However, real transformation of society whereby women liberate themselves along with other disadvantaged and exploited groups will depend on the combined contributions of grassroots and educated women and men.

KIT, Amsterdam [U 94-317]

137   Measurement and valuation of unpaid work

UN INTERNATIONAL RESEARCH AND TRAINING INSTITUTE FOR THE ADVANCEMENT OF WOMEN] - INSTRAW News (1994)20 p.30-32 [EN] ill., tabs

A short report is provided of an INSTRAW project to develop cost-effective measurement and valuation of work in the informal and domestic subsistence sectors, particularly that done by women, so that it can be included in national accounts. Based on the preliminary results of five country studies, INSTRAW has identified a group of work activities that are currently excluded from the System of National Accounts. A classification is proposed in order to include these activities in national accounts.

KIT, Amsterdam [K 2365-(1994)20]

138   Measures to integrate the employment, income and shelter needs of women in programmes and projects in the plantation sector : final evaluation report
ILO. Industrial Activities Branch, Geneva [34] p. 1992 [EN] ill., tabs

In collaboration with the Organization of Tanzanian Trade Unions (OTTU), ILO implemented a three-year project in 1989 to improve the working and living conditions of women on sugar, sisal and tea plantations by developing capacity for representing female plantation workers at national, regional and local levels. An evaluation was conducted in July 1992 which found that the immediate objectives of the project have been reached in varying degrees. The objectives of establishing a cadre of trained specialists concerned with women workers and increasing women's participation in workers' organizations have been fully achieved: the Women Workers Department of OTTU has been managing the project; the organizers-trainers have been posted in the regions and integrated into the OTTU structure; and committees of women workers have been established at all of the project's plantation sites. Donor support should be considered to extend project activities for a further three year period. The new phase should focus on: (1) continued consolidation of the organizational base of women's participation in the new union of agricultural workers; (2) establishment of a strong tripartite machinery in addressing the situation of women plantation workers and formulating appropriate policies and strategies; (3) policy-oriented research supporting and facilitating the above; and (4) specific action plans formulated and implemented with committees of women workers which have received appropriate training.

KIT, Amsterdam [U 93-485]

139   Poverty in the 1990's : the responses of urban women
MEER, FATIMA. UNESCO, Paris 289 p. 1994 [EN] ill., tabs. Includes lit.refs

Comparative analyses are presented of women's strategies to overcome poverty within the context of the economic crisis and structural adjustment policies in Costa Rica, Ecuador, Ghana, Guyana, India, Mexico, the Philippines, South Africa, and Zimbabwe. Women's responses to poverty include engaging in employment,

primarily informal sector activities and low paid, unskilled jobs. These productive activities are undertaken in addition to domestic work and social reproduction. Another survival strategy of women has been to organize themselves into cooperatives, solidarity networks and other forms of mutual support organizations in order to gain access to productive resources. A uniform picture emerges: women bear the bulk of the responsibility for the family and its values, under adverse economic conditions, and under male domination, no matter how significant the woman's contribution to the household economy. Traditional concepts of gender rights and obligations continue to restrict women's options to cope with poverty. Women in Asia and Africa should deal with male domination on their own terms by exercising pressure on specific persons, on fathers, husbands, brothers; and work through traditional concepts of women's rights and obligations, first within the family, extending into kinship and neighbourhood. Imposition of Western liberal formulas on Africa and Asia should be avoided. Women should be judged in their own context and not in terms of First World feminist and Eurocentric expectations.

KIT, Amsterdam [U 94-371]

140   Market reforms and women workers in Vietnam : a case study of Hanoi and Ho Chi Minh City
MOGHADAM, VALENTINE M. - *Working Papers / WIDER* 116. UNU. WIDER, Helsinki 35 p. 1994 [EN] ill., tabs. Includes lit.refs ISSN 0782-8233

The effects of economic restructuring on urban women workers in Vietnam are determined, drawing on fieldwork from factories in Ho Chi Minh City and Hanoi, Vietnam, during February 1994. Socio-demographic and economic background information, including information on the labour force and women's employment, is provided. Following an outline of Vietnam's manufacturing sector, the situation of women working in the textiles and garment industries in both cities is examined. A comparison is made with the situation in other countries which are undergoing market reform, particularly with Eastern Europe and Russia. The move towards market reform in 1989 and the emphasis on exports has had a differential impact across Vietnamese society. As in other countries, many women workers and particularly women in lower-status occupations and with lower skills have lost their jobs. However, the prospects for women workers seem promising. New employment opportunities have developed and new kinds of jobs and occupations have evolved in the private sector, manufacturing and services. These trends, together with Vietnam's development strategy which evinces a sensitivity to labour and to women in particular, provide a supportive environment for women's participation in the labour force.

KIT, Amsterdam   [K 2714-(1994)116]

141   A woman's place : household labour allocation in rural Kenya

NEITZERT, MONICA Department of Economics, Laurentian University, Sudbury - *Canadian Journal of Development Studies* 15(1994)3 p.401-427 [EN] ill., graphs, tabs 54 lit.refs. With French summary. ISSN 0225-5189

Many economic development policies implicitly target male heads of households on the assumption that benefits so conferred will improve the welfare of all household members. The literature, however, indicates that women are excluded or have gained less from economic development than men. A more equitable approach to economic development would include all members of specific households. Male and female household labour allocation and their respective contribution to household welfare are analysed. Selected literature relating to women's role and economic development is examined, together with evidence of female and male participation in the formal rural labour market in Kenya in 1988. The review suggests that women have tended to be excluded from the direct gains of economic development by virtue of development policies and by labour market imperfections which reinforce the existing sexual division of labour. The current labour market incentives in rural areas of Kenya prepare boys for labour market participation and girls for subsistence agriculture and domestic work. Institutional reform, particularly reform of labour market and educational institutions, is a necessary condition for spreading the gains of economic development more widely. Development policies ought to be based on a model of household provision rather than on one of individual choice. Such a model would recognize women's role in household welfare and would therefore lead to policies which promote advancement in the technology for non-market welfare production.

KIT, Amsterdam   [H 1847-15(1994)3]

142   Gender, exploitation development and agricultural transformation in sub-Saharan Africa

NINDI, B.C. - *Eastern Africa Economic Review* 8(1992)2 p.123-134 [EN] 61 lit.refs

An improvement in agricultural productivity in sub-Saharan Africa is not possible in the short term unless the productivity of women is also improved. According to Boserup and others, intensification in agricultural production is required. The processes of intensification and technological change generally, however, lead to a decrease in women's participation in agriculture, often displacing women from their means of material production. Development planning often fails to include women and, as a consequence, women farmers in Africa are being marginalized in the agricultural production process. Based on recent FAO reports which demonstrate that population pressure and land scarcity are unevenly distributed, it is argued that the rate of displacement of women will vary considerably both within and between developing countries. The displacement of women farmers will therefore be blocked or retarded in areas with lower population densities due to the high incidence of human and animal diseases, in areas experiencing male out-migration, and in the presence of gender-neutral incentives to production.

KIT, Amsterdam   [A 2754-8(1992)2]

143   Central American men and women in the urban informal sector

PÉREZ SÁINZ, J.P.; MENJÍVAR LARÍN, R. - *Journal of Latin American Studies* 26(1994)2 p.431-447 [EN] ill., tabs lit.refs in notes ISSN 0022-216X

The participation of women and men in the informal sector in urban areas of Central America is explored, drawing on data from a recent region-wide study. A brief description of some basic socio-economic features of the Central American countries is given to provide an historical context. The relationship between the economic crisis, poverty and urban informal activities is explored by discussing three hypotheses dealing with the logic of labour mobility, types of informal activity, and traditional domestic roles. Allowing for some qualifications in the Costa Rican case and excluding Panama, the predominance of subsistence informality in Central America is reconfirmed. Participation in the informal sector may represent a means of popular reproduction rather than the search for accumulation. However, the presence of men and women in the informal sector has a different motivation. For men, individualistic motivations and a small contribution to domestic labour allows them in some instances to become involved in dynamic informal activity. By contrast, domestic and family considerations seriously limit such possibilities for women and confine them in most cases to a subsistence informality. Thus, factors associated with gender differences, as expressed in the reproductive sphere, extend their influence to the informal sector.

KIT, Amsterdam   [C 2128-26(1994)2]

144   The report on rural women living in poverty : Summit on the Economic Advancement of Rural Women, Geneva, 25-26 February 1992
POWER, JONATHAN. IFAD, Rome 59 p. 1992 [EN] ill., maps, tabs. Includes lit.refs

The number of rural women living in poverty in developing countries has increased by almost 50% over the past 20 years to an estimated 565 million: 374 million of them in Asia; 130 million in Africa; 43 million in Latin America and the Caribbean; and 18 million in the Near East and North Africa. This growth is not just a consequence of population growth and reflects the sharp rise in the number of female-headed households. While poverty among rural men has increased over the last 20 years by 30%, among women it has increased by 48%. The status and situation of rural women in developing countries are reviewed, based on several case studies and issues addressed at the Summit on the Economic Advancement of Rural Women, held in Geneva, Switzerland, during 25-26 February 1992, and organized by the IFAD. Following overviews of women's situation in rural Asia, Latin America and the Caribbean, and Africa, an outline is given of IFAD's approach to reaching rural women through its rural and agricultural project assistance. Although most developing countries have signed the UN Convention on the Elimination of All Forms of Discrimination Against Women, there is still a long way to go before the words of the 1979 Convention are translated into tangible change. There are still many obstacles to overcome, and ways of removing them are suggested.
KIT, Amsterdam   [Br U 94-7]

145   Women's employment and pay in Latin America : overview and methodology
PSACHAROPOULOS, GEORGE; TZANNATOS, ZAFIRIS. World Bank, Washington, DC xv, 250 p. 1992 [EN] ill., graphs, tabs. Bibliogr.: p. 217-239. Includes index ISBN 0-8213-2270-2

This first of two volumes presents aggregate data on the evolution of labour force differentials and female participation in Latin America, showing that in some countries twice as many women participate in the labour force than 20 years ago. Female participation rates were, however, found to be among the lowest in the world. On aggregate, women were found to be more likely to participate in the labour force if they have more years of schooling. In addition, more educated women earn significantly more than less educated women. Women were found to be paid less than their male counterparts. Common factors that determine salaries paid to men and women are analysed in order to identify what part of the male/female earnings differential can be attributed to different human capital

endowments between the sexes, and what part is due to unexplained factors such as discrimination. Differences in human capital endowments were found to explain only a small proportion of the wage differential in most country studies. The remaining proportion thus represents the upper level of discrimination. It is concluded that current labour legislation often prevents women from reaching their full productive potential. The companion volume uses household survey data to analyse labour force participation rates and wages earned by men and women in similar positions, paying special attention to education as a factor influencing women's decision to work.
KIT, Amsterdam   [U 93-41]

146   Case studies on women's employment and pay in Latin America
PSACHAROPOULOS, GEORGE; TZANNATOS, ZAFIRIS. World Bank, Washington, DC ix, 480 p. 1992 [EN] ill., graphs, tabs. Includes lit.refs ISBN 0-8213-2308-3

Household survey data are used to analyse labour force participation rates and wages earned by men and women in similar positions in Central and Latin America, paying special attention to the role of education as a factor influencing women's decision to work. Some 21 contributions examine these issues in 16 countries. In some countries, twice as many women participate in the labour market than 20 years ago. Aggregate results are analysed in a companion volume.
KIT, Amsterdam   [U 93-110]

147   Women and work in South Asia : regional patterns and perspectives
RAJU, SARASWATI; BAGCHI, DEIPICA. Routledge, London xviii, 282 p. 1993 [EN] ill., graphs, tabs. Includes index. Bibliogr.: p. 252-272 ISBN 0-415-04249-6

The patterns of female labour participation in South Asia have distinct spatial dimensions that cannot be explained in terms of economic rationale alone. This book integrates different scales of analysis and the methodologies of indigenous and Western contributors to consider female labour participation in different states of India, Nepal, Pakistan, and Sri Lanka. Female labour participation at various levels is placed in the regional variation of agricultural-ecological, technological-environmental, economic, demographic, ethnic, caste and religious contexts. Highlighting the public and private domains of women's work, inadequacies of nationally published data at an aggregate level are revealed. Regional and local religious, cultural and societal constraints on gender relations are discussed. Given the biological and social construction of gender roles in South Asia, women tend to concentrate in jobs where they can combine their households duties and work. Once household conditions improve there generally exists a parallel process of withdrawal of females from the labour market due to patriarchal notions of the male as the primary breadwinner and of females as the custodians of the family's honour. Without structural social transformation, efforts to increase women's autonomy at the grassroots remain extremely vulnerable. The recent phenomena of women's entry into the so-called male domain of work and the threefold increase in female students enroling in higher education in India may be the beginning of a changing societal attitude and a disintegration of the patriarchal ideology.

KIT, Amsterdam   [N 94-529]

148   Review and appraisal 1990

DIVISION FOR THE ADVANCEMENT OF WOMEN - *Women 2000* (1990)2. Centre for Social Development and Humanitarian Affairs, Vienna 28 p. [EN] ill., graphs, tabs.

An assessment is presented of the progress in implementing strategies at national and international levels to advance the status of women in relation to the goals of equality, development and peace. It is compiled by the Commission on the Status of Women, charged with reviewing and appraising the progress made and measures implemented to advance women's status. Part of the data was obtained from national governments and intergovernmental and non-governmental organizations. Poverty, illiteracy, poor nutrition, lack of participation at all levels, high population growth rates, the economic crisis and structural adjustment measures are identified as constraints to the implementation of the strategies. International institutional coordination, staff, and the work of NGOs in the field of women and development are also addressed. The recommendations and conclusions that emerged from the thirty-fourth session of the Commission on the Status of Women in 1990 are included.

KIT, Amsterdam   [K 2605-(1990)2]

149   The invisible adjustment : poor women and the economic crisis

ROCHA, LOLA. UNICEF. The Americas and the Caribbean Regional Office. Regional Programme Women in Development, Santiago 262 p. 1989 [EN] ill., graphs, tabs. Includes lit.refs

The impact of the economic crisis and adjustment policies of the 1980s on poor women in Latin America and the Caribbean is documented in this book. A conceptual framework is presented which aims at analysis of the complex web of conditions affecting the position of poor women, encompassing both socio-cultural and economic determinants. Case

studies of Argentina, Bolivia, Brazil, Ecuador, Honduras, Jamaica and Mexico indicate that the recession and mechanisms of adjustment are reflected in women's daily lives in the excessive number of hours worked in order to ensure family survival. The lengthening of women's working day, whether waged or unwaged, in a situation of generalized uncertainty and vulnerability is outlined. The limitations on their participation in public affairs and the possibility that they draw back from involvement in public issues and the political sphere are some of the expressions of the recent crisis and adjustment policies in relation to women in low income sectors. Women are not provided with sufficient education to meet the urgent income needs and the increasing demands generated by the crisis. Violence against women, the breakdown of family, and physical and mental health disorders are also considered to be expressions of the crisis. Patriarchal and male attitudes prevalent in the region's political culture, and the sexual division of labour, mean that women have only a limited participation in the mechanisms for the distribution of power. The evidence suggests that the situation created by the crisis may make it still more difficult to achieve the aim of putting men and women on equal footing as citizens.

KIT, Amsterdam   [U 92-276]

150   Women's work, women's worth : women, economics and development

ROTHSTEIN, FRANCES ABRAHAMER; STEPHEN, LYNN; RUDOLF, GLORIA; VILLARREAL, MAGDALENA; BOLLES, A. LYNN; SULLIVAN, KATHLEEN; BABB, FLORENCE E.; FINCH, JOHN; GAILEY, CHRISTINE WARD; TRASK, HAUNANI KAY; TRASK, MILILANI; MENCHER, JOAN; KIM, SEUNG-KYUNG; DALSIMER, MARLYN; NISONOFF, LAURIE; DAVIS, DIANA; SAUNDERS, LUCY WOOD; UCHMAN, ELKA; RAMDANE, ZAHRA; LADUKE, WINONA; CLARK, GRACIA - *Cultural Survival* 16(1992)4 p.19-71 [EN] ill., photogr. 59 lit.refs

Case studies are presented illustrating the various ways in which poor and working class women cope with the economic crisis in urban and rural areas of developing countries. The 19 short articles cover the involvement of women in agriculture, trade networks, informal sector activities, such as domestic service and street vending, and the industrial sector in rural and urban areas. Other issues addressed are women's responses to the one-child population policy and the 'missing girls' phenomenon of the 1980s in China, and the status of women refugees in Afghanistan. Women play an important role in survival of culture and traditions and, at the same time, they are major actors in economic development. Gender hierarchies aggravated by ethnicity and class, however, restrict women's access to marketable skills and resources, and thereby women's potential economic role. Women depend on kin, workplace and community networks to have access to labour, resources, jobs and protection. These networks, however, are overlooked in development planning and have no power to affect local practice and national and international policies. Women's networks and women's proven ability to amass capital through them should be recognized as a powerful resource for change.

KIT, Amsterdam [D 2695-16(1992)4]

151 Rural women in Latin America : rural development, access to land, migration and legislation

HUMAN RESOURCES, INSTITUTIONS AND AGRARIAN REFORM DIVISION, REGIONAL OFFICE FOR LATIN AMERICA AND THE CARIBBEAN. FAO, Rome 257 p. 1992 [EN] ill., tabs. Includes lit.refs

Four studies consider key issues for the advancement of rural women in Latin America. The first study identifies the problems that women face with regard to access to land ownership, considering how these obstacles affect participation in rural development in the region. It also suggests specific measures to overcome these difficulties. Case studies from Colombia and Honduras provide more in-depth information to complement the regional analysis. The second study seeks to determine the extent to which female migration affects small agricultural units with case studies from Mexico and the Dominican Republic. The role of women in the migratory process is examined, as well as behaviour patterns adopted according to the various socio-productive contexts. The third study presents a detailed review of the constitutional, labour, agrarian, and credit legislation in Chile, the Dominican Republic, Guatemala and Peru, to determine the extent to which these factors affect rural women's participation in the development process. Legislative amendments are suggested. The final study considers the current characteristics and conditions of women's living and working environment to determine their implications for the design and implementation of rural development and women-targeted policies. This regional study, which also includes specific data for Brazil and Paraguay, highlights the emerging contradiction between the prevailing cultural patterns and the growing participation of women in agricultural production. Women-oriented programmes are needed which integrate both their reproductive and productive functions.

KIT, Amsterdam [U 94-543]

152 New technology for rural women : paradoxes of sustainability

SCHOONMAKER FREUDENBERGER, KAREN - *Development in Practice* 4(1994)1 p.13-22 [EN] ill. 10 lit.refs ISSN 0961-4524

The difficulties of reaching relatively poor populations with labour-saving technologies are discussed, taking the case of milling and dehulling technologies for coarse grains in Senegal and the Gambia. A simple analytical model is presented which helps to explain why the vast majority of labour-saving machines are underutilized in rural areas. Donors continue to support such projects, despite the fact that they only occasionally provide significant benefits to the broad population in the short term and that they are not sustainable in the longer term. The constraint which is a key limiting factor appears to be the shortage of cash (or payment-in-kind) needed to pay processing fees. This moderately affects milling demand and greatly affects dehulling demand because, both in Senegal and the Gambia, women who do not have enough money to both dehull and mill by machine give priority to milling. Women's inability to pay processing fees is a problem because in the time saved by using a machine to dehull or mill their grains, women cannot earn enough money to pay the fees for using the machine. It is argued that new approaches to introducing labour-saving technologies in rural areas are needed to reach those women who cannot afford the technology.

KIT, Amsterdam [D 2672-4(1994)1]

153 Role transition of women in agriculture : some issues

SEN, D. - *Journal of Rural Development* 12(1993)5 p.497-513 [EN] ill. 9 lit.refs ISSN 0970-3357

A framework is presented for changing the role of women in agriculture and related activities. Possible areas for intervention which provide alternative, productive employment opportunities are suggested. The role of technology and the need for agricultural extension to improve women's productivity are discussed. Experiences of using extension to address women's problems in Indian agriculture are outlined. A review is made of the institutional support to women provided by the government, financial institutions and voluntary organizations. The position of the female workforce can be improved by increasing its productive potential. Women should be treated as important economic actors not as dependent members of the family. Institutional interventions should provide women with productive resources. The ability of women to contribute more to the family income will in turn reduce the dependency syndrome under which they have traditionally been suffering. The basic issues surrounding appropriate income-generating activities, extension and institutional support need to be determined in a strategy which will enable women to become equal partners in the process of national development.

KIT, Amsterdam [A 3312-12(1993)5]

154 Women's contribution towards national development in Zambia

SIBALWA, DAVID - *Convergence* 26(1993)2 p.38-46 [EN] 9 lit.refs. With French and Spanish summary ISSN 0010-8146

A review is presented of women's roles in economic activities in Zambia. Tradition and legislation are shown to operate as influential factors in defining and shaping women's work. Although equal pay for equal work is being advocated, gender disparity in access to wage work should first be addressed. Enhancing women's access to education and training opportunities (formal, non-formal, vocational) is considered one vital way for women to gain status in society, to narrow the gender wage gap, and to improve their productivity. Policies that fail to encourage women's participation in formal and non-formal schooling may serve to keep women in marginal roles in the economy and the power structures of society, and will institutionalize their low status, low income gender-stereotyped jobs. Programmes should include awareness-raising and concentrate on critical issues that confront women and men in the political, social, economic and legal spheres, such as the women's legal rights, the educational system, health issues and credit facilities. Women's access to vocational training, formal and non-formal education and employment will eventually lead to changes in tradition and legislation.

KIT, Amsterdam [H 1967-26(1993)2]

155 Women in public enterprises in developing countries

SIPIC, GORANA; VRATUSA, ANTON; SISUL, NADA; RAMACHANDRAN, REENA; IYER, LALITHA; BAKHIR, MOHAMMED H.; LOH LEE LEE; FUBARA, BEDFORD A.; GABRIEL, A.O.I.; TOBY, A.J.; SHAIKH, KHALID M.; BARNOUTI, SOUAD N. - *Public Enterprise* 13(1993)3/4 p.147-313 [EN] ill., tabs 56 lit.refs. With Arabic, English, Spanish and French summary ISSN 0351-3464

This special issue presents some 10 of the papers prepared for the International Workshop on Women in Public Enterprises: Current Facts and Perspectives, held in New Delhi, India, in November 1991. These papers provide case studies from India, Iraq, Malaysia, Nigeria and Pakistan, focusing on the position of women at their salaried workplace as well as in the household. They provide data on the similarities and differences in the position of women resulting from the social or economic circumstances or from the historical, cultural, religious or political background. Furthermore, perspectives of women in public enterprises are highlighted. The basic conclusion is that the women's movement should rethink its organizational structure and identify issues rising in international importance which pose threats and must be turned into opportunities. The final contribution is a methodological study, jointly prepared by International Centre of Public Enterprises and the UN International Research and Training Institute for the Advancement of Women, which analyses trends in the social impact assessment of the investment/acquisition of technology projects with particular reference to the position of women. The annexes contain: (1) an approach to the system of indicators and data on the position of women in public enterprises in developing countries; and (2) two questionnaires on public enterprise performance in general and on the position of individual employees.

KIT, Amsterdam [K 2340-13(1993)3/4]

156 Mortgaging women's lives : feminist critiques of structural adjustment

SPARR, PAMELA. Zed Books, London x, 214 p. 1994 [EN] ill., tabs. Includes lit.refs, index ISBN 1-85649-102-1

The impact of structural adjustment policies and programmes on women is documented in this book. The case studies focus on the employment and income-generating effects of structural adjustment on women. They illustrate important differences in the way macroeconomic policies and corporate behaviour affect women and in women's responses to structural adjustment. Household characteristics such as size, composition, life-cycle stage, place of residence (urban/rural), access to land and other indicators of wealth and status determine the impact of public policy and people's responses to it. Other aspects of class, as well as race, ethnicity and culture, also need to be considered to understand gender dynamics. Two introductory chapters cover structural adjustment and feminist critiques of it. Case studies consider structural adjustment from the perspective of: the impact of privatization on women and their status in Egypt; women's employment in the public and informal sectors; employment implications for women of export-oriented manufacturing in Turkey; women's industrial employment opportunities in Sri Lanka; rural women's home production activities and crop production in the Philippines; rural women's production resources and quality of life; and women's livelihoods in Jamaica. In order to enter the policy and analytical debate on structural adjustment on an equal plane, gender analysis must demonstrate that it has significant economic ramifications for the entire society. Otherwise, women's concerns will be an add-on rather than integral to policy formation. It is suggested that the research base should be broadened to include gender analysis of macroeconomic issues and, subsequently, governments should be put under pressure to collect gender-differentiated statistics.

KIT, Amsterdam   [P 94-700]

157   The impact of crisis, stabilization and structural adjustment on women in Lima, Peru
TANSKI, JANET M. - *World Development* 22(1994)11 p.1627-1642 [EN] ill., tabs 35 lit.refs ISSN 0305-750X

Recent development literature has suggested that the negative effects of structural adjustment policies have been borne disproportionately by the poor of Latin America, and more specifically by poor women. Empirical studies are lacking, however, and the connection between the crisis and women is not always clear. The impact of the economic crisis and structural adjustment on the situation of urban women in Lima, Peru, is considered. National household survey data for 1979-1991 on the cost of living, poverty levels, unemployment and underemployment, job segregation and discrimination, and female wages relative to male wages are examined. Results show that women have disproportionately higher rates of unemployment, that the percentage of female-headed households is rising, and that households headed by females face much higher and increasing poverty rates than households with male heads. Females, and particularly female heads of households, work longer hours than males, tend to be concentrated in low wage occupations, are more seriously affected by rising costs for health care, and have lower levels of education than men. Structural adjustment policies force women to work even longer hours in the informal sector, where job and income security is very uncertain, and women face even higher rates of poverty and unemployment since they tend to lose their jobs faster than males, especially in the higher paid occupational categories.

KIT, Amsterdam   [E 1271-22(1994)11]

158   Women, work, and breastfeeding
VAN ESTERIK, PENNY - *Cornell International Nutrition Monograph Series* 23. Cornell University. Division of Nutritional Sciences, Ithaca, NY 92 p. 1992 [EN] ill., tabs. Includes lit.refs

The evidence available on women's work and breast-feeding is reviewed, with particular emphasis on noting the wide range of contexts in which work and breast-feeding are combined in both developed and developing countries and in both the formal and informal sector. The combination of work and breast-feeding is then considered from a feminist perspective. Strategies that have been pursued to assist women to breast-feed at the individual, workplace, community, national and international levels are highlighted. Recommendations to promote, support and protect breast-feeding among working women are made, including: conducting a situation analysis to determine women's work contexts; implementing existing laws relevant to working women and breast-feeding; strengthening the maternity entitlements; linking mother-to-mother breast-feeding support groups with working women's groups to assist working women in initiating and maintaining lactation; removing contradictions from government policies on infant feeding so that mothers receive clear and consistent messages about the value of breast-feeding; and developing programme linkages to family planning initiatives, environmental groups, women-in-development programmes, and national women's organizations, encouraging them to see how their agendas would be furthered by support for breast-feeding.

KIT, Amsterdam   [H 1889-(1992)23]

159   Micro-enterprise support and the double bind of gender in Jamaica
WINT, ELEANOR - *Labour, Capital and Society* 26(1993)2 p.182-202 [EN] ill. 27 lit.refs. With French summary ISSN 0706-1706

Policies designed to counter some of the difficulties which women have traditionally experienced in small businesses in Jamaica are described. The prevailing family situation and employment pattern are reviewed. Self-employment has become critical over the last two decades with the onset of the economic crisis in the 1970s and with adoption of stabilization and structural adjustment programmes. The policies and experiences of lending agencies which have concentrated their efforts on the small enterprise sector over the last decade are analysed. The limited success of these agencies and the failure of many women to move beyond the initial small enterprise level is discussed. Women entrepreneurs are constrained by restrictive definitions of female behaviour: to embark on new ventures which require aggressiveness, initiative and movement outside the traditional community is counter to prevailing norms and runs many risks. If her business grows, a women without a male protector may become more vulnerable to attack and robbery. Once she gains access to the formal credit system, she may be seen as a bad risk unless she can give evidence of male financial backing. Critical support systems, including child care and business management training, are needed to stimulate women to participate in the labour force and improve their economic position.

KIT, Amsterdam   [A 2301-26(1993)2]

160 Factors that impede and facilitate management careers of women in the Malaysian civil service

YOUSOF, JANAT MOHD - *Public Administration and Development* 14(1994)4 p.395-404 [EN] ill., tabs 40 lit.refs ISSN 0271-2075

Factors that have facilitated and hindered the careers of male and male managers in the Malaysian civil service are identified. Some 146 male and female managers were surveyed using a modified Hale and Kelly questionnaire. Differences between women and men in management jobs in general and at various management levels are examined. Many of the conditions which inhibit the careers of female managers elsewhere in the world were identified by the respondents. Family requirements and resulting role conflict were evident. Many women have not married which may reflect a need to choose between career and family. There was some evidence of sexual harassment. The women under study attributed their success primarily to luck; this may imply that they suffer from low self-esteem. However, despite a biased distribution of resources for higher education in favour of men, women have achieved career success as managers. This is largely associated with the educational and socio-economic status of women's parents and parents' apparent willingness to educate female offspring who were not necessarily the eldest child. Women were as likely as men to have male mentors but were more likely to have female mentors. Having a mentor is often identified as a key factor in female managers' success. Women managers acquisition of male mentors reflects the cosmopolitan nature of the civil service in Kuala Lumpur and is unexpected in a Muslim country.

KIT, Amsterdam   [E 1227-14(1994)4]

4 Sexual and reproductive health

A critical review of sexual and reproductive health[1]

Anita Hardon

Family planning was once seen as the crucial programme to achieve fertility decline but the 1990s have seen an important shift in population policies. The consensus is now that family planning should be implemented as part of a broader sexual and reproductive health approach. This shift in emphasis has its origin in two trends. The first is the increasing opposition of women's health advocates to target-oriented family planning programmes that primarily aim to achieve fertility decline and do not sufficiently respect women's reproductive rights. The second trend is the increasing recognition among family planning policymakers and administrators that although contributions to fertility decline have been made, there is still a large unmet need. Programme effectiveness is only likely to increase if the quality of care is enhanced and if existing family planning and health services also respond to women's and men's other reproductive and sexual health needs.

Reproductive and sexual health: the concepts

Reproductive health encompasses a set of health problems or diseases associated with the physical and social risks of human sexuality and reproduction. Germain and Ordway (1989) define a reproductive health approach as one which enables all women and men, including adolescents, to regulate their own fertility safely and effectively by conceiving when they desire, terminating unwanted pregnancies and carrying wanted pregnancies to term; to remain free of disease, disability or death associated with reproduction and sexuality; and to bear and raise healthy children. Graham (1993) states that reproductive health connotes an absence of infections, unwanted pregnancies or coercion; fertility regulation without dangerous side-effects; safe childbirth; and the raising of healthy children. The definition of reproductive health included in paragraph 7.2 of the final document of the UN International Conference on Population and Development, held in Cairo during 1994, reads as follows:

> 'Reproductive health is a state of complete physical, mental, and social well-being and not merely the absence of disease and infirmity, in all matters relating to the reproductive system and to its functions and processes. Reproductive health therefore implies that people are able to have a satisfying and safe sex life and that they have the capability to reproduce and the freedom to decide if, when and how often to do so' (UN 1994).

Increasingly reproductive health is seen in terms of sexual health. In addition to fertility regulation and the prevention and control of reproductive morbidity and mortality, sexual health refers to a satisfying sex life, free of violence, fear and unnecessary pain, and including mutually caring sexual relations. Sexual health was defined as early as 1975 by the WHO as 'the integration of the somatic, emotional, intellectual and social aspects of sexual being in ways that are positively enriching and that enhance personality, communication and love'. The report of the Cairo Conference refers to 'the enhancement of life and personal relations, and not merely counselling and care related to reproduction and sexually transmitted diseases' (UN 1994; paragraph 7.2).

Implementation of the reproductive and sexual health approach will require a revolution in health care. It requires family planning and health administrators to jointly plan the implementation of programmes and to define cost-effective packages of good quality, integrated services tailored to the specific needs of diverse clients in different settings and available to all who need them (Aitken and Reichenbach 1994).

The final document of the Cairo Conference states that health care in the context of primary health care should include:

> '...family planning counselling, information, education, communication and services; education and services for prenatal care, safe delivery, and postnatal care, especially breast-feeding, infant and women's health care; prevention and appropriate treatment of infertility: abortion as specified in paragraph 8.25[2], including prevention of abortion and the management of the consequences of abortion; treatment of reproductive tract infections; sexually transmitted diseases and other reproductive health conditions; and information, education and counselling, as appropriate, on human sexuality, reproductive health and responsible parenthood. Referral for family planning services and further diagnoses and treatment for complications of pregnancy, delivery and abortion, infertility, reproductive tract infections, breast cancer and cancers of the reproductive system, sexually transmitted diseases and HIV/AIDS should also be an integral component of primary health care including reproductive health care programmes.'

The programme of action formulated during the Cairo Conference sets a target for the implementation of reproductive health programmes:

> 'All countries should strive to make accessible, through the primary health care system, reproductive health to all individuals of appropriate ages as soon as possible and no later than the year 2015' (UN 1994).

Reproductive health and gender

Reproductive health is a gender issue. It is affected by societal norms and value systems which indicate ideal behaviours for men and women and which determine their different social roles, statuses and identities (Appelman and Reysoo 1994). These gender norms and values vary across cultures, although women are seen to be subservient to men in most societies. This chapter reviews recent literature on the various components of reproductive health[3], highlighting the ways women's unequal decision-making power and access to resources adversely affect their reproductive health, leading to problems such as unwanted pregnancies, unmet needs for contraception, lack of access to antenatal care, higher risks of maternal mortality and STD infection and female genital mutilation.

Reproductive health services have tended to focus on married women who, because of their biological function of childbearing, are more vulnerable in terms of their reproductive health. In doing so, these health services tend to perpetuate existing gender disparities. In many countries, family planning programmes concentrate on convincing married women of the need for family planning and offer most services to them. Men's concerns in this field are neglected although they are influential in couples' decisions concerning reproduction and fertility control. Male anxieties about vasectomies and condom use have, for example, great impact on decisions regarding which contraceptive method will be used. Often men determine whether their wives are able to use contraception and what method they should use. Mother and child health and family planning programmes have tended not only to ignore men, but also unmarried and childless women (MacFadden 1994). Most government health programmes emphasize services for the sick child, immunization and the prevention of maternal mortality. Other female sexual, gynaecological, mental and emotional problems related to women's reproductive and sexual health are not addressed. Issues that must be dealt with in gender-sensitive reproductive health programmes are examined below.

Contraception

The Cairo Conference reached a consensus, stating that reproductive health implies people are able to have a satisfying and safe sex life, and have the freedom to decide if, when and how often they will have children. Implicit in this condition is the right of men and women to be informed and to have access to safe, effective, affordable and acceptable methods of family planning of their choice, as well as other methods for regulating fertility which are not against the law. This right is not new; it has been part of all declarations issued since the first Conference on Population, held in Bucharest in 1974. Many countries have ratified the Convention on the Elimination of All Forms of Discrimination Against Women in which this right is included. The convention obliges the countries that have ratified it 'to eliminate discrimination against women in the field of health care in order to ensure ... access to health care services, including those related to family planning'. However, many states do not implement this right in practice (Cook 1994).

Barriers to contraceptive use

Since their inception, family planning programmes have been accompanied by studies which in general aim to describe barriers to contraceptive use and factors determining acceptance and continuation of use. An important socio-cultural barrier to contraceptive acceptance is the fact that, in many countries, the number of children is related to people's status and wealth (Ringheim 1993). Men are often seen to have authority in matters of family size and composition. Men want large families and are especially concerned about the number of sons born to them. Women gain status by having children. If they do not give birth to the desired number of children, particularly sons, women run the risk of being abandoned. Few field studies have dealt with these fertility issues from a gender perspective, elucidating both male and female perspectives and interests. One of the few exceptions is a study of gender ideology and fertility strategies among the Yoruba of Nigeria (Renne 1993). This study suggests that, in contrast to expectations, both men and women subscribe to the prevailing gender ideology. The number of children wanted varied more by the respondents' age than by sex.

A recent study from Bangladesh related worker-client family planning exchanges to contraceptive acceptance (Phillips et al. 1993). It concludes that visits from a female family planning worker were twice as effective as visits from a male worker. Women visited by female workers were 2.8 times more likely to be using contraceptives 90 days after the visit than women who had not received such a visit. Home visits by male workers increased contraceptive use by 1.4 times. The authors suggest that the principal effect of a home visit was to crystallize latent demand for contraception; female workers increased new demand by stimulating ideological change.

Another frequently studied barrier to contraceptive use is the fear of side-effects, a fear which is especially felt by women, who are usually the users of the contraceptive methods. A study in the Sudan found that only 14.3% of 305 married women in Khartoum used modern contraception (Swar Eldahab 1993). The total fertility rate was 5.1. Fear of side-effects was mentioned by 42.8% of all women not using contraceptives. Interestingly, only 25% of these women had actually experienced side-effects. About 50% of women in the highest class feared that side-effects would cause infertility, reflecting the socio-cultural emphasis on fertility. Religious disapproval of contraception was widespread among lower income women while it was virtually non-existent among upper class women. Dissatisfaction with contraceptives also leads to high discontinuation rates. Research from Peru reported that a relatively high percentage of women (46.6%) discontinued their accepted method of contraception within one year because they were dissatisfied with it (Kost 1993).

The fear of side-effects and the high rate of discontinuation indicate a need for new and improved contraceptives. Fathalla (1993) has reviewed contraceptive research, finding that innovation has occurred in phases. The first phase of the contraceptive revolution, he argues, consisted of male contraception: withdrawal and condoms. The second phase has emerged in the past decades and consists of contraceptives which women could use without their partner's cooperation, such as the pill. Intrauterine devices, injectable hormones and implants have further expanded women's choice. These methods are longer lasting and reversible but must be administered in clinics. Fathalla states that demographic concerns have driven the development of these new technologies. Even though these technologies benefit women, however, they do not always meet their concerns and needs. In his view, women's health advocates should be involved in the development of a new generation of contraceptives that better meet women's concerns and needs.

Men and contraceptive use
Very few studies deal with men's responsibility for and participation in family planning. Condom use and vasectomy are two existing forms of contraception for men, but men are unlikely to use these methods in most countries (Riedberger 1993). In Zimbabwe, the family planning programme has tried to change men's attitudes and behaviour (Piotrow et al. 1992). A media campaign was conducted, including a twice weekly radio soap-opera of 52 episodes, motivational talks and pamphlets. The campaign reached 52% of men aged 18-55 years. After completion of the campaign, condom use had increased from 5% to 10% among this group. In Colombia, the family planning association has taken a significant step by opening special male family planning clinics (Gutierrez 1995). Clients are offered gender counselling, STD/HIV diagnosis, vasectomies and a free telephone line for information. The programme has led to more early STD-related consultations and increased condom use.

Adolescent sexuality and contraception
As outlined above, traditional family planning programmes focus on married women. It is, however, increasingly recognized around the world that adolescents engage in sex at an early age and should have access to contraceptives, if only to prevent teenage pregnancies. Various studies in this field point to the lack of contraceptive use despite sexual activity in adolescence. Agyei et al. (1994) report that in Mbale District, Uganda, adolescents start having sexual intercourse at 15 years of age. Despite quite good knowledge of contraceptives, they still engage in unprotected sexual intercourse. Research in the Gambia found that only 21% of women and 7% of men had used contraception at their first time of intercourse (Kane et al. 1993). Almost half of sexually active adults had never used contraceptives: lack of knowledge and limited access to modern contraceptives were seen to be obstacles to their use of family planning. Attendance at family life (a euphemism for sexual health) education sessions at schools had a significant positive impact on knowledge and contraceptive use among the young people surveyed.

The Mexican family planning association set up a comprehensive *Gente Joven* (Young People) Project in 1986 to deal with the issue of adolescent sexuality. Peer educators provide sex education at sites where young people are already assembled, such as schools and recreation centres. This sex education deals not only with contraception but also with anatomy and physiology of reproductive organs, premarital sexual decision-making and STDs. The training models emphasize overcoming gender inequalities and promoting reciprocal relations (Lopez-Juarez 1993).

Abortion

If contraception fails, women need to have access to safe and effective abortion. Unsafe abortion is a major public health problem. It is estimated that each year approximately 100,000 women die as a result of unsafe abortions while 25 million suffer from related morbidity (Aitken and Reichenbach 1994). Access to safe abortion is one of the most controversial issues in the area of reproductive health, mainly due to opposition from conservative and religious groups. The Cairo Conference was dominated by discussions on this issue. The conference's final document considered 'prevention of abortion and the management of the consequences of abortion' only, stating that 'in cases where abortion is not against the law, it should be safe' (UN 1994).

A review from Mexico (Elu 1993) states that women's health advocates have been unsuccessful in calling for liberalization of the abortion law due to strong opposition from anti-abortion groups and other conservative forces. The current Mexican abortion law stipulates that legal abortion may only be performed when the mother's life is at risk, pregnancy has been the result of rape, and there is a risk of congenital abnormality.

In most countries of sub-Saharan Africa, abortion is restricted to specific therapeutic concerns. An important question in these countries is whether HIV infection or AIDS can be a legitimate reason for abortion. In practice, gynaecologists there do conduct abortions but they generally fear retribution and public controversy related to their services. Few data are available on the number of women requesting and undergoing legal abortions and how often they resort to traditional and informal providers. In Bangladesh, abortion is only available to save the life of the mother but menstrual regulation (an abortion procedure done when menstruation is delayed for a limited number of weeks, often without performing a pregnancy test) is legally available. Begum (1993) found that only 22% of abortions in Bangladesh are performed in menstrual regulation centres. At least one third of the 24,000 pregnancy-related deaths in Bangladesh are associated with septic abortions performed by untrained rural practitioners. Women in rural areas seem to be unaware of the availability of menstrual regulation.

Pregnancy-related mortality and morbidity

Safe motherhood is another important component of reproductive health care. Annually around 350,000 women die in childbirth while overall maternal morbidity is estimated to affect 35 million women per year. Most empirical studies of maternal mortality are hospital-based but in many developing countries the vast majority of women do not make use of health services; they deliver their child at home. One community survey conducted by trained birth attendants in Burkina Faso found the maternal mortality ratio to be as high as 4.5 deaths per 1000 births (Wollast et al. 1993). Obstructed labour was the main factor leading to complications and maternal death. Health centre records and field surveys demonstrated that the maternal death rate in India was 7.98 per 1000 live births (Bhatia 1993). Maternal deaths accounted for 36% of the mortality among women of reproductive age. Many of these deaths were considered to be preventable.

A problem in many settings is that women under-utilize existing services. In Ecuador, for example, public sector facilities should serve 54% of the population but only 18% of women use them (Smith 1993). In Pakistan, women prefer a female health worker during delivery; this is most common during home deliveries. Women often prefer giving birth at home where they are supported by trusted people with whom they feel comfortable. Heywood (1991) describes how women who deliver at the clinic are considered lazy in the Atacora region of Benin. Bravery is a characteristic that a woman must show during delivery. Sometimes however, such bravery has dire consequences. Heywood describes arriving at a village for routine supervision and being called to a house only 100 metres from a health post. There he found a grossly dehydrated woman, lying moribund in faeces, with a baby dead in the uterus. The woman had been in labour for four days but no one had informed the trained birth attendant at the clinic.

The main intervention in this area is pre-natal care, which is intended to identify high risk pregnancies. It is generally a component of primary health care. Community-based approaches to pre-natal care, including family planning and midwife training, have greatly contributed to the reduction of maternal mortality in countries such as Bangladesh, Ethiopia and Guatemala (Tinker et al. 1993). Nevertheless, such screening and care alone cannot reduce maternal mortality: emergency obstetric care is needed to treat obstetric complications (Freedman and Maine 1993). Distance, cost and inadequate quality of care are major obstacles to decisions to seek care; disease severity, gender and socio-economic status also affect these decisions. Those who decide to seek help in a timely fashion may still be delayed due to difficulties in accessing care facilities. Further delays may be encountered at health facilities themselves due to shortages of qualified staff, drugs and supplies, administrative delays and clinical mismanagement (Thaddeus and Maine 1994). An integrated approach to preventing maternal mortality should pay attention to adolescent nutritional status, women's knowledge about contraception, danger signs during pregnancy, STDs, and access to health care facilities, including emergency transport (Tinker et al. 1993).

Reproductive tract infections and STDs

Treatment of reproductive tract infections and STDs is another important component of reproductive health. The majority of recent publications deal with the prevention and treatment of HIV/AIDS. These studies show that, overall, women are more vulnerable to HIV/STD infection than men due to physiological, socio-cultural and economic factors which decrease control over their lives and increase exposure to risk (Women and Autonomy Centre 1993). Marital infidelity is usually not a matter of discussion between partners, making insistence on faithfulness and monogamy difficult. Economic dependence on men or lack of sufficient income lead considerable numbers of women to trade sex for money. The biggest problem for women, however, is that men's cooperation is needed for condom use. Men may use condoms when visiting sex workers but even then not uncommonly pay more for unprotected sex. They tend not to use condoms at all with their wives or regular partners. This may be related to the dominant epidemiological model on which health care policies and prevention programmes have been based. It focuses on female sex workers and their role in HIV transmission and not on men or the general female population (Seidel 1993). Yet all women and men who engage in unprotected sex are at risk. Women may be able to refuse sexual intercourse for limited periods of time if they think their partner has an STD or has been unfaithful (see for example Orubuloye et al. 1993) but their ability to sustain this for a long period of time is limited.

HIV prevention and coping strategies
A limited number of studies have involved women themselves in assessing their HIV transmission risk, developing interventions for preventing HIV transmission, and coping with infection and AIDS. One study in Rwanda (Keogh et al. 1994) considered the needs of HIV-positive women. The women identified food, housing and money as their current needs, and food, child care and money as their future needs in the event that they become ill. The preferred sources of support were individual counselling and women's support groups. Almost 75% of the women did not expect a supportive reaction from their partners after disclosure of test results. Schoepf (1993) has described how in Kinshasa, Zaire, culturally appropriate community-based empowerment workshops were developed as an HIV prevention strategy. While significant changes were observed in the participating women's knowledge and action, economic necessity and inequality limited their ability to avoid sexual risk.

A major problem for HIV-positive women is the risk of vertical transmission to their children. In Kenya, Temmerman et al. (1993) determined the effects of antenatal counselling on women living with HIV and their subsequent behaviour. Of 94 women who tested positive for HIV, only two returned to the clinic for further counselling. Follow-up 12 months later showed that most of the women were not using oral contraceptives or condoms to prevent further transmission. Very few had told their husbands of their HIV status, partly due to fear of abandonment.

Morbidity burden of STDs
Most studies related to STDs and other reproductive morbidity deal with AIDS, probably because of its high mortality. Other STDs tend to be approached as co-factors for HIV transmission. Still, it is important to realize that the morbidity burden of STDs themselves, such as gonorrhoea and chlamydia, is very high. Annually, about 225 million new cases of STDs occur, more than 90% of these in developing countries. WHO estimates that there are nearly 330 million cases of treatable STDs worldwide at any one time. Some 20 million people suffer from gonorrhoea and 50 million from chlamydia. Women more often suffer from STD-related complications because the initial symptoms are internal, unrecognized and therefore untreated. Untreated STDs are apt to lead to acute pelvic inflammatory disease in 5%-10% of women which, in turn, can cause ectopic pregnancy, chronic pelvic pain, adverse pregnancy outcomes and infertility (Aitken and Reichenbach 1994).

Disease burdens differ from country to country and between rural and urban areas. In Egypt, one study of 509 women in two villages measured reproductive morbidity (Zurayk et al. 1993). Questionnaires were administered using local terms for reproductive morbidity; these were accompanied by clinical and laboratory investigations. An estimated 50% of the women had reproductive tract infections, particularly vaginitis; 56% had a prolapsed uterus; and 63% were anaemic. Only 5% of the women had no reproductive morbidity.

A Nigerian study reported reproductive tract infections and STDs among Yoruba women (Erwin 1993). Candidiasis, occurring in 37% of women, was reportedly most common, followed by trichomoniasis (16%), bacterial vaginosis (11%), gonorrhoea (4%), chlamydia (3%) and syphilis (2%). Common signs noted were lower abdominal pain, abnormal vaginal discharges, genital sores and ulcers. The women feared that these infections would temporarily or permanently affect their fertility. Women sought help for these conditions from private physicians or pharmacists.

One factor that is seen to contribute to the risks of STD and HIV transmission is the use of substances, such as powders, pumice or leaves, to make the vagina dry and tight. This practice is carried out for two reasons: it is believed to increase sexual pleasure for men; and it is considered a home remedy for vaginal complaints (Brown et al. 1993 and Williams 1993). These products can cause inflammatory lesions which foster trauma during intercourse and facilitate HIV/STD infection. Irwin et al. (1993) interviewed 124 Zairian women and men and found that all kinds of substances are used to mask abnormal vaginal discharges.

Reproductive cancers

As in the industrialized countries, reproductive cancers of women and men are becoming a leading cause of death in many developing regions, including Latin America, India and China. The screening, diagnosis and treatment of reproductive cancers (breast, cervical and prostate cancers) should ideally be part of a reproductive health approach in all countries. There is a tendency to ignore the subject altogether possibly because of the extreme costs of such programmes.

Genital mutilation

Perhaps the most controversial form of reproductive health morbidity is that related to female genital mutilation. Of the girls and women living today, an estimated 85 to 114 million have undergone genital mutilation (Toubia 1993). It is most common in Africa. Female genital mutilation is the collective name given to several different traditional practices that involve the cutting of female genitals and/or removal of the external sexual organs. The WHO finds this practice to be seriously harmful and argues that it should be abolished. Complications include severe bleeding, infections, pain, urine retention, pregnancy complications, infertility, psychological stress and shock (Toubia 1993). In Egypt a strong correlation between educational level and female genital mutilation was found: only 35% of girls with secondary school education had undergone genital mutilation, compared to 89% of those with only primary school education (Hussein 1993). Based on these findings, a programme to eradicate this practice has been set up by the Egyptian Council for the Prevention of

Traditional Practices Harmful to Women. Bartels (1993), reporting on the Sudan and Senegal, proposes a culturally-sensitive approach to female genital mutilation. Women should, in her view, not be conceptualized simply as victims of culture but as active participants. Many women themselves see genital mutilation as a form of ritual marking which determines their gender and ethnic affiliation. Programmes aiming to eradicate the practice should take this into account.

Infertility

STDs, primarily gonorrhoea and genital chlamydia infection, are one of the main causes of infertility. An estimated 60 million couples experience this problem annually, a figure in the same order as the 80 million unwanted pregnancies (Aitken and Reichenbach 1994). Among selected populations in Central Africa, STD-induced infertility is estimated to affect as many as one-third to one-half of all couples (Mtimavalye and Belsey 1987). Nevertheless, little research is devoted to infertility, even though it can cause great distress among women and men, especially in 'pro-natalist' cultures. One study (Neff 1994) conducted in Kerala, India, shows that infertility is not only of individual concern. Social responsibility and consequences are included in Nayar constructions of infertility. It is the duty of matrilineal kin to foster progeny in the best interests of the group. When this responsibility is not met, powerful negative consequences, viewed as curses of family fertility gods, may transpire for all lineage members.

   In Egypt, Inhorn and Buss (1994) have done some innovative work on the issue of infertility. She describes how the urban and rural poor often attribute infertility to *kabsa*, a form of 'boundary crossing' by symbolically polluted individuals into the rooms of reproductively vulnerable women. Women who have been reproductively restricted by *kabsa* must overcome its effects or they will be barred from achieving normal adult 'personhood', according to widely accepted normative standards. Women bear the major burden of infertility in terms of blame, social ostracism and the relentless search for therapies which can be painful and even harmful.

An integrated approach

The literature suggests a number of reproductive health issues which could be better addressed by using an integrated approach to the varied elements of health care. For example, recent studies show that women may discontinue contraceptive use because they fear side-effects will cause infertility. STDs, when untreated, contribute to infertility as well. Infertility is greatly feared by both men and women, particularly in societies where women's status is related to their reproductive capacities. Reducing the immense morbidity burden of STDs should be a priority of health programmes, given their relation to infertility and HIV transmission. HIV/STD prevention via condom use is another urgent need. Community-based approaches which consider women and, more importantly, men to be active partners in health care can lead to increased condom use. Increased attention should also be paid to making the female condom accessible and affordable, while microbicides which permit pregnancies still need intensified research. The problem of vertical transmission of HIV means that women need access to safe abortion facilities if they choose to terminate their pregnancy. Crucial to all efforts in the domain of reproductive health is sexual health education. Such education should not only deal with bio-technical aspects of sexuality but also with ways people can have a satisfying sex life, mutually caring relations, and sexual rights.

The integrated reproductive and sexual health concept faces a number of problems in implementation. The concept is not being promoted together with a strategy unlike the primary health care approach accepted at Alma Ata. The process involved is not clear, nor is the way in which priorities should be set. There is no consensus regarding whether the implementation of reproductive health care should be top-down, as has generally been the case with family planning, or whether it calls for a participatory approach. Ways of involving men should also be explored. There also needs to be discussion on whether a multi-sectoral approach, involving other relevant sectors such as education, is required or whether initiatives should be restricted to family planning and health fields. The principles to be followed require clarification. A consensus is needed on whether making services available is sufficient or whether equitable distribution should have priority, with its implications for the reallocation of scarce resources.

The setting of priorities faces particular difficulties. There is an increasing tendency to base priorities on cost-benefit analysis although the setting of priorities in a more participatory way in dialogue with communities could be preferable. The World Bank (1993), following a cost-benefit approach, has defined priorities based on a short list of programme components : (1) AIDS prevention as a priority public health intervention; (2) services to ensure pre-natal, childbirth and antenatal health care in order to prevent maternal deaths; (3) improved access to family planning services which could prevent 850,000 child deaths per year and eliminate 100,000 maternal deaths; and (4) control of STDs, which account for more than 250 million cases of debilitating and fatal diseases each year. The World Bank considers these clinical interventions to be highly cost effective, often costing less than US$ 50 per disability for each year of life gained. Treatment of infertility, the provision of safe abortions, and the treatment of other reproductive morbidity, such as cervical cancer, are not mentioned in the list of essential services. If the World Bank strategy is followed, these would not be included in the government-based health programmes.

Implementing reproductive health care at national and district levels

Until the reproductive health care approach can be brought into operation, policy-makers and programme managers in developing countries will find it difficult to implement the revolutionary changes required to provide and implement services. Some steps, however, could be taken. First, they will need to review the services currently being offered and reflect on which services are missing. The extent to which family planning is integrated with other health care services at the district and community level needs to be taken into account. In some countries, family planning is still a vertical programme, in others it is integrated into the mother and child health care component of primary health care. Reproductive health care policies will need to be developed that specify national aims and implementation strategies.

Achieving a consensus regarding reproductive health will be difficult. When fertility was the primary issue in the population arena, an initial tendency to implement coercive technological fixes through contraception was replaced by an understanding that family planning will only work if people *want* to have fewer children. The need to improve women's status, with attention to education, employment and autonomy issues, came to the forefront of population debates and was included in policies. Socio-economic and political issues were at stake. Now, the emphasis on reproductive health could lead to 'medicalization' of population policies and programmes. Education, employment and autonomy are not components of reproductive health programme. Instead, emphasis is upon medical terms such as STDs, reproductive tract infections and cancers. If attention to reproductive health results in a narrowing and 'medicalizing' of the approach chosen in population programmes, this will most likely be counterproductive for women, men and society at large.

In practice, governments and international agencies continue to consider population growth to be an important development issue. Fertility decline, to be achieved by expanding the coverage of family planning programmes, is seen as the solution. Women's employment status and educational levels are put forward as important determinants of fertility. Contraceptive prevalence rates are the presented outcome measures, and socio-cultural factors are seen as barriers to contraceptive acceptance. Recent IPPF country reports for Pakistan (1994) and India (1994), for example, state that the governments of these countries continue to regard population growth as too high and a barrier to reducing poverty. These reports mention the need to expand contraceptive acceptance rates as the solution, rather than a way to meet the reproductive health needs of women.

Recent reports on population indicate that the analytical frameworks of demographers who develop population policies have not yet changed. They have still not put reproductive health problems at the core of their policies. In their analysis, reproductive health is not a determinant of population growth nor is a reproductive health programme likely to be a cost-effective approach to fertility decline. On the other hand, they see improving literacy levels is important as well as providing contraceptives to those who want to regulate their fertility.

It is thus likely that when the reproductive health approach is implemented at national and international levels, conflicts will emerge between demography-oriented experts and health experts. Changing policies and programmes will not be enough; a re-shuffling of actors will be required. At the international level, WHO is likely to become more important as this agency has the required expertise in the field of reproductive health. At the national level, ministries of health will become more important in implementing population programmes. At the district level, health teams and primary health care programme managers will need to implement reproductive health care policies concerning the specific problems of their regions.

A review of the literature shows that empirical studies dealing with reproductive health as a whole are rare. Most focus on specific components, with special emphasis on contraception and HIV/AIDS. Given the lack of data on reproductive health, it is essential that tools be developed to facilitate rapid appraisal of reproductive problems at the district and community levels, making it possible to set priorities for intervention. Such appraisals should follow the approach chosen in the Egyptian reproductive health study (Zurayk et al. 1993). Local terms for common reproductive health problems were used in a simple questionnaire developed to assess disease burdens, accompanied by some essential laboratory and clinical tests. Such studies should deal with common problems such as vaginal discharge (as an indicator of reproductive tract infection), abdominal pain, uterine prolapse and maternal anaemia. In addition to such medical problems, it should assess gender-based issues which determine the power of women to deal with their health problems and to control their fertility and infection risks. Such surveys can lead to simple indicators which can be included in existing management information systems as outcome measures of reproductive health care interventions. In most health services at present, routine information is only collected on issues such as maternal mortality and contraceptive acceptance.

Community-based approaches

Although few of the studies reviewed deal with people's views on all of these issues, those that do make it clear that effective, community-based approaches are required which involve both women and men in defining problems and deciding what course of action to take. Timmermans (1995), for example, reports how a large family planning programme in Mali found that village midwives (and not the community-based distributors trained in the family planning programme) were in a good position to implement family planning at the community level. Being in touch with pregnant women and their husbands, they could discuss issues of contraception with both partners and thus increase male responsibility.

Ideally, reproductive health efforts at the community level should include training in the field of sexual health. A needs assessment in Mali (Prochaska and Traoré 1995) revealed that people have great difficulty in talking about sexual health. People indicated that it is prohibited to talk about sexual activity between wives and husbands. A local saying is 'People who talk about such things don't live long'. However, anthropological field work showed that women are obliged to acquiesce to men's sexual wishes. Women complain that they find it difficult to enjoy sexual intercourse after a hard working day. Some men in the field study acknowledged that they do not engage in foreplay with their wives.

Innovative participatory training initiatives, developed by the IPPF, encourage community health workers and their clients to discuss sexual health and rights (Visser 1994). The training initiatives reveal attitudes towards sexuality, such as the unwillingness of men to take responsibility for contraception, that pose problems for reproductive health. Such community-based approaches can incorporate subtle approaches to dealing with gender-based inequities at the local level.

The capacity of district health services to deal with the identified reproductive health problems is likely to be the greatest constraint to effective implementation of a reproductive health programme. If infertility proves to be a big problem in communities, the district health team should aim to prevent STD infections, which are an important cause of infertility, and to provide some simple fertility tests and counselling on fertile periods. Insemination could be provided as a form of treatment. Most governmental health programmes in developing countries cannot afford to make expensive treatments such as in vitro fertilization available to their clients. Likewise, if cervical cancer proves to be a problem, the question is whether the programme should start screening with pap-smears for women who are at risk. It is unlikely that such a programme will be able to afford to treat cervical cancer.

Identifying feasible and appropriate reproductive health interventions is perhaps one of the most serious problems confronting the reproductive health care approach when it is put into practice. Before we reach that point, many barriers to implementation must be overcome. If this can be achieved, effective, integrated reproductive health programmes can become a major asset for women and men, and for the community as a whole.

Notes

1 The author acknowledges with thanks the series of literature searches provided by Henk van Dam and Minke Valk. Dia Timmermans has commented on and given suggestions on the initial framework and the resulting analysis; her support was inspiring.

2 Paragraph 8.25 was controversial during the Cairo conference. It states that in no cases should abortion be promoted as a method of family planning and refers to national sovereignty in this field.

3 The literature searches for 1993/1994 covered the following topics: contraception, abortion, maternal mortality and antenatal care, STDs, other reproductive morbidity and infertility.

Bibliography

Agyei, W.K.A. and J. Mukiza-Gsapere and E.J. Epema, 'Sexual behaviour, reproductive health and contraceptive use among adolescents and young adults in Mbale District, Uganda'. *Journal of Tropical Medicine and Hygiene*, vol. 97, no. 4 (1994), pp. 219-227.

Aitken, I. and L. Reichenbach, 'Reproductive and sexual health services: expanding access and enhancing choice.' In: Sen G. et al. (ed.) *Population policies reconsidered: health empowerment and rights*. Harvard, Harvard University Press, 1994.

Appelman, S. and F. Reysoo (ed.), *Everything you always wanted to know ... : lexicon and comments on the new population concepts from a gender perspective*. Oegstgeest, Vrouwenberaad Ontwikkelingssamenwerking, 1994.

Bartels, E., 'Vrouwenbesnijdenis als markeringsritueel'. *Antropologische Verkenningen*, vol. 12, no. 1 (1993), pp. 1-19.

Begum, S.F., 'Saving lives with menstrual regulation'. *Planned Parenthood Challenges*, no. 1 (1993), pp. 30-31.

Bhatia, J.C., 'Levels and causes of maternal mortality in southern India'. *Studies of Family Planning*, vol. 24, no. 5 (1993), pp. 310-318.

Brown, J.E., O.B. Ayowa and R.C. Brown, 'Dry and tight: sexual practices and potential AIDS risk in Zaire'. *Social Science and Medicine*, vol. 37, no. 8 (1993), pp. 989-994.

Cook, R.J., *Women's health and human rights: the promotion and protection of women's health through international rights law*. Geneva, World Health Organization, 1994.

Elu, M.C., 'Abortion yes, abortion no, in Mexico'. *Reproductive Health Matters*, no. 1 (1993), pp. 58-66.

Erwin, J.O., 'Reproductive tract infections among women in Ado-Ekiti, Nigeria: symptoms recognition, perceived causes, and treatment choices'. *Health Transition Review*, vol. 3 Supplement (1993), pp. 135-149.

Fathalla, M.F., 'Contraceptive research and development: the unfinished revolution'. *Populi*, vol. 20, no. 9 (1993), pp. 8-10.

Freedman, L.P. and D. Maine, 'Women's mortality: a legacy of neglect.' In: Koblinsky, M. et al. (ed.), *The health of women: a global perspective*. Oxford, Westview Press, 1993.

Germain, A. and J. Ordway, *Population control and women's health: balancing the scales*. New York, International Women's Health Coalition, 1989.

Graham, W., 'Reproductive health in developing countries: measurement, determinants and consequences. Overview.' In: *International Population Conference/Congres International de la Population, Montreal 1993, 24 August-1st September*. Liege, International Union for the Scientific Study of Population, 1993, pp. 571-577.

Gutierrez, A., 'Man, hombre, homme: meeting male reproductive health care needs in Colombia.' Presented at a meeting on Effective Approaches for the Prevention of HIV/AIDS in Women, held at WHO/GPA, Geneva, February 1995.

Heywood, A., *Primary health care in the Atacora, Benin: success and failures*. (Bulletin no. 322) Amsterdam, Royal Tropical Institute, 1991.

Hussein, A., 'Female genital mutilation: the road to success in Egypt'. *Planned Parenthood Challenges*, no. 2 (1993), pp. 40-42.

Inhorn, M.C. and K.A. Buss, 'Ethnography, epidemiology and infertility in Egypt'. *Social Science and Medicine*, vol. 39, no. 5 (1994), pp. 671-686.

International Planned Parenthood Federation, *Pakistan, South Asia Region*. (IPPF Country Profiles) New York, 1994.

International Planned Parenthood Federation, *India, South Asia Region*. (IPPF Country Profiles) New York, 1994.

Irwin, K., N. Mibandumba, K. Mbuyi, R. Ryder and D. Sequeira, 'More on vaginal inflammation in Africa'. *New England Journal of Medicine*, vol. 328, no. 12 (1993), pp. 888-889.

Kane, T.T., R. de Buysscher, T.T. Taylor, T. Smith and M. Jeng, 'Sexual activity, family life education, and contraceptive practice among young adults in Banjul, The Gambia'. *Studies in Family Planning*, vol. 24, no. 1 (1993), pp. 50-61.

Keogh, P., S. Allen, C. Almedal and B. Temahagili, 'The social impact of HIV on women in Kigali, Rwanda: a prospective study'. *Social Science and Medicine*, vol. 38, no. 8 (1994), pp. 1047-1053.

Kost, K., 'The dynamics of contraceptive use in Peru'. *Studies in Family Planning*, vol. 24, no. 2 (1993), pp. 109-119.

Lopez-Juarez, A., 'Gente Joven: meeting needs'. *Planned Parenthood Challenges*, no. 2 (1993), pp. 31-33.

MacFadden, P., 'Health is a gender issue'. *Southern Africa, vol. 7*, no. 3-4 (1994), pp. 59-61.

Mtimavalye, L.A. and M.A. Belsey, *Infertility and sexually transmitted disease: major problems in maternal and child health and family planning*. (Technical background paper for the International Conference on Better Health for Women and Children through Family Planning) Nairobi, Population Council, 1987.

Neff, D.L., 'The social construction of infertility: the case of the matrilineal Nayars in South India'. *Social Science and Medicine*, vol. 39, no. 4 (1994), pp. 475-485.

Orubuloye, I.O., P. Caldwell and J.C. Caldwell, 'The role of high-risk occupations in the spread of AIDS: truck drivers and itinerant market women in Nigeria'. *International Family Planning Perspectives*, vol. 19, no. 2 (1993), pp. 43-48.

Piotrow, P.T. et al, 'Changing men's attitude and behavior: the Zimbabwe male motivation project'. *Studies in Family Planning*, vol. 23, no. 6 (1992), pp. 365-375.

Phillips, J.F., M.B. Hossain, R. Simmons and M.A. Koenig, 'Worker-client exchanges and contraceptive use in rural Bangladesh'. *Studies in Family Planning*, vol. 24, no. 6 (1993), pp. 329-342.

Prochaska, R. and C.K.C. Traoré, *Femme et santé à San, Mali*. Amsterdam, Royal Tropical Institute, 1995 (Forthcoming).

Renne, E.P., 'Gender ideology and fertility strategies in an Ekiti Yoruba village'. *Studies in Family Planning*, vol. 24, no. 6 (1993), pp. 343-353.

Riedberger, I., *Einstellung von Männern zur Familienplanung und Möglichkeiten ihrer stärkeren Einbeziehung in Familienplanungsprogramme*. (Forchungsberichte der Bundesministeriums für wirtschaftliche Zusammenarbeit und Entwicklung no. 108) Köln, Weltforum, 1993.

Ringheim, K., 'Factors that determine prevalence of use of contraceptive methods for men'. *Studies in Family Planning*, vol. 24, no. 2 (1993), pp. 87-99

Schoepf, B.G., 'Gender, development and AIDS: a political economy and culture framework'. *Women and International Development Annual*, no. 3 (1993), pp. 53-85.

Seidel, G., 'Women at risk: gender and AIDS in Africa'. *Disasters*, vol. 17, no. 2 (1993), pp. 133-142.

Smith, D.G., 'Safe motherhood: listening to women'. *Tropical Doctor*, vol. 23, no. 1 (1993), pp. 1-2.

Swar Eldahab, A.M., 'Constraints on effective family planning in urban Sudan'. *Studies in Family Planning*, vol. 24, no. 6 (1993), pp. 366-374.

Temmerman, M. et al, 'Post-partum counselling of HIV infected women and their subsequent reproductive behaviour'. In: M. Berer and S. Ray (ed.), *Women and HIV/AIDS: an international resource book; information, action and resources on women and HIV/AIDS, reproductive health and sexual relationships.* London, Pandora, 1993, pp. 104-105.

Thaddeus, S. and D. Maine, 'Too far to walk: maternal mortality in context'. *Social Science and Medicine*, vol. 38, no. 8 (1994), pp. 1091-1110.

Timmermans, D., Personal communication, 1995.

Tinker, A., M.A. Koblinsky and P. Daly, *Making motherhood safe.* (Discussion Papers no. 202) Washington DC, World Bank, 1993.

Toubia, N., *Female genital mutilation: a call for global action.* New York, Population Council, 1993.

United Nations, *Report of the International Conference on Population and Development (Cairo, 5-13 September 1994).* Geneva, 1994.

Visser, T., *Report of three training workshops on sexual health needs in Iringa Region, Tanzania.* Amsterdam, Royal Tropical Institute (with the IPPF), 1994.

Williams, A.O., 'More on vaginal inflammation in Africa'. *New England Journal of Medicine*, vol. 328, no. 12 (1993), p. 888.

Wollast, E. et al, 'Detecting maternal morbidity and mortality by traditional birth attendants in Burkina Faso'. *Health Policy and Planning*, vol. 8, no. 2 (1993), pp. 161-168.

Women and Autonomy Centre, 'Women and AIDS'. *VENA Journal*, vol. 5, no. 1 (1993), pp. 1-45.

World Bank, *Investing in health*, New York, 1993.

World Health Organization, *Education and training in human sexuality: the training of health professionals.* (Technical Report Series no. 572) Geneva, WHO, 1975.

Zurayk, H., H. Khattab, N. Younis, M. El Mouelhy and M. Fadle, 'Concepts and measures of reproductive morbidity'. *Health Transition Review*, vol. 3, no. 1 (1993), pp. 17-39.

Annotated bibliography

Sexual and reproductive health

161   Socio-economic, cultural, and legal factors affecting girls' and women's health and their access to and utilization of health and nutrition services in developing countries
ACSÁDI, GEORGE T.F.; JOHNSON-ACSÁDI, GWENDOLYN - *Women's Health and Nutrition Work Program*. World Bank. Population, Health and Nutrition Department, Washington, DC [105] p. 1993 [EN] ill., tabs. Includes lit.refs
An analysis is presented of the aspects of culture and the socio-economic factors that negatively affect women's and girls' health and wellbeing. Factors affecting the health of female infants and girls include a preference for boys and low valuation of girls. Factors affecting access to and utilization of family planning, health and nutrition services are examined. Legal, institutional and policy measures, and other instruments concerned with marriage and family, reproduction, mortality, and gender equality in society, are described. Priorities and options for the design of programmes aimed at creating an environment conducive to overall gains in the health and wellbeing of females are suggested. Disadvantages in the allotment of food and food supplements should be eliminated. Health interventions should be implemented with due consideration of cultural issues and barriers. Men should be made aware of the plight of women and should be involved in programmes to improve the health, nutrition and wellbeing of girls and women.
KIT, Amsterdam   [U 94-545]

162   AIDS and its effects on the advancement of women
BRANCH FOR THE ADVANCEMENT OF WOMEN - *Women 2000* 1. Centre for Social Development and Humanitarian Affairs, Vienna 16 p. 1989 [EN] ill., tabs. Includes lit.refs
The impact of AIDS on women is substantial: it is estimated that in 1989 at least 1.5 million women were infected whereas an incalculable number of women are affected by the consequences of the disease. Having reviewed the spread of AIDS, including estimates of the number of HIV-infected women, the adverse economic and social effects of AIDS on women and the factors making women particularly vulnerable to HIV infection are discussed. Women who are infected with HIV or AIDS can transmit the disease to their children. In addition, a woman with AIDS may be denied medical assistance, rejected by her family and friends, and forced to leave her job and home. A woman can be stigmatized even when she has been infected through a monogamous relationship with her husband or through rape. Women's property and other rights are often not protected by law, making them more vulnerable to prejudice and to being stigmatized. Women who are not infected can also be affected by HIV/AIDS by the extra demands on their time and energy posed by fulfilling their role as carers of people, including children, with AIDS. In the effort to reduce the spread of HIV and AIDS, women's groups can provide effective self-help and support mechanisms for women with HIV/AIDS. National groups can work together to share resources, thus enhancing international cooperation and cooperation between agencies, professions and interests.
KIT, Amsterdam   [K 2605-(1989)1]

163   Gender and population policies : some reflections
BARBIERI, TERESITA DE - *Reproductive Health Matters* (1993)1 p.85-92 [EN] ill. lit.refs in notes
The impact of gender on sexuality, reproduction and the social division of labour is examined. Gender is defined as the social construction that defines and gives meaning to sexuality and human reproduction. The entrenched position of gender norms and behaviour is the reason that there have been slow changes in fertility, marriage and, to some extent, mortality. Population policies want to reduce population growth without changing social relations or inequalities in wealth and income. Women have only recently been involved in the planning and development process, and it is too soon to say what the effect of this will be. Gender is also discussed in relation to family planning programmes, sexuality, and childbearing.

Redefinition of sexual roles would provide opportunities for a more complete quality of life for present and future generations. The right to have children is an inalienable and essential right with obligations and responsibilities for both mothers and fathers. A newborn also has an essential and inalienable right to be nurtured with love, fed, educated and cared for, and to know its ancestors.

KIT, Amsterdam   [D 3099-(1993)1]

164   Women's roles and gender gap in health and survival

BASU, ALAKA MALWADE - *Economic and Political Weekly* 28(1993)43 p.2356-2362 [EN] ill. 39 lit.refs ISSN 0012-9976

Gender differences in health and mortality in India are examined by analyzing the health risks women face in their productive/economic, domestic and reproductive roles, relative to the risks men face. Determinants of women's health are divided into determinants affecting exposure to illness, and determinants affecting the outcome of illness. Male mortality is also compared with female mortality. A general finding is that where women are economically active, not restricted to the domestic domain and not defined primarily by the number of children they bear, the gender gap in health and survival is smaller it is for women who are economically inactive, imprisoned in the domestic world, and dependent on their reproductive success for their status. However, women's participation in productive activities and modernization may adversely affect their health and thereby narrow the gap between male and female mortality. For example, although female employment may result in more equal treatment of sons and daughters, it may increase the gender gap in the exposure to and intensity of several diseases among adults. Gender differences in health are often small compared to differences caused by other factors such as caste, place of residence and education. The fact that much of the current gender difference in health and mortality is still preventable justifies a continuation of efforts to attain gender equality in health opportunities and treatment.

KIT, Amsterdam   [B 3057-28(1993)43]

165   Saving lives with menstrual regulation

BEGUM, SYEDA FEROZA - *Planned Parenthood Challenges* (1993)1 p.30-31 [EN] ill.

Although Bangladesh law permits induced abortion only to save the life of the mother, menstrual regulation is legally available. A large menstrual regulation training programme was organized in 1978 for government physicians and health visitors. By 1983, there were 11 menstrual regulation centres and the procedure had become incorporated into the National Family Planning Programme. At present, 22% of abortions are performed in menstrual regulation centres. At least one third of the 24,000 maternal deaths each year are associated with septic abortions performed by untrained abortionists in the rural areas. Menstrual regulation offers a means to prevent many of these deaths. However, rural women are largely unaware of the availability of menstrual regulation and must be reached by field-level health and family planning workers with information about the safety of this method. In addition, women must be made aware that menstrual regulation can be performed only up to the tenth week of pregnancy, and only up to 8 weeks if performed by a health visitor.

KIT, Amsterdam   [D 3027-(1993)1]

166   Women's groups, NGOs and safe motherhood

BERER, MARGE - *WHO/FHE* 92.3. WHO. Division of Family Health. Maternal Health and Safe Motherhood Programme, Geneva iv, 76 p. [EN] ill. Includes lit.refs

Ideas and examples of efforts that can be undertaken by individuals, grassroots women's groups, women's organizations and other NGOs in developing countries to prevent and reduce maternal mortality and morbidity within the broader context of women's reproductive health are described. A wide range of maternal health issues can be addressed through such efforts, including: pregnancy and childbirth; unwanted pregnancy; abortion; adolescent sexuality and pregnancy; quality of care; counselling; reproductive tract infections; women's rights; and HIV/AIDS. The efforts described take many forms: community-based research; education, information and awareness-raising materials for women as well as for men; media campaigns; public education programmes; health service delivery; local and international events, meetings and workshops; and campaigns for better laws and policies.

KIT, Amsterdam   [K 2433-(1992)3]

167   Dry and tight : sexual practices and potential AIDS risk in Zaire

BROWN, JUDITH E.; AYOWA, OKAKO BIBI; BROWN, RICHARD C. - *Social Science and Medicine* 37(1993)8 p.989-994 [EN] ill., tabs 7 lit.refs ISSN 0277-9536

Both men and women in central Zaire express a preference for a 'dry, tight' vagina, claiming that it increases pleasure during sexual intercourse. Focus group interviews established that wiping and washing procedures, as well as 30 different substances, mostly leaves and powders that women insert into the vagina, were used to produce the desired effects. Women who use leaves said they crush them, insert them for several hours, then remove them before intercourse. Women who insert powders leave them in place during intercourse. Individual interviews with 99 women (half of them unmarried prostitutes and half married women) showed that over one third of each group had used vaginal 'drying' or 'tightening' substances at some time. Vaginal examinations by a physician revealed that several of the substances cause inflammatory lesions of the vagina and cervix. Furthermore, some products cause extreme dryness that could foster epithelial trauma during coitus, both for the woman and for her partner. Breaks in the epithelium may promote the passage of organisms that cause AIDS and other STDs. Thus, the sexual practices of drying and tightening the vagina may be increasing the risk of infection.

KIT, Amsterdam   [E 2085-37(1993)8]

168   Women and AIDS in developing countries
BRUYN, MARIA DE - *Social Science and Medicine* 34(1992)3 p.249-262 [EN] Bibliogr. ISSN 0277-9536

Following a brief indication of the HIV/AIDS epidemiological situation in developing countries, the relatively greater impact of HIV/AIDS on women is discussed. Stereotypes related to HIV/AIDS have meant that women are either blamed for their spread or not recognized as potential patients, resulting in delayed diagnosis and treatment, stigmatization, loss of income and violations of human rights. Women are at increased risk of exposure to HIV infection for reasons related to their gender. Further, the psychological and social burdens are greater for women than for men in a similar situation because of problems related to pregnancy and motherhood, and because of potential rejection by their marital partners. The frequently low socio-economic status of women and their lack of power make it difficult for them to undertake preventive measures. It is suggested that prevention programmes are needed to support women in coping with the HIV/AIDS epidemic, and that HIV/AIDS related research regarding women should be increased.

KIT, Amsterdam   [E 2085-34(1992)3]

169   Marital status and abortion in sub-Saharan Africa
CALDWELL, JOHN CHARLES; CALDWELL, PAT *In: Nuptiality in sub-Saharan Africa : contemporary anthropological and demographic perspectives* ed. by Caroline Bledsoe and Gilles Pison. - Oxford : Clarendon, 1994 p.274-295 [EN] 46 lit.refs

Abortion among single and married women in sub-Saharan Africa is examined, based on a variety of secondary sources. Despite its minimal impact on overall fertility, abortion can be an important means for individual women to achieve their wider life and marital goals. Except on very

limited medical grounds, induced abortion is illegal nearly everywhere in sub-Saharan Africa. Whatever its actual prevalence, abortion is undoubtedly understated. It appears to be most common among urban and educated women. Three options for abortion comprise: expensive, doctor-induced abortions; abortions performed by non-medically trained practitioners; and proprietary pills and medicines. Abortions are largely undergone by childless women because bearing children might force marriage or the cessation of schooling or training. Although abortion is less common in married women, it appears to be widely used to space children. The results of the Nigerian segment of the Changing African Family Project from 1973 indicated that abortions among married women in Ibadan had little to do with the problems of raising large families but were more the result of attempting to maintain the expected minimum interval between births, to suppress evidence of adultery, and to prevent births which might strain a weak relationship.

KIT, Amsterdam   [N 94-1930]

170   The impact of marriage change on the risks of exposure to sexually transmitted diseases in Africa
CARAËL, MICHEL *In: Nuptiality in sub-Saharan Africa : contemporary anthropological and demographic perspectives* ed. by Caroline Bledsoe and Gilles Pison. - Oxford : Clarendon, 1994 p.255-273 [EN] ill., tabs 60 lit.refs

The epidemic of AIDS in Africa and its implications for public health are explored. The association of STDs and marriage status is examined, emphasizing the importance of casual sexual relations for the diffusion of STDs and HIV infection. Data covering the spread of HIV and other STDs in the city of Kigali, Rwanda, were collected to illustrate the importance of commercial sexual relations and to examine the relationship of the epidemic to marriage status. Observations from Rwanda and from other cities in East and Central Africa suggest that the greater the imbalance of sexual freedom between men and women, the more rapid the progress of the HIV epidemic. In a situation where women have less sexual freedom, single men with no access to women through marriage commonly seek the services of prostitutes. Once they are married, moreover, a large percentage may continue to frequent prostitutes. The rapid spread of HIV infection among prostitutes is intensified by numerous sexual partners (500-1500 per year) and by the high prevalence of STDs. This high prevalence in turn increases the rates at which prostitutes infect a variety of clients of different ages and social networks, resulting eventually in the contamination of clients' regular female partners. A comparison of cultural contexts indicates that sexual liberty for both sexes limits the spread of HIV infection.

KIT, Amsterdam   [N 94-1930]

171   Women and AIDS in Africa : demographic implications for health promotion
DECOSAS, JOSEF; PEDNEAULT, VIOLETTE - *Health Policy and Planning* 7(1992)3 p.227-233 [EN] ill., tabs 20 lit.refs ISSN 0268-1080

The population pyramid in most countries of Africa is symmetrical with a broad base. In urban areas there is, however, a prominent one-sided bulge caused by the migration of young males (aged 18-35) from rural areas into the cities for employment. The prevalence of HIV infection in urban populations in Africa is highest in the 25-35 year old age group in males and in the 15-25 age group in females. This difference is due to the fact that, on average, sexual partnerships are formed between older men and younger women. The distortion of the urban population profile, caused by male migration, results in an overall 1:1 female:male prevalence ratio of infection. As the epidemic spreads into the larger rural population, the absolute size of the most severely affected younger female population is larger than the size of the older male population which will eventually lead to a higher number of infections in women.

KIT, Amsterdam   [E 2772-7(1992)3]

172   Cutting the rose : female genital mutilation : the practice and its prevention
DORKENOO, EFUA. *Minority Rights Publications.* MRG, London xi, 196 p. 1994 [EN] ill., maps. Includes index, lit.refs ISBN 1-873194-60-9

The book argues that female genital mutilation (FGM) has a negative effect on both the physical and psychological health of millions of women, not just in Africa but also in Europe, North America and other parts of the world. Wide variations of mutilation are performed on the normal vulva, including circumcision, excision of the clitoris, and infibulation. The age at which this takes place varies from a few days old among the nomads of the Sudan to shortly before marriage among the Ibo of Nigeria. Short-term complications include violent pain, haemorrhage, and post-operative shock. Longer term complications include lack of sensation or pain during intercourse, painful menstruation, the development of tumours, cysts and scar-tissue, complications during childbirth, and psychological consequences. FGM is part of a continuum of patriarchal repression of female sexuality. Women are generally the direct perpetrators of the practice but they have ended up performing FGM as a result of their powerlessness in male dominated societies. The

history of the campaign for FGM's abolition indicates that there have been varying levels of activity undertaken by individuals, NGOs, and the UN over a long period of time. Some general lessons are drawn from past efforts which might be useful for planning future programmes. Case studies of initiatives against FGM in many African countries are provided. A strategy for the prevention of the practice among immigrants to Western countries is also outlined.

KIT, Amsterdam   [N 95-525]

173   Inter-relationship between gender relations and the HIV/AIDS epidemic : some possible considerations for policies and programmes
DU GUERNY, JACQUES; SJÖBERG, ELISABETH - *AIDS* 7(1993)8 p.1027-1034 [EN] ill. 29 lit.refs ISSN 0269-9370

Over 90% of newly infected adults have acquired HIV infection from heterosexual intercourse. The heterosexual spread of the epidemic is greatly facilitated by the inability of many women to protect themselves owing to their lower status and their lack of influence over sexual relations. It is suggested that HIV/AIDS policies and programmes should go beyond addressing health issues and should incorporate measures to alter the socio-economic and cultural situation. These strategies involve, first, raising women's status, particularly through empowerment, and, second, redesigning gender relations. Interrelated and complementary strategies with both short and long-term goals are needed to combat AIDS more effectively by incorporating the gender dimension. Gender analysis should provide the information base for AIDS policies and programmes. By identifying the strong and weak points of each gender role, focal points for intervention may be identified. Two examples are given to illustrate how different components of HIV/AIDS programmes could be made more effective using gender analysis: information, education and communication (IEC) programmes; and the issue of caring for AIDS patients, including a tentative checklist.

KIT, Amsterdam   [E 2963-7(1993)8]

174   Sexual behaviour and networking : anthropological and socio-cultural studies on the transmission of HIV
DYSON, TIM. Derouaux-Ordina, Liège 385 p. 1992 [EN] ill., graphs, tabs. Includes lit.refs ISBN 2-87040-046-2

In the context of the spread of AIDS, this volume contains 18 papers that approach the study of human sexuality from a variety of anthropological and population perspectives. These include: mathematical modelling; historical investigation of past epidemics of STDs; national surveys of sexual behaviour; longitudinal surveys; and anthropological research involving participant observation, case studies, action research, sexual diaries, focus group discussions and related approaches. All main types of sexual interaction (heterosexual, homosexual and bisexual) are addressed. Circumstances in both developed and developing countries are reviewed. The papers cover a range of situations: urban Brazil; rural Sudan; evolving patterns of heterosexual interaction in India and Africa; and behavioural change among homosexual men in France and the USA. Some of the populations which are considered (Uganda, Kenya) have become heavily affected by HIV, others (rural Senegal) have much lower levels of infection. Knowledge about the variety and diversity of sexual behaviour is important to understand the future course of the epidemic and to identify preventive measures.

KIT, Amsterdam   [N 93-5367]

175   The influence of spouses over each other's contraceptive attitudes in Ghana

EZEH, ALEX CHIKA - *Studies in Family Planning* 24(1993)3 p.163-174 [EN] ill., graphs, tabs 10 lit.refs. ISSN 0039-3665

The extent to which spouses in Ghana affect each other's attitudes towards family planning is examined. Quantitative evidence from the 1988 Demographic Health Survey and qualitative information from focus group research, undertaken during 1991, are analysed. Although husbands report slightly more favourable attitudes towards family planning than their wives, they show less enthusiasm for stopping childbearing. Some 75% of couples had the same attitude towards family planning. A woman's attitude towards contraception depends not only on her individual characteristics but also on the characteristics of her husband. Her characteristics do not, however, affect her husband's attitude towards family planning. Men's influence over their wives' contraceptive attitude seems to operate both through their comparative advantage in mate selection and through cultural norms which subjugate women to men. Marriage patterns and cultural norms were found to strip women of any right to their preferred reproductive behaviour and may account for their childbearing patterns.

KIT, Amsterdam   [H 1677-24(1993)3]

176   Women's perspectives on reproductive health research

GERMAIN, ADRIENNE; FAUNDES, A. *In: Challenges in reproductive health research : biennial report 1992-1993 UNDP/UNFPA/WHO/World Bank Special Programme of Research, Development and Research Training in Human Reproduction* ed. by J. Khanna, P.F.A. Van Look, P.D. Griffin.

- Geneva : WHO, 1994 p.58-65 [EN] 20 lit.refs

During the last decade an international women's health movement has emerged through which women are asserting their rights to reproductive choice and basic health services. The approach incorporates women and women's perspectives in all levels of decision making regarding reproductive health research and services. Within the context of changing sexual relations and reproduction, major benefits of including women's experiences and perspectives in reproductive health research and services are reviewed, and implications for the research and service agendas are suggested. A process of dialogue and constructive collaboration between scientists, women's health advocates, policymakers, and service providers at national and international levels is required to deal with the challenges ahead: developing the capacity for communication among various actors, enhancing women's organizational strength and scientists' commitment, and ensuring that dialogue and collaboration actually occur.

KIT, Amsterdam   [U 94-451]

177   AIDS and women in Brazil : the emerging problem

GOLDSTEIN, DONNA M. Department of Anthropology, University of California, Berkeley - *Social Science and Medicine* 39(1994)7 p.919-929 [EN] 39 lit.refs ISSN 0277-9536

The public discourse on AIDS and sexuality is compared with the private discourse of low income, urban women in Brazil. Data were collected during interviews with 60 male and female factory workers and with 18 women's groups in favelas (urban shantytowns) of Rio de Janeiro and in poor neighbourhoods of Sao Paulo. Women's perspectives on sexuality are explored by examining what they say about anal sex, virginity and fidelity, and what are seen as approximating culturally scripted ideals for sexual behaviour. AIDS discourses that are being proposed by the Brazilian government, AIDS activist groups and the women's movement are examined in the light of these perspectives. It is argued that AIDS is politicized in Brazil but that the most pressing needs of women and their children have remained relatively untouched. In the present structure of AIDS discourse, male sexual freedom is protected in the name of sexual freedom for all, while women's sexuality, protected in the private sphere, remains unchanged and locked into cultural norms. The inequality of sexual ideology among men and women requires re-examination of AIDS campaigns. HIV/AIDS prevention and education should not be limited to condom literacy which has been central to the Brazilian AIDS campaigns. Campaigns that allow women to reconstitute themselves as sexual subjects, empowered to renegotiate sexual practices and safe sex arrangements with their partners, are urgently needed.

KIT, Amsterdam   [E 2085-39(1994)7]

178   Gender, women, and health in the Americas
GÓMEZ GÓMEZ, ELSA - *Scientific Publication / Pan American Health Organization, WHO* 541. WHO. PAHO, Washington, DC xix, 280 p. 1993 [EN] ill., graphs, tabs. Includes lit.refs ISBN 92-75-11541-9
  Women and health issues are examined in this collection of papers. The emphasis is on the situation that women occupy vis-à-vis men in specific health contexts and within particular social groups. Conceptual elements for the interpretation and re-examination of the links between women, health and development are provided. The health problems that women face in the different stages of their life-cycle, from infancy to old age, and in different classes and countries are discussed, highlighting the gender factors associated with their incidence and with the way in which these problems are approached. The use of medical technologies in the health care of women, the role of women as providers of health, and the relationship between women's health and the law are also dealt with.

KIT, Amsterdam   [K 1741-(1993)541]

179   New approaches for male motivation
GREENE, PAMELA A.S. *In: Family planning : meeting challenges, promoting choices : the proceedings of the IPPF Family Planning Congress, New Delhi, October 1992* ed. by Pramilla Senanayake and Ronald L. Kleinman. - Lancs : Parthenon, 1993 p.437-444 [EN] 3 lit.refs
  Concern for the involvement of men in family planning over the past decade has resulted in the design of programmes to increase male responsibility in fertility regulation. Recent studies on the knowledge, attitudes and practice of men suggest that male attitudes towards family planning are beginning to change in Africa. Many innovative approaches that have been pursued to involve men in family planning have concentrated heavily on information, education and communication strategies, and a number of factors which have contributed to their success are identified. Social marketing, an approach which hinges on community participation in decision-making, can be used to understand the problems and practices in the cultural and social setting of the persons involved, and to motivate behaviour change. It is concluded that male involvement in family planning is crucial to the promotion of family planning and responsible parenthood in Africa. Approaches should continue to focus on adopting innovative interventions that combine a mix of socially and

culturally appropriate communication materials and channels. Such communication efforts need to be professionally planned, carefully targeted, and supported by personal counselling to meet individuals fears and uncertainties.

KIT, Amsterdam   [N 94-678]

180   Women, men, and AIDS in Brazil : the visible and the invisible
GUIMARAES, CARMEN DORA. Rio de Janeiro 12 p. 1992 [EN] Includes lit.refs
  Since its onset in the early 1980s, AIDS in Brazil has largely been associated with homosexual and bisexual men. An important epidemiological shift was observed from the late 1980s onwards with increasing numbers of women and children being infected. The 'bisexual bridge' metaphor was coined which assumes that women were infected through contact with a bisexual male. This metaphor, however, tends to ignore certain aspects of Brazilian sexuality in which some men have sexual relations both with women and other men without identifying themselves as bisexual or even homosexual. The moral codes embedded in Brazilian gender relations contribute to exclude women who are not prostitutes from the epidemic, making them unaware of the risks they are running and placing them at particular disadvantage in the prevention, early diagnosis, and treatment of HIV/AIDS. Measures and strategies of prevention and control for women can only be effective if they are based on women's specific biomedical characteristics and social needs. Condom use has become the main focus of STD/AIDS prevention strategies. Condoms, however, are short-term solutions and will only be used for casual encounters and when a couple first get to know each other.

KIT, Amsterdam   [Br G 94-99]

181   Women, the HIV epidemic and human rights : a tragic imperative
HAMBLIN, JULIE; REID, ELIZABETH. Sydney ii, 22 p. 1991 [EN] Includes lit.refs
  Women are disproportionately affected by and at risk of HIV infection as a result of their social, economic and sexual subordinate status. The vulnerability of women to AIDS must be understood in the broader context of deeply embedded social and gender inequalities which lie at the heart of women's inability to deal effectively with the risks and needs created by the epidemic. Unless the interaction between HIV infection, cultural values and the rights and needs of women is recognized, the fundamental changes required to stem this epidemic will not be attainable. Preventive measures advocated to date have offered women no protection from infection as women lack the power to act accordingly. The most effective prevention strategy for women is

behaviour change in men. National-level policies and research should be directed at improving women's status and developing HIV prevention measures that women themselves can use such as barrier protection methods. The international HIV policy framework should also be modified to account for the interrelationship between women's status and women's risk of HIV infection. In addition, mechanisms must be established to uphold human rights for women as a reality and to impose sanctions for abuses of rights. Laws must be put in place to change structural factors that deny women equal status with men.

KIT, Amsterdam [G 94-520]

182   Safe motherhood

HOFVANDER, YNGVE - *NU* 7(1993)1 Uppsala University. Department of Pediatrics. ICH Unit, Uppsala 46 p. [EN] ill., graphs, maps, tabs. Includes lit.refs ISSN 0283-9164

Problems related to pregnancy and childbirth are a major cause of maternal death in developing countries. The majority of these deaths are preventable at a low cost. The WHO Safe Motherhood Initiative aims to improve maternal health significantly by the year 2000. This issue covers a number of the Safe Motherhood components, including prenatal screening, emergency obstetrics with limited resources, family planning, induced abortion and midwife training. A case study examines the auditing of perinatal infant and maternal mortality as an indicator of obstetric care in Maputo Central Hospital, Mozambique. Finally, the signs of a fertility transition to smaller families in sub-Saharan Africa are examined.

KIT, Amsterdam [D 2826-7(1993)1]

183   Priorité à la santé familiale pour toucher les hommes : planification familiale

ILBOUDO, MARCELINE; KOALGA, OSCAR - *Pop Sahel* (1994)20 p.8-11 [FR] ill., photogr. ISSN 1010-8246

Family planning policies and programmes in sub-Saharan Africa have generally been directed at women. Men, as target group, have been ignored whereas they play a major role in family matters, including family planning. It is argued that men should be incorporated into family planning efforts, and encouraged to assume responsibility for family planning. A few family planning/health initiatives directed at men have been launched in sub-Saharan African which may provide lessons for future efforts.

KIT, Amsterdam [K 2540-(1994)20]

184   From fertility reduction to reproductive choice : gender perspectives on family planning

KABEER, NAILA - *Discussion Paper / IDS, University of Sussex* 299. IDS, Brighton BN1 9RE. 38 p. 1992 [EN] Includes lit.refs ISBN 0-903715-64-3

The narrow focus of past population policy on fertility reduction gave rise to ineffective family planning programmes, frequently coupled with coercive measures and human rights' violations. As women's rights and responsibilities assume greater importance in the international development community, family planning programmes centred on enhancing reproductive choice are likely to be more equitable and, in the long run, more sustainable than those which aim at fertility reduction. Having reviewed arguments for broadening the focus of population efforts, a number of principles, guidelines and measures that could assist in formulating a population policy guided by a concern with women's reproductive choice and wellbeing, rather than with fertility reduction, are offered. Health policy measures suggested are: expansion of reproductive choices through comprehensive provision of safe contraceptive methods; a greater involvement of men in the responsibilities of planned reproduction and parenthood; and a greater concern for maternal health to complement the present focus on family planning and children's welfare. Additional non-health sector recommendations relate to the field of education, paid employment and organization of women workers.

KIT, Amsterdam [E 2206-(1992)299]

185   Bridging the divide

KABEER, NAILA - *People and the Planet* 2(1993)1 p.27-28 [EN] ill., photogr.

Family planning programmes are unlikely to succeed where women's bodies and reproductivity are treated as pawns among struggling states, religions, male heads of households, and private corporations. Women's needs and interests must be taken into account. There are substantial differences in how these needs are interpreted. Feminists would understand that a woman's need for reproductive technology is part of a broader right to control over her own body and life. The population establishment interprets women's needs in the context of slowing down fertility, and secondarily as individual reproductive choice. Many family planning programmes function from a top down approach of implementing population control. Coercion is practised routinely in some countries, either directly or indirectly, through incentives and targets, linking acceptance with provision of other goods and services. Discontinuation rates continue to remain high as a result of the inattention to women's needs. Monitoring and evaluation of family planning programmes emphasize quantitative indicators such as targets reached, clients recruited, rates of acceptance, and other measures. The quality of interaction between provider and user and the satisfaction of user needs is rarely measured. Feminists' perspectives on family planning would promote women's involvement in the conceptualization, formulation, and implementation of programmes. Men's reproductive responsibilities would not be neglected or denied. A feminist population policy is needed, together with a shift away from policy that is resource dependent.

KIT, Amsterdam [D 2681-2(1993)1]

186   Women and the AIDS epidemic : an impending crisis for the Americas
KIMBALL, ANN MARIE; GONZÁLEZ, ROXANE SALVATIERRA; ZACARÍAS, FERNANDO - *Scientific Publication / Pan American Health Organization* (1993)541 p.178-183 [EN] ill., tabs 10 lit.refs

Factors that contribute to increased prevalence of AIDS among women, and what can be done to contain or control the epidemic are examined. Women become infected with HIV through the same routes as their male counterparts, namely blood transfusion and sexual transmission. However, women seem to be at greater risk of HIV infection than men. Women have a higher exposure to blood transfusions as a result of complications of pregnancy and childbirth, and women seem to be at much greater risk of HIV infection through heterosexual intercourse with an infected male partner than vice versa. In Latin America and the Caribbean, women with bisexual partners, women who engage in prostitution, and women who have STDs have higher HIV seroprevalence than other groups of women and men. Women who have partners who are HIV-positive or who are intravenous drug abusers are also at higher risk. Public health interventions can help prevent women becoming infected by securing a safe and adequate blood supply, and through the promotion of safe sex, including the use of condoms. Attention should also given to vertical maternal/infant HIV transmission, considering issues such as the termination of pregnancy.

KIT, Amsterdam [K 1741-(1993)541]

187   Family planning and the Malawian male
KISHINDO, PAUL - *Journal of Social Development in Africa* 9(1994)2 p.61-69 [EN] 10 lit.refs ISSN 1012-1080

The fertility rate in Malawi is a cause for concern, indicating the need for adoption of contraceptive and family planning methods. However, there is a low contraceptive acceptance rate among women and a consequent high degree of risk concerning pregnancy. The consequences of high fertility have a negative effect at both the family and wider societal levels. Efforts to bring down the population should involve both men and women. The present system which has tended to

concentrate on women as change agents is inadequate because women, particularly married women, who are most exposed to the risk of pregnancy, do not really control their own reproductive capacities. Rather, it is men as husbands and brothers who take decisions about fertility. Since men have such a crucial role in fertility, it is important that they appreciate the value of family planning for the quality of life of their families. This implies that any family planning programme should include activities directed at both women and men.

KIT, Amsterdam [A 2698-9(1994)2]

188   The health of women : a global perspective
KOBLINSKY, MARJORIE A.; TIMYAN, JUDITH; GAY, JILL. Westview, Boulder, CO viii, 291 p. 1993 [EN] ill., tabs. Includes index. Includes lit.refs ISBN 0-8133-8500-8

Every year millions of women suffer preventable illnesses and 500,000 die from pregnancy-related complications. Too many die because they lack the information and resources to care for themselves. In 1991 the Conference on Women's Health: the Action Agenda was organized out of a growing recognition of the need for improvements in women's health. This book, reflecting the formal and informal discussions at the conference, addresses the information and services women need to improve their health and the context in which they live their lives, suggesting concrete ways to redress international inattention to women's health. Having provided a broader perspective on women's health, the chapters address: women's nutrition through the life-cycle; reproductive tract infections and STDs, including HIV/AIDS; family planning; abortion; mortality; violence against women; mental health; and access to and quality of health care. Guiding principles are drawn: gender-specific data are essential for resource allocation; health providers, planners and advocates must confront gender discrimination; women's health begins in infancy, implying that policies and programmes should include the nutrition, health care and education of girls and young women as well as mothers; and although female mortality and morbidity are the gross indicators of women's health, the quality of women's lives is an indicator of their ability to develop and maximize their potential. Women must be empowered by training, education and participation to seek prevention and treatment of diseases which maim and kill them. They must determine for themselves how many children they want because it is they who take the risks of fertility and the responsibilities of motherhood.

KIT, Amsterdam [N 93-6304]

189   Family and gender issues for population policy
LLOYD, CYNTHIA B. Population Council, United Nations, 1 Dag Hammarskjold Plaza, New York, NY - *Working papers / Research Division, Population Council* 48. Population Council. Research Division, New York, NY 41 p. 1993 [EN] ill., tabs Includes lit.refs

Population policy and the collection and analysis of demographic data rely on a number of assumptions about the nature of family: decisions about childbearing are made exclusively within the family; improvements in women's work status outside the family contribute to less reliance on children and family members for economic support; fathers share jointly with mothers in the responsibility for child maintenance and upbringing; and parents support each child equally. The singular emphasis on women as agents of change is misplaced. More needs to be known about the extent of men's reproductive and familial roles and how costs and benefits of children are distributed. Discussion and tables are devoted to several distinctive features of families. Statistical tables pertain to selected countries in sub-Saharan Africa, Asia, North America, and Latin America and the Caribbean. The data reflect a diversity in family forms which could be further amplified by analysis of parent-child links and membership in multiple families. Stability and economic cohesiveness of families appear to be important factors influencing family size goals but insufficient data prevent a better understanding of the nature and extent of their influence. When women have a fair share of their economic gains for personal benefit, there will be a direct and immediate impact on fertility in male dominant societies. Economic prospects for girls must be comparable to those for boys. Empirical analysis of gender relations and the structure and organization of families is required in place of assumptions.
KIT, Amsterdam   [H 2015-(1993)48]

190   What is the family (and who does the planning)?
LLOYD, CYNTHIA B. Population Council, UN, 1 Dag Hammarskjold Plaza, New York, NY - *Populi* 20(1993)4 p.8-11 [EN] ISSN 0251-6861

Governments tend to base their population policies on an unrealistic assumption of what constitutes a family. They define the family as a closed physical, economic and emotional unit: the basic unit within society. Migration, polygamy, divorce, remarriage, and childbearing outside of marriage are relatively common in developing countries; many children do not live with both parents. Fathers often migrate to earn money to support their families but women do not consistently receive remittances, particularly when the parents are not married to each other. Sexual relations occur outside marriage, often resulting in pregnancy. Pre-marital and extramarital sexual relations imply the need for individuals to decide on contraceptive use. Sexual relations within marriage should involve joint decision-making about contraception. In reality, spouses do not always have the same fertility goals and, when they do, they may not agree on contraception. Most family planning programmes concentrate on currently married women and operate as though unmarried women do not have sexual intercourse. Such programmes should also target men because in those cases when husbands approve of contraception, contraceptive use increases. The costs of rearing children are increasing worldwide but this does not necessarily decrease the desire for children. Women's education and improved status result in decreased desire for children. The changing family highlights the need for research to focus on men and on family structures.
KIT, Amsterdam   [K 1507-20(1993)4]

191   Health is a gender issue
MACFADDEN, PATRICIA - *Southern Africa* 7(1994)3/4 p.59-61 [EN] ill.

The definition of women's health is linked to their reproductive health. The Safe Motherhood Initiative, mother and child health, and primary health care are existing health programmes that reinforce the assumption that women have no health needs besides those determined by motherhood and the medical community. Health programmes in developing countries do not target women who are not pregnant or not lactating. Many women do not perceive health holistically. Most African women are the least healthy in their communities. The medical community also ignores unmarried women who are not mothers, reflecting a pressing need to develop a new concept of health for women. Health workers and health centres tend to cater only for pregnancy and children, even though the workers tend to be women themselves. African women therefore only seek medical care for conditions linked to childbirth and practice self-care for other conditions or tolerate pain and discomfort. Their gynaecological, mental, and emotional needs are marginalized. The Ford Foundation has committed US $125 million to address the health needs of urban and rural women, especially poor women, throughout the reproductive cycle. Patriarchal African states reinforce the gender biases in the health and educational systems. Women tend to have a negative and self-marginalizing perception of their own health. A woman-centred concept of health uses wellbeing instead of health to affirm the right of women to a healthy existence. Adoption of this holistic concept sets in motion very important processes: rejection of the stereotypical image of African women and construction of a new, positive image.

KIT, Amsterdam   [A 2748-7(1993)3/4]

192   Private decisions, public debate : women, reproduction & population
MIRSKY, JUDITH; RADLETT, MARTY. Panos, London vi, 185 p. 1994 [EN] ill. Includes lit.refs ISBN 1-870670-34-5

The book comprises 13 studies which address subjects related to women's reproductive health and choice. Women's health needs go beyond family planning, and should be met by a wide range of reproductive health services and concerns, including family planning services. In addition, legal, policy and cultural constraints on women's exercise of reproductive choice and health should be removed. A study from India highlights the lack of services available to both women and men in the field of prevention and treatment of STDs and other reproductive tract infections. Health hazards associated with unsafe induced abortion in Tanzania, and the health consequences for women of son preference in Egypt and Pakistan are examined. A study from the Philippines outlines the contraceptive benefits of breast-feeding. Other subjects discussed are: female genital mutilation in Burkina Faso; HIV and its relation to reproductive health in Thailand; the politics of reproduction in Pakistan; obstetric fistulae, a major health hazard of neglected childbirth, in Ethiopia; the relationship between education and employment, and reproductive choice in Pakistan; and the role of midwives in reproductive health in Ghana. Constraints on women's reproductive choice are demonstrated by a report from Pakistan on the politics of reproduction; a study on the influence of the Catholic church on women's reproductive choice in Chile; the increasing incidence of childbirth by Caesarean section and sterilizations in Brazil; and an examination of social forces and women's reproductive rights in Egypt.

KIT, Amsterdam   [P 94-440]

193   Women's access to health care in developing countries
NASH OJANUGA, DURRENDA; GILBERT, CATHY School of Social Work, University of Alabama, P.O. Box 870314, Tuscaloosa - *Social Science and Medicine* 35(1992)4 p.613-617 [EN] 27 lit.refs ISSN 0277-9536

Gender specific analysis of health and health care utilization in developing countries reveals significant disparities between men and women. Women often suffer poorer health and consume fewer health care resources than their male counterparts. In addition to adverse health conditions, such as infectious diseases and

inadequate water supplies and sanitation, these women are frequently confronted with a myriad of factors which negatively impinge upon their physical wellbeing and access to health care services. Most of the health hazards faced by women during their reproductive life are either preventable or curable. Women's access to and use of health care is restricted by institutional, economic and cultural barriers, including distance to health centres, lack of health facilities, women's lack of control over income, and patrilineal ideology. It is argued that women must become agents of change to improve their situation and gain control of their own lives, particularly in the area of reproductive health and behaviour. Factors such as access to income, legal rights, social status, and education may prove far more important in determining women's access to health care than technological distribution and governmental strategies.

KIT, Amsterdam   [E 2085-35(1992)4]

194   Gender exploitation and violence : the market in women, girls and sex in Nepal : an overview of the situation and a review of the literature
O'DEA, PAULINE. UNICEF, [New York, NY] iv, 90 p. 1993 [EN] Bibliogr.: p. 58-90 ISBN 92-806-3007-5

Drawing on the available literature, a review is made of prostitution and women and girl trafficking in Nepal. The evidence suggests a vast market which can be divided into: women and girls trafficked mainly to India; prostitution associated with cultural and religious traditions; and local sex workers. It is estimated that tens of thousands are actively involved in this illegal and, in terms of forced prostitution, inhuman behaviour. Findings suggest that about 100,000 Nepali girls and women work in Indian brothels. Key factors maintaining and expanding the sex market include poverty and the low status of women and girls. Although the sex market provides an income to the sex workers, major profits are not made by the sex workers themselves but by those who control the sex market. Major negative consequences include brutalization of family relationships, social isolation, and increased risk of STDs, HIV infection and AIDS. The sex market poses new threats to a society built on collective responsibility and group work. Action undertaken by NGOs and other development agencies to provide girls and women with alternative income and employment opportunities is reviewed, together with suggestions for future action. An annotated bibliography is presented on the issue in general, cultural and religious-based forms of prostitution, STDs and AIDS, and Indian literature on the Nepali situation.

KIT, Amsterdam   [U 94-320]

195   Impact of AIDS on the patterns of AIDS-related risk and preventive behaviours among married men in a Nigerian town
ODEBIYI, A.I. - *Scandinavian Journal of Development Alternatives* 11(1992)2 p.5-14 [EN] 17 lit.refs ISSN 0280-2791

The sexual behaviour of 90 married men from indigenous and transitional areas of the university town of Ile-Ife, Nigeria, was surveyed during 1991. Although all of the men had heard about AIDS, only 66% perceived it to be an STD. Some attributed AIDS to evil forces and God's punishment for men's excesses. Although most of the respondents were aware that the use of condoms could prevent AIDS, they did not use them, largely because condoms were perceive to reduce enjoyment of sexual acts. Analysis of men's attitudes towards other AIDS-related risk behaviours, such as the practice of polygyny, extramarital relations and contact with sex workers, revealed that the majority (64.4%) were opposed to polygyny but that many (54.4%) supported and justified the habit of having extramarital affairs. The respondents were against contact with sex workers because they associated this group of women with STDs. It is concluded that the sexual behaviour of respondents has not changed, despite the publicity about AIDS and its prevention. Interventions that involve interaction with AIDS patients are suggested as a strategy to bring about behavioural change, together with efforts to promote the use of condoms.
KIT, Amsterdam   [E 2562-11(1992)2]

196   Gender inequalities of health in the Third World
OKOJIE, CHRISTIANA E.E. - *Social Science and Medicine* 39(1994)9 p.1237-1247 [EN] 48 lit.refs ISSN 0277-9536

Health hazards are present at every stage of a woman's life-cycle in developing countries, including: reproductive health problems, excess female mortality in childhood, violence against girls and women, occupational and environmental hazards, and cervical and breast cancer. Many of these lead to maternal mortality which is commonly used as an indicator of women's health in the literature. Gender inequalities in health originate in the traditional society where definitions of health status and traditional medical practices all reflect the subordinate social status of women. Gender inequalities are manifested in traditional medical practices which attribute women's illnesses to behavioural lapses by women; and in the differential utilization of modern health care services by women and girls, including maternal care, general health care, family planning and safe abortion services. Reasons for gender inequalities include: emphasis on women's childbearing roles resulting in early and excessive childbearing; sex preference manifested in discrimination against female children in health and general care; women's workloads which not only expose them to health hazards but also make it difficult for them to take time off for health care; women's lack of autonomy leading to a lack of decision-making power and access to independent income; and early marriage which exposes women to the complications of early and excessive childbearing. Gender inequality in health is one of the social dimensions in which gender inequality is manifested in developing countries. Strategies to eradicate gender inequalities in health must therefore involve policies to improve the status of women, increase their autonomy, and policies to improve availability of health services and quality of care.
KIT, Amsterdam   [E 2085-39(1994)9]

197   African women's control over their sexuality in an era of AIDS : a study of the Yoruba of Nigeria
ORUBULOYE, I.O.; CALDWELL, JOHN CHARLES; CALDWELL, PAT. Faculty of the Social Sciences, Ondo State University, Ado-Ekiti - *Social Science and Medicine* 37(1993)7 p.859-872 [EN] ill. 60 lit.refs ISSN 0277-9536

Very little knowledge is available about African women's control over their sexual relations with husbands or other stable partners in situations where there is a high risk of STDs and HIV/AIDS. Such control must be seen as encompassing women's control over their sexuality and reproduction as well as the broader areas over which they can make decisions. A study was undertaken among the Yoruba people in Ado-Ekiti town of Ondo State, Nigeria, during 1991. Women's ability to control marital sexual relations when their husbands are infected with STDs is explored, together with the implications for HIV infection. STDs were the focus of attention because the AIDS epidemic is still at an early stage in Nigeria. Yoruba women were found to be able to refuse sexual relations for a limited time. They are placed at greater risk of STD infection by their ignorance of whether their partner is infected than by a lack of ability to control the situation when STDs have been identified. This ability may be more limited in the case of AIDS because of its longer duration. If women know that their husband is suffering from STDs or AIDS, they can demand sexual abstinence, safe sex or leave the marriage. The fundamental situation was found to be different from that in East and Southern Africa because of lineage structures to which women also belong.
KIT, Amsterdam   [E 2085-37(1993)7]

198 Adolescent motherhood : problems and consequences
PATHAK, K.B.; RAM, F. International Institute for Population Sciences, Deonar, Bombay 400 068 - *Journal of Family Welfare* 39(1993)1 p.17-23 [EN] tabs 9 lit.refs

An estimated 13 million female adolescents under 18 years of age are married in India. The widespread existence of the phenomenon of early marriage reflects the cultural norm encouraging married couples to raise many sons to provide for the security and wellbeing of parents throughout their later years. Parents can maximize the production of offspring by starting young. Most young women are subject to this traditional outlook on child wealth and they are also overwhelmingly ignorant about family planning methods. Young women should be provided with educational and economic alternatives to early childbearing. In so doing, fertility, maternal mortality and child mortality will decrease. Since early marriage is strongly related to the schooling of girls, especially those aged 10-14 years, it is further suggested that the education of girls should be made compulsory to the tenth standard.
KIT, Amsterdam   [B 2797-39(1993)1]

199 Maternal mortality in Africa : 1980-87
PAUL, BIMAL KANTI. Department of Geography, Kansas State University, Manhattan - *Social Science and Medicine* 37(1993)6 p.745-752 [EN] ill., graphs, tabs 40 lit.refs ISSN 0277-9536

African women of reproductive age have the highest death risk from maternal causes of any women in the world. The lifetime chance of maternal death is 1 in 21 in Africa as compared to 1 in 54 in Asia which ranks second highest. Published data are used to examine the level and correlates of the maternal mortality ratio (MMR) in Africa. The data indicate that MMR greatly differs among the countries of Africa from 40 to 2000 per 100,000 live births. High MMR is found in most countries of sub-Saharan Africa, while countries of Northern Africa are characterized by relatively low levels of maternal death. Reasons for high MMR in sub-Saharan Africa are strongly influenced by population size, crude birth rate, crude death rate, calorie supply as a percentage of requirements, access to safe water, and percentage of urban population. Some cultural and behavioural factors, such as female circumcision and infibulation, are also associated with a high MMR. Findings suggest that maternal mortality will decline given an increase in the food supply and lowering of both birth and death rates. Further, the cultural status of women needs to be improved and cultural practices, such as female genital mutilation, should be stopped.
KIT, Amsterdam   [E 2085-37(1993)6]

200 Changing men's attitudes and behavior : the Zimbabwe male motivation project
PIOTROW, PHYLLIS T.; KINCAID, D. LAWRENCE; HINDIN, MICHELLE J.; LETTENMAIER, CHERYL L.; KUSEKA, INNOCENT; SILBERMAN, TERRY; ZINANGA, ALEX; CHIKARA, FLORENCE; ADAMCHAK, DONALD J.; MBIZVO, MICHAEL T.; LYNN, WILMA; KUMAH, OPIA MENSAH; KIM, YOUNG. MI Center for Communication Programs, Johns Hopkins University, 527 St. Paul Place, Baltimore - *Studies in Family Planning* 23(1992)6 p.365-375 [EN] ill., graphs, tabs 28 lit.refs ISSN 0039-3665

A multimedia communication campaign was conducted during 1988-1989 to promote family planning among men in Zimbabwe. The campaign consisted of a 52-episode, twice weekly radio soap opera, some 60 motivational talks, and two pamphlets about contraceptive methods. Changes over time were measured by comparing a sub-set of a follow-up survey conducted from October to December 1989 to a baseline survey conducted from April to June 1988. Men exposed to the campaign were also compared to men who were not. The follow-up survey revealed that the campaign reached 52% of men aged 18-55. Among married Shona-speaking men, use of modern contraceptive methods increased from 56% to 59% during the campaign. Condom use increased from 5% to 10%. Men exposed to the campaign were significantly more likely than other men to make the decision to use contraceptives and to say that both spouses should decide how many children to have.
KIT, Amsterdam   [H 1677-23(1992)6]

201 Women and access to health care
PUENTES-MARKIDES, CRISTINA Health Policies Development Programme, Pan American Health Organization, 525 23rd Street NW, Washington, DC 20037 - *Social Science and Medicine* 35(1992)4 p.619-626 [EN] ill. 40 lit.refs ISSN 0277-9536

Women's access to health care in developing countries is assessed, with specific reference to Latin America and the Caribbean. Available literature on the concept of access as it relates to variables such as accountability, ability to pay, and acceptability of health services, considering both the socio-economic crisis of the last decade and equity objectives, is reviewed. Various approaches to defining variables affecting access to health care are found in the literature. The ability to pay for services is an important determinant of access to health care. Other studies point to behavioural issues including motivation, health-seeking behaviour and perception of illness as a deterrent to women in the low socio-economic strata, while others indicate that socio-cultural issues such as values, education, religion or demographic variables related to age influence access to health care. Lessons from past policies and strategies to secure access to health care suggest a need to move away from traditional solutions that have proven to be insensitive to the needs of the disadvantaged, and to women's needs in particular, towards health policies which include women's perspectives and allow for women's participation in decision-making processes regarding their own health. The instrument of participatory planning appears the preferred method to ensure that all segments of society participate.

KIT, Amsterdam   [E 2085-35(1992)4]

202   Young women : silence, susceptibility and the HIV epidemic
REID, ELIZABETH. UNDP. HIV and Development Programme, [New York, NY 9 p. 1992] [EN] ill., graphs. Includes lit.refs

Women in developing countries are increasingly becoming infected with HIV. Proportionally more girls and young women are becoming infected in their teens and early twenties than women in any other age group. They are generally being infected 5-10 years earlier than men. The extent of the early and easy infection of young women indicates a particular susceptibility to infection in this group. This susceptibility cannot be adequately explained by the cultural, social or economic conditions under which young women have intercourse, nor by the presence of infections and lesions, frequency of intercourse or nutritional status. The possibility of physiological vulnerability as a contributory factor should be urgently explored. The genital tract of young women might be a less effective barrier to virus penetration than that of older women due to less proficient mucous production and the presence of cervical damage. This biological vulnerability could be reinforced by the more likely participation of young women in non-consensual, hurried or frequent intercourse. Strategies must be found to lengthen the time before first intercourse for young women, increase the age at first pregnancy, and which increase the ability of young girls to control the situations in which they are sexually active. Families, schools and groups should represent sanctuaries from HIV infection for young women. The urgency of the situation may well necessitate the use of sanctions: laws against rape and incest, and family law relating to the age of marriage.

KIT, Amsterdam   [Br U 94-252]

203   Gender, knowledge and responsibility
REID, ELIZABETH. UNDP. HIV and Development Programme, New York, NY [15] p. [1992] [EN] Includes lit.refs

Prevention strategies developed in response to the HIV/AIDS epidemic have not, to their cost, been based on an understanding of women's life situations. Most women are at risk of HIV infection by sexual transmission as a result of cultural and sexual practices. The prevention strategies advocated to prevent sexual transmission have offered women little or no protection from infection because they failed to increase women's ability to protect themselves. Strategies which are able to protect women must be based on the contexts in which women's sexuality is expressed and, at the level of the individual, they must be strategies that women can control. Among the few possible options that fulfil these conditions are: the use of diaphragm plus spermicide which may protect both women and men from HIV infection and which can, if necessary, be used clandestinely by women; the female condom; and collectively talking to men about the importance of protecting themselves from HIV infection and the consequences of HIV infection for their families. It is argued that strategies which rely on behavioural change should be based on an understanding of men's sexuality, life situations and communities. Women's gender specific experiences and knowledge can be made accessible by ensuring that women as well as men shape and determine the agendas, by first person narratives or by the devolution of responsibility for interventions to women and their communities.

KIT, Amsterdam   [U 94-238]

204   Women's living conditions and maternal mortality in Latin America
RENDÓN, LISA; LANGER, ANA; HERNÁNDEZ, BERNARDO University of North Carolina, POB 2688, Chapel Hill, NC - *Bulletin of the Pan American Health Organization* 27(1993)1 p.56-64 1993 [EN] ill. 31 lit.refs ISSN 0085-4638

The living conditions of women in Latin America and the relationship of these conditions to maternal mortality are reviewed. One obstacle to this review is the lack of valid data on maternal mortality and influential factors. Several methods of analysis, such as use of death registers and census data, are required. Maternal mortality, defined as death from obstetric causes, is deceptive because mortality is also indirectly affected by other factors. Scarce medical care resources, poor social circumstances, and the multiple roles of women place them at high risk of maternal death. Treatment, such as abortion, may not even be available. Social pressures to have large families, discrimination against women and poor working conditions can place women at a disadvantage and endanger their health. Distance, transport difficulties, cost and poor quality of available care also effect maternal health. Women in rural areas seek midwives who are respected community members but they may lack the training to cope with a high-risk delivery. In cities, transport, ability to pay and quality of care are most important. The lack of family planning also affects the level of risk, as do socio-economic factors, such as income, education, housing, sanitation, and nutrition. The maternal health care model proposed by Dixon-Mueller is described. It advocates the integration of maternal health and family planning services into existing primary health care. Interventions are also required to reduce death from induced, illegal abortions.

KIT, Amsterdam [K 2428-27(1993)1]

205 Reproductive health : towards a brighter future
World Health Forum 15(1994)1 p.1-8 [EN] ill. ISSN 0251-2432

In 1972 the WHO initiated the Special Programme of Research, Development and Research Training in Human Reproduction. Now co-sponsored by the UNDP, the UNFPA, the World Bank and WHO, the programme has become the main instrument of research in reproductive health in the UN system. The programme recognizes that human reproduction influences the health of women and children, the status of women, population levels, socio-economic development and the global environment. The pillars of reproductive health are identified as family planning, maternal and child care, and the prevention of STDs. The progress that has been made, and the prospects for the future, are reviewed, focusing on the programme's approach, developments in contraceptive technologies, epidemiological and social science research, and the programme's resources, including finance. Since 1972, international, regional and national structures for research, research training and support have been created. As a result of research studies on the service aspects of fertility regulation, changes in national family planning programmes and even in legislation have been made by India, Indonesia, Kenya, Pakistan, the Philippines, Thailand, Turkey and other WHO member states.

KIT, Amsterdam [K 1884-15(1994)1]

206 Factors that determine prevalence of use of contraceptive methods for men
RINGHEIM, KAREN Spec. Prog. of Research, Development and Research Training in Human Reproduction, WHO, 1211 Geneva 27 - *Studies in Family Planning* 24(1993)2 p.87-99 1993 [EN] Bibliogr. p.96-99 ISSN 0039-3665

Globally, men have not shared equally with women the responsibility for fertility regulation. While family planning efforts have been directed almost exclusively towards women, the lack of male involvement may also reflect the limited options available to men. Current methods for men are either coitus-dependent, such as the

condom or withdrawal, or permanent, such as vasectomy. The 20 year history of social science research on male contraceptive methods is examined in terms of the human and method factors related to the acceptability of hypothetical methods and the prevalence of use of existing methods. Aside from recent innovations in the technique, vasectomy is the only new male method that has been added to men's contraceptive options in the past 25 years. Acceptability and use of a contraceptive method are determined by human factors including motivation, life-style, and knowledge, as well as by safety, efficacy and convenience. Men are more likely to accept a reversible, non-coitus dependent and long-acting contraceptive method such as injectable and implanted hormones which are currently being researched. The anticipated development of new methods of male fertility regulation, particularly hormonal methods, will provide opportunities to study communication between spouses, a couple's decision-making process, and issues of gender dominance and gender identification as expressed through sexuality and procreation.

KIT, Amsterdam [H 1677-24(1993)2]

207 Reaching women in Latin America and the Caribbean : an integrated approach to safer sex
ROITSTEIN, FLORENCIA; BECKER, JULIE. IPPF/WHR HIV/STD Prevention Program, [London] 13 p. 1994 [EN] ill., tabs. Includes lit.refs

The International Planned Parenthood Federation, Western Hemisphere Region (IPPF/WHR) initiated an HIV/STD prevention programme with the principal objective of integrating HIV/STD prevention into existing programmes and services of family planning associations. Family planning programmes are considered key settings for incorporation of HIV/STD prevention activities because they reach large numbers of sexually active people, and because such programmes are often the only contact women in developing countries have with organized health programmes. The integrated strategy comprised three major strategic components to achieve safe sex: behaviour change; condom promotion; and STD control (rather than HIV). The history of integrating the HIV/STD prevention strategy into programmes and services of IPPF/WHR affiliates in Latin America and the Caribbean are described. The application of this model in Jamaica is examined, including collection of baseline and follow-up data on staff knowledge, skills and practice. The Jamaican case and experience in Brazil suggest that integrating HIV/STD prevention into national family planning programmes can enhance the quality of such programmes and services so that they meet a broad range of clients' reproductive and sexual health needs by offering fully integrated HIV/STD prevention and family planning counselling sessions, by improving method mix through increased condom distribution, and by strengthening STD referral and follow-up systems.

KIT, Amsterdam   [Br G 94-98]

208   Sexual behaviour and the acceptability of condoms to Ugandan males
RWABUKWALI, CHARLES B. - *Eastern Africa Social Science Research Review* 8(1992)1 p.33-45 [EN] ill., tabs 11 lit.refs

Sexual behaviour and condom acceptability among urban and rural men was examined in Uganda. Data were collected from 601 males in Kampala and the rural Masaka and Kabarole Districts during 1989. Some 23% of the respondents reported using condoms, representing a much higher percentage than found by previous studies. More widespread use of condoms may be associated with a campaign by the AIDS control programme which had been conducted in the study areas. The most important factors associated with condom use were residing in an urban area and education. Condom use was not significantly related to number of wives or children. The pattern of cultural beliefs and practices, including sexual practices, suggests that only moderate levels of condom use can be achieved. However, with greater efforts at public education and rationalization of delivery systems for contraceptives, and for condoms in particular, the level of condom use among Ugandan males may be increased.

KIT, Amsterdam   [D 2893-8(1992)1]

209   Social roles and physical health : the case of female disadvantage in poor countries
SANTOW, GIGI - *Social Science and Medicine* 40(1995)2 p.147-161 [EN] 92 lit.refs ISSN 0277-9536

Literature on the effect of women's inferior status on their health and that of their children is reviewed. The geographical and cultural scope was dictated by the available research with many examples coming from South Asia, Arab countries and sub-Saharan Africa and fewer from Latin America. Women's culturally and socially determined roles impair their health and that of their children through a complex web of physiological and behavioural interrelationships and synergies that pervade every aspect of their lives. Women's roles also affect their use of health services since modern health care has been absorbed so successfully into traditional structures that families tend to allocate it, like food, according to characteristics such as sex and age. Some basic underlying differences between the health risks facing women and men are discussed. Health risks facing women and girls include: female infanticide; inequitable distribution of food and poor nutrition;

childbearing and contraception; STDs and HIV/AIDS; female genital mutilation; and the dependence of children on women. Female education and the redefinition of familial relationships can both operate to improve women's position and hence their health and that of their children. In addition, health interventions and services can contribute to improving women's health through revising their view of women as the natural guardians of their family's health and by drawing other family members, and particularly husbands, into their orbit.

KIT, Amsterdam   [E 2085-40(1995)2]

210   Sex, gender and society in Zaire
SCHOEPF, BROOKE GRUNDFEST *In: Sexual behaviour and networking : anthropological and socio-cultural studies on the transmission of HIV* ed. by Tim Dyson. - Liège : Derouaux-Ordina, 1992 p.353-375 1992 [EN] 89 lit.refs

Sexual culture in Zaire is explored in different time periods, based primarily on secondary sources. Changing gender relations, the consequence of increasing social inequality, have altered the meanings with which sex is invested, as well as rules of sexual behaviour and penalties for breaking rules. The picture of a homogeneous African sexual culture must be rejected and other grounds sought for the epidemic spread of HIV. These are to be found in the fields of biological and socio-cultural interaction; the political ecology of disease; social inequality; and the prolonged, deepening economic crisis. Gender inequality and the poverty that circumscribes many people's daily lives render most women unable to negotiate safer sex. Thus, prevention begins with changes in men's behaviour. However, since the spread of HIV is linked to the economic crisis, even relatively effective behavioural interventions will be limited by constraints in the socio-economic and political structures that shape both culture and people's struggles to change their own lives. Women need access to other means of support if they are to stop using sex as an economic resource. As long as women are denied access to alternative employment opportunities, some will continue to use sexual services as their main means of economic support. New economic opportunities can only occur in the context of sustained growth, making sexual transmission of HIV/AIDS a development issue.

KIT, Amsterdam   [N 93-5367]

211   Credit programs, women's empowerment, and contraceptive use in rural Bangladesh
SCHULER, SIDNEY RUTH; HASHEMI, SYED M. JSI Research and Training Institute, Empowerment of Women Program, 1616 N. Fort Meyer Dr., Arlington - *Studies in Family Planning* 25(1994)2

p.65-76 [EN] tabs 29 lit.refs ISSN 0039-3665
Findings of research addressing the question of how women's status affects fertility are presented, based on data obtained from 1305 married women in rural Bangladesh at two points in time, mid-1991 and late 1992. The effects on contraceptive use of women's participation in rural credit programmes and on their status or level of empowerment were examined. A woman's level of empowerment is defined here as a function of her relative physical mobility, economic security, ability to make various purchases on her own, freedom from domination and violence within her family, political and legal awareness, and participation in public protests and political campaigning. The main finding is that participation in both of the credit programmes studied, those of the Grameen Bank and the Bangladesh Rural Advancement Committee (BRAC), is positively associated with women's level of empowerment. A positive effect on contraceptive use is discernible among both participants and non-participants in Grameen Bank villages. Participation in BRAC does not appear to affect contraceptive use.

KIT, Amsterdam   [H 1677-25(1994)2]

212   Women at risk : gender and AIDS in Africa
SEIDEL, GILL - *Disasters* 17(1993)2 p.133-142
[EN] 64 lit.refs ISSN 0361-3666
AIDS in Africa is a gender, development and rights issue involving power and differential access to resources. The risk situations for women in stressed development contexts of war, destabilization and displacement, and the many contexts of transactional sex, are poorly understood by policymakers and the medical community. The dominant epidemiological paradigm has focused on female prostitutes in a number of African cities. The limitations of this approach are discussed, as are the different contextualized meanings of sexual exchange. The importance of women's experience of STDs and HIV, and their perceptions of risk are stressed. There is a need for non-judgemental services linked to primary and comprehensive health care, and for sensitive, qualitative research. All women who engage in unprotected, penetrative sex are at risk. Most health promotion messages, however, construct an image of women as prostitutes or seek to mobilize women as carers and educators of families and communities.

KIT, Amsterdam   [E 2813-17(1993)2]

213   The competing discourses of HIV/AIDS in sub-Saharan Africa : discourses of rights and employment vs discourses of control and exclusion
SEIDEL, GILL - *Social Science and Medicine* 36(1993)3 p.175-194 [EN] Bibliogr. ISSN 0277-9536
The competing discourses of HIV/AIDS

circulating in sub-Saharan Africa are identified. These are medical, medico-moral, developmental (distinguishing between women-in-development and gender perspectives), legal, ethical, and the rights discourse of groups living with HIV/AIDS and of African pressure groups. The analytical framework is that of discourse analysis as exemplified by Foucault. The medical and medico-moral discourses are identified as dominant. They shape the perceptions of the pandemic, and responses to it and to those living with HIV/AIDS. However, dissident activists are gradually changing the dominant frameworks, and are mobilizing a struggle for meaning around definitions of gender, human rights, and development.

KIT, Amsterdam   [E 2085-36(1993)3]

214   Population policies reconsidered : health, empowerment, and rights
SEN, GITA; GERMAIN, ADRIENNE; CHEN, LINCOLN C. - *Harvard Series on Population and International Health*. Harvard School of Public Health, Boston, MA xiv, 280 p. 1994 [EN] ill., graphs, tabs. Includes index, lit.refs ISBN 0-674-69003-6
New directions for population policy and family planning programmes are proposed based upon the universally accepted goals of reproductive and sexual health, women's empowerment and human rights. These directions represent a shift from passive concepts of women's education and status to promotion of social changes, including sustained leadership and organization by women; generation of political will; provision of basic infrastructure and social services to reduce women's triple workloads; and fundamental changes in the power dynamics between women and men, as well as among women themselves. Key actions required to improve family planning programmes and make them more effective in providing reproductive and sexual health services are discussed, including redefining objectives of family planning programmes; expanding their coverage; improving fertility regulation technologies; and enhancing resource allocation. Population policies should be part of human development approaches that create an enabling environment within which people can attain their health and rights.

KIT, Amsterdam   [N 95-937]

215   'Getting AIDS is like breaking your shaft in the shamba' : energy, disease, and changing concepts of manhood in Kilimanjaro
SETEL, PHILIP - *Working Papers in African Studies* 168. Boston University. African Studies Center, Boston, MA i, 10 p. 1993 [EN]
Changes in ideas of male labour and sexuality among the Chagga of northeastern Tanzania are studied. Perspectives on productive adulthood and adult sexuality in connection with AIDS are

presented. The relevant themes are the interconnections of work, money and sexuality; the mechanism by which they are related; and different modes of expressing these issues among people of different generations, and among men and women. Fieldwork was undertaken in Chagga areas of northern Kilimanjaro region, particularly in the regional capital of Moshi and in villages and a market town nearby. In the late 1980s, people in Kilimanjaro region began noticing AIDS in their midst. By 1990, AIDS had entered the public consciousness to a significant degree. Many people believe that AIDS came to Chagga via businessmen who went to Dar es Salaam, Nairobi and Mombasa, and through prostitutes and bar-girls in Moshi. The young men of the region are immersed in both of these worlds, thereby leaving the traditional shamba and kihamba lands. This transformation is occurring in the context of economic decline for many and the simultaneous spread of AIDS, illustrating both the present and past arrangements of productive and reproductive relations.

KIT, Amsterdam   [A 2477-(1993)168]

216   Husband and wife communication and decision-making in family planning : Sri Lanka
SIVASUBRAHAMANIAM, S.; KANE, THOMAS T. *In: Population transition in South Asia* ed. by Ashish Bose and M.K. Premi. - Delhi : BR Publishing Corporation, 1992 p.327-339 [EN] ill., graphs, tabs

Husband and wife communication is an important criterium for contraceptive behaviour. Existing patterns of communication and decision-making in family planning matters between spouses in Sri Lanka were examined using data from the 1985 Sri Lanka Contraceptive Survey. The analysis revealed that there is a high degree of family planning communication between husbands and wives. The husband-wife communication varies, however, according to education, age, place of residence, number of living children, desire for more children, and the wife's employment status. The degree of family planning communication was higher among educated and younger couples, among couples desiring no more children, and in urban and rural areas than in tea estates. Both husband and wife appeared to be important sources of information on family planning and contraception. The data suggest that wives initiate family planning discussions more often than their husbands. For most methods it appears that the decision to use a particular method is frequently made jointly by both the husband and the wife.

KIT, Amsterdam   [P 94-808]

217   HIV seroprevalence trends among women in developing countries
STANECKI, KAREN A.; WAY, PETER O.. US Bureau of the Census, Washington, DC [17] p. [1994] [EN] ill., graphs.

Information and statistical tables on HIV seroprevalence trends are provided for: pregnant women in selected urban areas of Africa, Latin America and the Caribbean, and Asia; and commercial sex workers in sub-Saharan Africa, in capital cities of 9 Latin American countries, and in Asia, India and Thailand. Statistics are also provided on HIV prevalence rates of STD clinic patients, by sex, in selected Latin American sites; of the general population of Mali by region and sex; and of the general population of Uganda by age and sex. The emerging pattern of excess female morbidity and mortality from HIV/AIDS has significant implications for the social and economic wellbeing of society.

KIT, Amsterdam   [Br G 94-100]

218   Methods women can use [to protect themselves against contracting HIV infection by the sexual route]
STEIN, ZENA A. [s.l.], [s.n.] [27] p. 1994 [EN] ill., graphs, tabs

The socio-economic constraints placed on many individuals make reliance on lifelong mutual monogamy an imperfect strategy, on its own, to stem the spread of the HIV/AIDS epidemic. While awaiting the development of long-term microbicides or vaccines, options to prevent HIV infection by the sexual route are behavioural change and the use of barrier methods. Options available for women to protect themselves from HIV infection, with or without the support of their partner, are the female condom and chemical barriers, or spermicides. Two reviews of epidemiological studies of Nonoxynol-9, initially developed as a contraceptive spermicide, are presented, one dealing with its effectiveness against HIV, the other addressing the issue of safety. Despite their imperfections, barrier methods may have a positive impact on HIV prevention. The dissemination of information and education on what is available, how to use barrier methods, and when to acquire them is a necessary beginning in a process of instituting behavioural changes to achieve AIDS prevention.

KIT, Amsterdam   [G 94-519]

219   Modern contraception use in Ethiopia : does involving husbands make a difference?
TEREFE, ALMAZ - *American Journal of Public Health* 83(1993)11 p.1567-1571 [EN] ill., tabs 14 lit.refs ISSN 0090-0036

A randomized field study was conducted to determine the efficacy of home visits with and without husband participation on family planning education in Ethiopia. The use of modern contraceptives by more than 500 couples was surveyed during August 1990-December 1991 in Kotobe District, Addis Ababa. A greater proportion (25%) of couples in the experimental group who had received visits with husbands being present were practising modern contraception two months after the visit than in the control group (15%) who had received a home visit without the husband being present. Some 12 months after the visit, 33% of couples in the experimental group were practising modern contraception, compared with 17% in the control group. The inclusion of husbands in family planning programmes was found to result in increases in the use of modern contraception. There exists an important 'sleeper' effect to the education intervention, reflected in a delay of greater than two months in the initiation of modern contraception for most couples.

KIT, Amsterdam   [H 1605-83(1993)11]

220   Too far to walk : maternal mortality in context

THADDEUS, SEREEN; MALINE, DEBORAH Center for Communication Programs, Johns Hopkins School of Public Health, 111 Market Place, suite 310, Baltimore - *Social Science and Medicine* 38(1994)8 p.1091-1110 1994 [EN] ill. Bibliogr. ISSN 0277-9536

A multidisciplinary literature review of research on maternal mortality was undertaken as part of the Prevention of Maternal Mortality Programme. Literature about developing countries is examined with an emphasis on Africa. About 500,000 women worldwide die annually from complications associated with pregnancy and childbirth. Factors contributing to maternal mortality between the onset of obstetric complication and its outcome are examined. Such outcomes are most adversely affected by delayed treatment. The provision of treatment may, however, be delayed by a lengthy decision-making process over whether or not to seek care, identifying and reaching a medical centre, and/or receiving adequate and appropriate treatment once at the chosen centre. Distance, cost, and quality of care are major obstacles to the decision to seek care but these factors are also affected by disease severity, gender, and socio-economic status. Those who decide in timely fashion to seek help may still be delayed as a result of difficulties in accessing care facilities. Further delays may be encountered at health centres due to shortages of qualified staff, drugs and supplies, administrative delays, and clinical mismanagement. Options for change are discussed.

KIT, Amsterdam   [E 2085-38(1994)8]

221   Making motherhood safe

TINKER, ANNE; KOBLINSKY, MARJORIE A.; DALY, PATRICIA Health and Nutrition Department, World Bank, 1818 H Street, N.W., Washington - *World Bank Discussion Papers* 202. World Bank, Washington, DC xv, 143 p. 1993 [EN] ill., graphs, tabs. Includes lit.refs ISSN 0259-210X ISBN 0-8213-2468-3

More then 150 million women become pregnant in developing countries each year and an estimated 500,000 of them die from pregnancy-related causes, the major causes being haemorrhage, unsafe abortion, infection, hypertensive disorders and obstructed labour. In 1987, a number of international and national organizations launched the Safe Motherhood Initiative to reduce maternal morbidity and mortality by half by the year 2000. Lessons for reducing maternal mortality derived from experience and research in the context of this initiative in both developing and developed countries are discussed, showing that community-based approaches such as family planning and training and the deployment of midwives have helped reduce maternal deaths in high mortality settings. Prenatal care and delivery services are among the most cost-effective interventions for improving maternal and child health. Priorities and programme strategies for making family planning services and maternal health more effective by improving quality, increasing access, and educating the public about the importance of such services are recommended. The following issues need to be considered in the development of safe motherhood policies and programmes: a needs assessment of the health infrastructure, adapting existing health systems to women's needs, strengthening the health infrastructure, upgrading health facilities, upgrading the skills of health providers and delegating responsibility, and intra- and inter-sectoral coordination should be strengthened.

KIT, Amsterdam   [K 2481-(1993)202]

222   Male approval and acceptance of condoms in diverse cultural settings : the SOMARC social marketing experience

TIPPING, SHARON[s.n.], [s.l.] [18] p. 1991 [EN] ill., tabs. Includes lit.refs

Social Marketing for Change (SOMARC) is an initiative, funded by development aid, to deliver reduced price contraceptives to consumers in developing countries using commercial intervention, marketing and advertising. The SOMARC experience with achieving male approval and acceptance of condoms in four countries over the past 7 years is considered. The SOMARC Panther Condom Project in Barbados was aimed at young, unmarried men in an effort to reduce the high level of teenage pregnancy. In Indonesia, the Dualima condom was advertised in order to introduce the condom to the family market. The SOMARC-managed condom project in Morocco aimed to enhance the image of the condom as a contraceptive method which offers married men the opportunity to share responsibility for family planning. The programme in Ghana had a target audience of married men, aged 26-35 years, with a secondary school education and in the middle and lower-middle social classes. Research was conducted to evaluate how effective the interventions had been. Attitudes towards and usage of condoms were found to have improved in each case, despite the various cultural settings and different approaches. The SOMARC projects were effective in desensitizing reactions to a controversial product with a bad image by emphasizing positive product attributes using creative and culturally acceptable means.

KIT, Amsterdam   [G 94-536]

223   Female genital mutilation : a call for global action
TOUBIA, NAHID. Women Ink., New York, NY 48 p. 1993 [EN] ill., maps, tabs. Includes lit.refs
    Female genital mutilation is the collective name given to several different traditional practices that involve the cutting of female genitals. It is being practised all over the world, particularly in Africa, as one of the traditional rituals that prepare girls for womanhood. The age at which it is practised varies widely but it is often between 4-8 years of age, at a time when girls can be made aware of the social role expected of them as women. Having described the different types of female genital mutilation, attention is paid to the medical complications and sexual and psychological impact of the practice. The prevalence and extent of female genital mutilation is reviewed. The role of religion and the cultural significance are explored. The practice is also discussed from the perspective of children's rights. Legal measures to eradicate it at international and national level are suggested, together with recommendations for action.

KIT, Amsterdam   [Br N 94-140]

224   Young Ugandans know condoms prevent STDs, but disagree on whether use shows respect for partner
TURNER, R. - International Family Planning Perspectives 19(1993)2 p.76-77 [EN] ISSN 0162-2749
    The Adolescent Fertility Survey covering six districts of Uganda (Jinja, Kampala, Masaka, Kabale, Hoima, and Mbale) was conducted during 1988-1990. A probability sample of households was selected from rural sub-parishes and urban administrative divisions. Some 4510 participants, aged 15-24 years, were chosen on the basis of age, regardless of marital status. Approximately 82% of the males and 80% of the females had had

a sexual partner in the last three years. Two thirds of the males had had more than one sexual partner while most young women had had only one sexual partner. Some 79% of urban males and 82% of urban females used no contraception compared with 92% and 97% of rural respondents, respectively. Condom use was reported among 18% of urban males and 5% of rural males; less than 1% of females in both areas reported condom use. Most respondents agreed that using a condom helps prevent STDs. Some 12% of urban females were using oral contraceptives. Sex education offered in the school system may be inappropriate to meet the needs of the adolescents and young adults. The establishment of health clinics for young adults that would combine sex education, STD treatment and family planning services is recommended.

KIT, Amsterdam   [H 1795-19(1993)2]

225   Gender inequalities in health in the Third World : uncharted ground
VLASSOFF, CAROL - Social Science and Medicine 39(1994)9 p.1249-1259 [EN] 53 lit.refs ISSN 0277-9536
    Gender differences in health in developing countries have, until recently, received little attention from researchers, health programmes and international development efforts. Several issues related to gender and health care in developing countries on which information, in particular of an empirical nature, is inadequate are highlighted. It is suggested that certain health conditions and diseases such as leprosy and tuberculosis may have differential effects on women and men. Diseases may affect physical appearance and be associated with social stigma, illustrated by a case study from Nigeria which found social stigma associated with skin disease. Gender inequalities in health and health-related technology, including contraceptive methods, drugs, tropical disease prevention and control, are examined. The lack of gender-sensitivity in the provision of health services, in particular in patient-client communication, interpersonal relations and follow-up, is discussed. Women should participate in health policy making and research because women have a central role to play in various health activities. Improvements in research are suggested, including the incorporation of a sex variable in future studies in order to reduce data gaps and increase the gender-sensitivity of health policy and interventions.

KIT, Amsterdam   [E 2085-39(1994)9]

226   Women, Health and Development : progress report
BY THE DIRECTOR-GENERAL. WHO, Geneva 33 p. 1992 [EN] ill., graphs, tabs

The principles and goals of the UN Decade for Women (1976-1985) have been translated by the WHO into practical activities for the programme on Women, Health and Development (WHD). The programme, which is consistent with the WHO's mandate on broad aspects of health, focuses on: the promotion of women's health; women as both beneficiaries and providers of health care; and women's education and overall status as a means to enhance their contribution to health and socio-economic development. This progress report provides a background to the programme and gives a situation analysis of WHD, outlining the particular health concerns of women in developed and developing countries from infancy to old age, and stressing health-related gender differentials in mortality between women and men. Particular attention is paid to maternal health and family planning, and to women's role in health care. The many WHO programmes aimed at achieving better health for women are described. An overview is given of action in the six major regions of the world. Approaches for the 1990s include measures in all regions to reduce the gender gap between men and women, the development of indicators to monitor progress towards the goals of women's health, and women's participation in development. A unifying goal for the future is needed, requiring enhancement of women's status, equipping them with basic knowledge and skills and access to services, and bringing them into the mainstream of development as full partners.

KIT, Amsterdam   [Br U 93-54]

227   Tave kuzvigamuchira sezvazviri (We take it as it is) : consequences of HIV and AIDS for women in Zimbabwe, coping behaviour and support provided
WOUDENBERG, JUDITH VAN. Utrecht vi, 134 p. 1994 [EN] ill., tabs. Includes lit.refs
    The consequences of HIV infection and AIDS for HIV-positive women in Zimbabwe are assessed. The support provided by the Mashambanzou Care Trust for HIV-positive women in Harare is explored. The main psychological consequences for HIV-positive women concern uncertainty about the future, and most women are worried about their children's future. Women at Mashambanzou employed different coping strategies. They often managed through emotion-focused coping: religion, positive reinterpretation, acceptance, seeking emotional social support, and denial. Most women realized that they were not victims and that they could do something about their own situation by taking care of themselves and showing a positive attitude. The project is valuable because it helps HIV-positive women to find individual coping strategies. The majority of

the women at Mashambanzou discussed HIV/AIDS with each other, but not with others at home or in their community. This was due to an either real or perceived low understanding of HIV/AIDS by the society, and perceived low acceptance and tolerance for people with HIV/AIDS. Measures recommended to improve the support for HIV-positive women include stimulating women to talk with close relatives and friends and other people in their community about their HIV status. Recommendations for organizations involved in HIV/AIDS work and for further research are provided, together with an overview of lessons learned.

KIT, Amsterdam   [G 94-102]

228   Concepts and measures of reproductive morbidity
ZURAYK, HUDA; KHATTAB, HIND; YOUNIS, NABIL; EL-MOUELHY, MAWAHEB; FADLE, MOHAMED - *Health Transition Review* 3(1993)1 p.17-40 [EN] ill., tabs 40 lit.refs ISSN 1036-4005
    A conceptual and methodological framework is developed to determine the extent of the problem of reproductive morbidity at the community level in the Middle East. Data were collected using questionnaires from two villages in rural Giza, Egypt. Field workers visited 509 women's homes to collect information on household characteristics and on reproductive morbidity. Researchers also went with the women to the health centre where they underwent a gynaecological examination. Some 50% of the women had reproductive tract infections, commonly vaginitis; 56% had prolapse of the uterus, and prevalence increased significantly with age; 63% were anaemic, particularly those 14-19 years of age (76%). Only 24 women (5%) had no reproductive morbidity. About 50% had at least three reproductive conditions. The leading problems reported by the women were vaginal discharge (77%), dysmenorrhoea (71%), perceived delay in conception (48%), stress incontinence (37%), and pain during intercourse (36%). Some 41% had been pregnant in the last two years. Some 77% of deliveries took place at home. Common complaints during pregnancy were headache (59%) and vaginal discharge (45%). After the birth of the child, fever and discharge/inflammation (30% for both) were common. It was concluded that similar research should be conducted in other communities and that reproductive health services should be expanded at the community level. Changes are suggested for the training programmes of health professionals and social scientists.

KIT, Amsterdam   [D 2613-3(1993)1]

5 A list of reference publications and resources

Reference publications and resources

229　Abortion : a tabulation of available data on the frequency and mortality of unsafe abortion
MATERNAL HEALTH AND SAFE MOTHERHOOD PROGRAMME - *WHO/FHE/MSM* 93.13. WHO. Division of Family Health, Geneva 114 p. 1993 [EN] ill., graphs, tabs. 1990 Bibliogr.: p. 90-114
KIT, Amsterdam   [K 2433-(1993)13]

230　Is there a distinct African sexuality? : a critical response to Caldwell
AHLBERG, BETH MAINA - *Africa* 64(1994)2 p.220-242 [EN] Bibliogr. With French summary
ISSN 0001-9720
KIT, Amsterdam   [A 1671-64(1994)2]

231　An annotated bibliography of documents produced by the Division of family health
[WHO/FHE] 94.6. WHO, Geneva 61 p. 1994 [EN]
KIT, Amsterdam   [K 2446-(1994)6]

232　Everything you always wanted to know... : lexicon and comments on the new population concepts from a gender perspective
APPELMAN, SIMONE; REYSOO, FENNEKE. Vrouwenberaad Ontwikkelingssamenwerking, Oegstgeest 35 p. 1994 [EN] Includes lit.refs ISBN 90-801068-8-7
KIT, Amsterdam   [G 94-471]

233　Occupational segmentation by sex in the world
BARBEZAT, DEBRA - *Equality for women in employment : an Interdepartmental Project Working Paper* 13. ILO, Geneva v, 95 p. 1993 [EN] ill., graphs, tabs. Includes lit.refs ISBN 92-2-109131-7
KIT, Amsterdam   [U 94-548]

234　Women and HIV/AIDS : an international resource book : information, action and resources on women and HIV/AIDS, reproductive health and sexual relationships
BERER, MARGE; RAY, SUNANDA. Pandora, London 383 p. 1993 [EN] ill., graphs. Includes index, lit.refs ISBN 0-04-440876-5
KIT, Amsterdam   [N 93-5348]

235　The family and sexual networking in sub-Saharan Africa : historical regional differences and present-day implications
CALDWELL, JOHN CHARLES; CALDWELL, PAT; ORUBULOYE, I.O. - *Population Studies* (1992)46 p.385-410 [EN] ill. lit.refs in notes. With summary (p.381)
KIT, Amsterdam   [E 2073-(1992)46]

236　Contraceptive method mix : guidelines for policy and service delivery
WHO, Geneva viii, 143 p. 1994 [EN] ill., graphs, tabs. Includes lit.refs ISBN 92-4-154459-7
KIT, Amsterdam   [U 94-537]

237　Coverage of maternity care : a tabulation of available information
MATERNAL HEALTH AND SAFE MOTHERHOOD PROGRAMME - *WHO/FME/MSM* 93.7. WHO. Division of Family Health, Geneva 143 p. 1993 [EN] ill., maps, tabs. Bibliogr.: p. 105-137
KIT, Amsterdam   [K 2433-(1993)7]

238　Creating common ground in Asia : women's perspectives on the selection and introduction of fertility regulation technologies : report of a meeting between women's health advocates, researchers, providers and policy-makers, Manila, 5-8 October, 1992
UNDP/UNFPA/WHO/WORLD BANK SPECIAL PROGRAMME OF RESEARCH, DEVELOPMENT AND RESEARCH TRAINING IN HUMAN REPRODUCTION. WHO, Geneva 45 p. 1994 [EN]
KIT, Amsterdam   [Br U 94-243]

239　Directory of national focal points for the advancement of women in Asia and the Pacific 1993
ECONOMIC AND SOCIAL COMMISSION FOR ASIA AND THE PACIFIC. UN. ESCAP, Bangkok x, 163 p. 1993 [EN] ill. 1987
KIT, Amsterdam   [U 93-438]

240   An end to debt : operational guidelines for credit projects
UNIFEM, New York, NY vii, 104 p. 1993 [EN] ill., tabs. Includes lit.refs
KIT, Amsterdam   [U 94-265]

241   Entrepreneurial skills for young women : a manual for trainers
WOMEN AND DEVELOPMENT PROGRAMME. Commonwealth Secretariat. Human Resource Development Group, London xv, 205 p. 1992 [EN] ill., tabs
KIT, Amsterdam   [N 94-2179]

242   Gender indicators of developing Asian and Pacific countries
CENTER FOR INTERNATIONAL RESEARCH. ADB, Manila xiv, 350 p. 1993 [EN] ill., graphs, tabs. Bibliogr.: p. 299-350 ISBN 971-561-043-9
KIT, Amsterdam   [U 94-86]

243   A gender-disaggregated data base on human resources in agriculture : data requirement and availability
FAO, Rome 77 p. 1993 [EN] ill., tabs. Includes lit.refs
KIT, Amsterdam   [U 94-586]

244   Women and work in developing countries : an annotated bibliography
GHORAYSHI, PARVIN - *Bibliographies and Indexes in Women's Studies* 20. Greenwood, Westport, CT xix, 223 p. 1994 [EN] Includes index ISSN 0742-6941 ISBN 0-313-28834-8
KIT, Amsterdam   [N 94-2654]

245   Statistical indicators of female participation in education in sub-Saharan Africa
HARTNETT, TERESA; HENEVELD, WARD - *AFTHR Technical Note* 7. World Bank, Washington, DC 46 p. 1993 [EN] ill., tabs. Includes lit.refs
KIT, Amsterdam   [Br U 94-126]

246   Salud integral para la mujer, Mexico
HERNÁNDEZ CÁRDENAS, ANA MARÍA *In: Women and HIV/AIDS : an international resource book : information, action and resources on women and HIV/AIDS, reproductive health and sexual relationships* ed. by Marge Berer with Sunanda Ray. - London : Pandora, 1993 p.289-290 1993 [EN]
KIT, Amsterdam   [N 93-5348]

247   Home-based maternal records : guidelines for development, adaptation and evaluation
WHO, Geneva viii, 85 p. 1994 [EN] ill., graphs, tabs. Includes lit.refs ISBN 92-4-154464-3
KIT, Amsterdam   [U 94-146]

248   Integrating women's issues into population education (a handbook)
UNESCO PRINCIPAL REGIONAL OFFICE FOR ASIA AND THE PACIFIC - *Population Education Programme Service*. UNESCO. PROAP, Bangkok iii, 206 p. 1992 [EN] ill.
KIT, Amsterdam   [U 93-335]

249   Gender relations of pastoral and agropastoral production : a bibliography with annotations
JOWKAR, FOROUZ; ABZAKH, SAMIR - *IDA Working Paper* 79. Institute for Development Anthropology, Binghamton, NY xii, 485 p. 1991 [EN] Includes index
KIT, Amsterdam   [H 1975-(1991)79]

250   Reproductive health : a key to a brighter future : biennial report 1990-1991
KHANNA, J.; LOOK, P.F.A. VAN; GRIFFIN, P.D.. WHO, Geneva xiii, 171 p. 1992 [EN] ill., graphs, tabs. Includes lit.refs ISBN 92-4-156153-X
KIT, Amsterdam   [U 92-295]

251   Women's health issues in Nigeria
KISEKKA, MERE NAKATEREGGA. Tamaza, Zaria xix, 234 p. 1992 [EN] ill., tabs. Includes lit.refs, index ISBN 978-30834-6-5
KIT, Amsterdam   [P 92-4480]

252   Rural women : annotated bibliography
KUBISZ, KRYSTYNA M.. CAB International, Wallingford 264 p. 1992 [EN] Includes index ISBN 0-85198-829-6
KIT, Amsterdam   [G 92-636]

253   Work and non-work in the official statistical system : issues concerning data base and research on women in India
KUNDU, AMITABH; PREMI, MAHENDRA K. *In: Population transition in South Asia* ed. by Ashish Bose and M.K. Premi. - Delhi : BR Publishing Corporation, 1992 p.63-82 1992 [EN] ill., tabs 7 lit.refs
KIT, Amsterdam   [P 94-808]

254   Methods to involve women in rural water supply, sanitation and water resource protection : using a gender approach
IRC, The Hague 34 p. 1992 [EN] Includes lit.refs
KIT, Amsterdam   [Br U 94-247]

255   Progress report on the World Bank's activities on women in development
MINH CHAU NGUYEN; STEELE, DIANE E. *In: Development issues : presentations...* Development Committee. - Washington, DC 1993 p.85-102 1993 [EN] 10 lit.refs
KIT, Amsterdam   [U 93-425]

256 Family planning and reproductive health services in Ghana : an annotated bibliography
OHENEBA-SAKYI, YAW - *African Special Bibliographic Series* 18. Greenwood, Westport, CT xix, 147 p. 1994 [EN] Includes index ISSN 0749-2308 ISBN 0-313-28900-X
KIT, Amsterdam   [D 2935-(1994)18]

257 ILO standard setting, policy studies and technical cooperation relating to population issues and women
OPPONG, CHRISTINE - *World Employment Programme Working Paper. Labour and Population Series* 185. ILO, Geneva viii, 73 p. 1993 [EN] Includes lit.refs ISBN 92-2-108789-1
KIT, Amsterdam   [U 94-35]

258 Population policies and programmes : proceedings...
UN. Department of Economic and Social Information and Policy Analysis, New York, NY x, 267 p. 1993 [EN] ill., graphs, tabs. Includes lit.refs ISBN 92-1-151252-2
KIT, Amsterdam   [U 94-168]

259 The prevalence of anaemia in women : a tabulation of available information
NUTRITION PROGRAMME, MATERNAL HEALTH AND SAFE MOTHERHOOD PROGRAMME - *WHO/MCH* 92.2, [Suppl.] WHO. Division of Family Health, Geneva 100 p. 1992 [EN] ill., maps, tabs. Bibliogr.: p. 74-100
KIT, Amsterdam   [K 2433-(1992)2]

260 Programming through the lens of gender
UNDP. Gender in Development Programme, New York, NY 1 portf. (8 vols) [1994] [EN] Includes lit.refs
KIT, Amsterdam   [U 94-539]

261 Resources for women in Zimbabwe : a directory
DEVELOPMENT INNOVATIONS AND NETWORKS, EAST AND SOUTHERN AFRICA. IRED, Harare vi, 176 p. 1992 [EN]
KIT, Amsterdam   [N 95-531]

262 Einstellung von Männern zur Familienplanung und Möglichkeiten ihrer stärkeren Einbeziehung in Familienplanungsprogramme
RIEDBERGER, IRMELA - *Forschungsberichte des Bundesministeriums für wirtschaftliche Zusammenarbeit und Entwicklung* 108. Weltforum, Köln ix, 181 p. 1993 [DE] Bibliogr.: p. 149-181 ISBN 3-8039-0412-9
KIT, Amsterdam   [E 2518-(1993)108]

263 Family planning : meeting challenges, promoting choices : the proceedings of the IPPF Family Planning Congress, New Delhi, October 1992
SENANAYAKE, PRAMILLA; KLEINMAN, RONALD L. Parthenon, Lancs xxiv, 744 p. 1992 [EN] ill., graphs, tabs. Includes lit.refs, index ISBN 1-85070-514-3
KIT, Amsterdam   [N 94-678]

264 Anthology on women, health and environment
SIMS, JACQUELINE. WHO, Geneva xi, 162 p. 1994 [EN] ill., graphs, tabs. Includes lit.refs
KIT, Amsterdam   [U 95-58]

265 South Asian women
UNFPA - *Report / UNFPA* New York, NY 38 p. 1992 [EN] ill., tabs. Includes lit.refs ISBN 0-89714-161-X
KIT, Amsterdam   [Br U 94-53]

266 Literature summary : women in fisheries development
STEELE, S. - *Inshore Fisheries Research Project Technical Document* (1993)5 p.39-48 [EN] 30 lit.refs ISSN 1018-3116
KIT, Amsterdam   [K 2745-(1993)5]

267 Training course in women's health
Institute of Development Training, Chapel Hill, NC 1993 [EN] ill. Includes lit.refs
KIT, Amsterdam   [N 94-310/313]N 94-1212/1217N 94-1765

268 Annotated bibliography gender and irrigation and soil and water conservation
VERKRUYSSE, B.. Agricultural University, Wageningen 204 p. 1992 [EN] Includes index ISBN 90-6754-216-4
KIT, Amsterdam   [N 92-7352]

269 Women's studies in India : information sources, services and programmes
VYAS, ANJU; SINGH, SUNITA. Sage, New Delhi 257 p. 1993 [EN] Includes index ISBN 81-7036-294-6
KIT, Amsterdam   [N 93-5810]

270 Gender issues sourcebook for the Water & Sanitation Sector
WAKEMAN, WENDY. UNDP-World Bank Water & Sanitation Program, [Washington, DC] iv, 110 p. 1993 [EN] ill. Includes lit.refs
KIT, Amsterdam   [U 94-182]

271   Women and development : an annotated bibliography 1990-1992
DEPARTMENT OF INFORMATION AND DOCUMENTATION - *An annotated bibliography / Department of Information and Documentation, Royal Tropical Institute*. Royal Tropical Institute, Amsterdam 206 p. 1992 [EN] Based on: Abstracts on rural development in the tropics (vol. 5, no. 1 - vol. 7, no. 4). Includes index ISSN 0924-9745 ISBN 90-6832-704-6
KIT, Amsterdam   [N 93-803]

272   Women and development and gender profiles in 54 developing countries : an inventory
CONTRIB. BY MATRIX CONSULTANTS, WOMEN AND DEVELOPMENT SPECIALISTS AT THE EMBASSIES, SPECIAL PROGRAMME WOMEN AND DEVELOPMENT. Ministry of Foreign Affairs. Directorate General for International Cooperation. Special Programme Women and Development, The Hague xiii, 135 p. 1993 [EN]
KIT, Amsterdam   [G 93-457]

273   Women, conservation and agriculture : a manual for trainers
WOMEN AND DEVELOPMENT PROGRAMME. Commonwealth Secretariat. Human Resource Development Group, London x, 199 p. 1992 [EN] ill., tabs. Includes lit.refs
KIT, Amsterdam   [N 94-2178]

274   Women and AIDS : agenda for action
WHO AND UNDP ; IN CONSULTATION WITH THE UNITED NATIONS DIVISION FOR THE ADVANCEMENT OF WOMEN. WHO, Geneva [14] p. 1994 [EN] ill., maps
KIT, Amsterdam   [Br U 94-99]

275   Women and AIDS
VENA Journal 5(1993)1 p.1-45 [EN] ill., photogr. lit.refs in notes ISSN 0925-9333
KIT, Amsterdam   [D 2412-5(1993)1]

6 Indexes to the annotated bibliographies

Subject index

(figures refer to abstract numbers)

appropriate technology
    transport, gender roles, women in agriculture, 114
attitudes
    abortion, marriage, fertility decline, family planning, 169
    AIDS, disease prevention, women's status, women's rights, sexual behaviour, 274
    contraceptives, contraceptive usage, men, marketing, family planning, cross-cultural analysis, 222
    family planning, men, 183
    family planning, men, 179
    family planning programmes, contraceptive usage, men, married women, 175
    family planning programmes, contraceptive usage, men, urban areas, 219
    family planning programmes, men, contraceptive usage, evaluation, 200
    health care delivery, women's status, social conditions, nutrition, family planning, 161
    men, family planning, 262
    school attendance, girls, public schools, private schools, women's status, 71
    sexual behaviour, sexually transmitted diseases, AIDS, contraceptive usage, 224
    women, men, women-in-development, guidelines, UNDP, reference materials, 260
    women workers, public administration, management, labour market, 26
    women's status, women workers, gender division of labour, 7

basic needs
    women, health conditions, environmental health, occupational health, 264
bibliographies
    employment, women, 244
    family health, primary health care, family planning, WHO, maternal health services, 231
    family planning, human reproduction, maternal health services, 256
    livestock industry, animal husbandry, gender roles, 249
    rural water supply, community participation, water resources development, sanitation,
        women-in-development, 254
    social research, women, women's status, 269
    women in agriculture, soil conservation, water conservation, 268
    women-in-development, fisheries, women workers, 266
    women-in-development, rural development, abstracts, tropical areas, 271
    women's status, women in agriculture, women-in-development, rural population, 252
birth control
    women-in-development, feminism, sexual behaviour, households, population policy, 22
breast-feeding
    disease prevention, bacteriology, family planning, female genital mutilation, teaching materials,
        health personnel, health, 267
    women workers, 158
    women workers, maternity leave, child care services, laws and regulations, 59
business
    entrepreneurship, management development, women, women-in-development, manuals, 84
business management
    entrepreneurship, vocational training, women, informal sector, training programmes, cost-benefit
        analysis, 90

career development
    women managers, women's status, civil service, 160
child care services
    women workers, breast-feeding, maternity leave, laws and regulations, 59
child development
    girls, women-in-development, international instruments, 3
child health
    maternal health services, questionnaires, health information, guidelines, manuals, 247
child survival
    maternal welfare, fertility, motherhood, 198
childbirth
    pregnancy, motherhood, pre-natal care, maternal health services, maternal and child health, 182
civil service
    women managers, career development, women's status, 160

cooperatives
women-in-development, training programmes, manuals, 82
communication media
women-in-development, 27
community development
group relations training, women-in-development, gender roles, women's status, manuals, 102
women-in-development, community participation, women's status, 100
women-in-development, law, 95
community participation
rural water supply, water resources development, sanitation, women-in-development, bibliographies, 254
women-in-development, community development, women's status, 100
women-in-development, water supply, sanitation, project activities, data collection, guidelines, information sources, reference materials, 270
women-in-development, water supply, sanitation, teacher training, manuals, 96
women workers, gender roles, social development, economic development, 150
women's status, project evaluation, institution-building, employment creation, 8
women's status, gender roles, democracy, international relations, 38
conflict
violence, women, 14
contraception
abortion, sterilization, gender preference, sexually transmitted diseases, AIDS, female genital mutilation, women's rights, 192
family planning programmes, guidelines, manuals, 236
human reproduction, sexually transmitted diseases, population policy, health services research, 176
contraceptive usage
AIDS, ethics, human rights, gender roles, 213
attitudes, contraceptives, men, marketing, family planning, cross-cultural analysis, 222
family planning programmes, attitudes, men, married women, 175
family planning programmes, attitudes, men, urban areas, 219
family planning programmes, men, attitudes, evaluation, 200
male contraception, 206
sexual behaviour, attitudes, sexually transmitted diseases, AIDS, 224
sexual behaviour, men, male contraception, 208
women's status, family planning, economic indicators, credit policy, 211
contraceptives
attitudes, contraceptive usage, men, marketing, family planning, cross-cultural analysis, 222
human reproduction, family planning programmes, health, women, recommendations, research, 238
cost-benefit analysis
entrepreneurship, vocational training, women, informal sector, business management, training programmes, 90
credit
financing, private enterprises, savings, women workers, financial institutions, financial assistance, 129
small enterprises, women, family responsibilities, 159
women, credit policy, 120
women-in-development, 130
women-in-development, project implementation, guidelines, manuals, 240
credit policy
contraceptive usage, women's status, family planning, economic indicators, 211
women, credit, 120
criminal law
domestic violence, gender crimes, abortion, prostitution, sterilization, women's rights, 64
cultural aspects
higher education, women, educational systems, social aspects, educational policy, 69
cultural values
social change, gender roles, social values, 55
culture
sexual behaviour, disease prevention, AIDS, 210

curriculum development
  teaching materials, women, health education, family planning education, project evaluation, 77
customary law
  inheritance and succession, rural areas, parent-child relations, econometrics, 47
customs and traditions
  fisheries, women workers, gender roles, 135

data bases
  women in agriculture, data collection, information sources, statistical data, 243
data collection
  employment, unemployment, women, labour statistics, statistical data, 253
  manpower, women workers, manpower statistics, statistical data, 106
  women in agriculture, information sources, statistical data, data bases, 243
  women-in-development, water supply, sanitation, project activities, community participation, guidelines, information sources, reference materials, 270
  women workers, labour market, domestic workers, informal sector, statistics, 112
death
  women, marriage customs, violence, marriage, marriage law, inheritance and succession, 66
decision-making
  family planning, gender roles, marriage, demographic analysis, 190
  interpersonal communication, gender roles, family planning, 216
declarations
  Palestine question, women's rights, human rights, UN, 52
  women-in-development, 104
democracy
  women's status, political systems, 51
  women's status, gender roles, community participation, international relations, 38
demographic analysis
  AIDS, women, health policy, 171
  family planning, decision-making, gender roles, marriage, 190
  women-in-development, rural development, women workers, women's status, family welfare, rural employment, fertility, family planning, 105
demographic statistics
  socio-economic indicators, women's status, reference materials, 242
development assistance
  entrepreneurship, women, income sources, small enterprises, 121
development models
  gender roles, women's status, 42
  women's status, population policy, environmental policy, women's advancement, 20
development planning
  agricultural development, gender roles, women's status, women workers, 142
  feminism, information management, women-in-development, gender roles, 18
  gender roles, gender discrimination, women-in-development, 79
  gender roles, women-in-development, education, 78
  women-in-development, rural development, 93
  women's advancement, gender roles, 101
development policy
  poverty, women-in-development, 46
  women, social groups, non-governmental organizations, 122
  women-in-development, education, employment, women's status, World Bank, 124
development strategies
  women-in-development, international decades, women's status, conferences, UN, meeting records, international instruments, 48, 49
  women-in-development, socio-economic indicators, 9
  women's status, UN, women's rights, women's advancement, non-governmental organizations, 61
  women's status, women's advancement, 148
directories
  women-in-development, 261, 239
disaster relief
  disaster preparedness, disaster prevention, gender roles, women-in-development, 65

disease prevention
AIDS, health education, family planning programmes, 207
AIDS, women, 218
AIDS, women, sexual behaviour, 203
AIDS, women's status, attitudes, sexual behaviour, programmes of action, 274
epidemiology, AIDS, girls, women, 202
epidemiology, AIDS, women's status, human rights, 181
family planning, breast-feeding, female genital mutilation, teaching materials, health personnel,
health, 267
gender roles, women's status, sexual behaviour, AIDS, 180
sexual behaviour, AIDS, men, 195
sexual behaviour, culture, AIDS, 210
domestic violence
criminal law, gender crimes, abortion, prostitution, sterilization, women's rights, 64
domestic workers
women workers, labour market, informal sector, data collection, statistics, 112
women workers, labour relations, trade unions, 115
women workers, workers' education, trade unions, working conditions, 134

economic conditions
Muslim women, women's status, social conditions, social change, 34
women's status, women-in-development, public health, women workers, 63
economic development
science and technology, women scientists, women's status, social conditions, 88
women-in-development, 60
women workers, community participation, gender roles, social development, 150
economic indicators
AIDS, health programmes, health education, sexually transmitted diseases, women, 246
contraceptive usage, women's status, family planning, credit policy, 211
mortality, maternal welfare, health services, 220
economic policy
structural adjustment, poverty, women, 107
structural adjustment, women in agriculture, women-in-development, 127
education
gender roles, women-in-development, development planning, 78
girls, school attendance, 245
women, development, labour, gender discrimination, 154
women-in-development, 99
women-in-development, employment, women's status, development policy, World Bank, 124
women-in-development, women's status, 83
women's advancement, 73
women's rights, population aspects, guidelines, population education, 76
educational policy
educational systems, women, 97
higher education, women, educational systems, social aspects, cultural aspects, 69
literacy, women, rural education, 75
educational systems
educational policy, women, 97
higher education, women, social aspects, cultural aspects, educational policy, 69
employment
unemployment, women, data collection, labour statistics, statistical data, 253
women, bibliographies, 244
women-in-development, education, women's status, development policy, World Bank, 124
women workers, public enterprises, social aspects, households, 155
women's status, labour market, structural adjustment, women workers, 25
employment creation
women's status, project evaluation, project implementation, institution-building, community
participation, 8
employment security
women, agricultural workers, gender roles, agricultural extension, 153

entrepreneurship
  business, management development, women, women-in-development, manuals, 84
  small enterprises, women, 119
  small enterprises, women-in-development, training programmes, manuals, 241
  vocational training, women, informal sector, business management, training programmes,
    cost-benefit analysis, 90
  women, income sources, small enterprises, development assistance, 121
environmental health
  women, health conditions, basic needs, occupational health, 264
environmental management
  women in agriculture, women-in-development, training programmes, manuals, 273
environmental policy
  development models, women's status, population policy, political aspects, women's advancement, 20
ethics
  AIDS, human rights, contraceptive usage, gender roles, 213
evaluation
  family planning programmes, men, attitudes, contraceptive usage, 200

family
  gender roles, population policy, 189
  kinship, gender roles, social change, 41
  women's rights, women-in-development, 58
family budget
  gender discrimination, girls, household surveys, 44
family health
  primary health care, family planning, bibliographies, WHO, maternal health services, 231
  women's status, health, gender roles, use studies, 209
family law
  women's rights, women's status, Islamic law, women, 43
family planning
  abortion, marriage, attitudes, fertility decline, 169
  attitudes, contraceptives, contraceptive usage, men, marketing, cross-cultural analysis, 222
  attitudes, men, 262
  contraceptive usage, women's status, economic indicators, credit policy, 211
  decision-making, gender roles, marriage, demographic analysis, 190
  disease prevention, bacteriology, breast-feeding, female genital mutilation, teaching materials,
    health personnel, health, 267
  family health, primary health care, bibliographies, WHO, maternal health services, 231
  fertility, men, gender roles, women, 187
  health care delivery, women's status, social conditions, nutrition, attitudes, 161
  human reproduction, 250, 263
  human reproduction, maternal health services, bibliographies, 256
  interpersonal communication, decision-making, gender roles, 216
  men, attitudes, 183
  men, attitudes, 179
  social change, women in agriculture, rural population, 16
  women-in-development, rural development, women workers, women's status, family welfare, rural
    employment, fertility, demographic analysis, 105
  women's status, population policy, 265, 184
family planning education
  curriculum development, teaching materials, women, health education, project evaluation, 77
family planning programmes
  attitudes, contraceptive usage, men, married women, 175
  attitudes, contraceptive usage, men, urban areas, 219
  contraception, guidelines, manuals, 236
  disease prevention, AIDS, health education, 207
  human reproduction, contraceptives, health, women, recommendations, research, 238
  men, attitudes, contraceptive usage, evaluation, 200
  women's status, economic aspects, maternal welfare, 185
  women's status, gender roles, population policy, 163

family responsibilities
    national accounts, time-use statistics, women workers, informal sector, income, statistical
        methodology, 137
    small enterprises, credit, women, 159
family welfare
    women-in-development, rural development, women workers, women's status, rural employment,
        fertility, demographic analysis, family planning, 105
farming systems
    women in agriculture, land rights, gender division of labour, 116
female genital mutilation
    contraception, abortion, sterilization, gender preference, sexually transmitted diseases, AIDS,
        women's rights, 192
    disease prevention, bacteriology, family planning, breast-feeding, teaching materials, health
        personnel, health, 267
    rights of the child, women's rights, 172, 223
feminism
    information management, women-in-development, development planning, gender roles, 18
    Muslim women, women's status, Islam, social conditions, 2
    gender roles, 33
    structural adjustment, women workers, 156
    women-in-development, political economy, 131
    women-in-development, gender division of labour, human geography, 36
    women-in-development, sexual behaviour, households, birth control, population policy, 22
    women-in-development, women's status, social conditions, gender roles, social policy, 89
    women's status, gender roles, history, 17
    women's status, gender roles, subsaharan literature, 40
    women's status, women's rights, women's advancement, 29
fertility
    family planning, men, gender roles, women, 187
    maternal welfare, child survival, motherhood, 198
    women-in-development, rural development, women workers, women's status, family welfare, rural
        employment, demographic analysis, family planning, 105
fertility decline
    abortion, marriage, attitudes, family planning, 169
    abortion, mortality, maternal welfare, 165
financial assistance
    financing, private enterprises, credit, savings, women workers, financial institutions, 129
financial institutions
    financing, private enterprises, credit, savings, women workers, financial assistance, 129
    small enterprises, women-in-development, project activities, World Bank, 113
financing
    private enterprises, credit, savings, women workers, financial institutions, financial assistance, 129
fisheries
    women workers, gender roles, customs and traditions, 135
    women-in-development, women workers, bibliographies, 266

gender crimes
    criminal law, domestic violence, abortion, prostitution, sterilization, women's rights, 64
gender discrimination
    family budget, girls, household surveys, 44
    gender division of labour, households, labour market, rural areas, 141
    gender roles, development planning, women-in-development, 79
    health services, women, 225, 193
    health services, women, mortality, morbidity, 196
    treaties, international instruments, women's rights, UN, 12
    violence, women, cross-cultural analysis, 54
    women, development, labour, education, 154
    women workers, salaries, labour market, 145, 146
gender division of labour
    households, labour market, gender discrimination, rural areas, 141

refugees, women's status, 30
women in agriculture, 21
women in agriculture, farming systems, land rights, 116
women-in-development, human geography, feminism, 36
women workers, wages, labour market, comparative analysis, 233
women workers, women's status, women in agriculture, cross-cultural analysis, 147
women's rights, women's status, women in agriculture, land rights, 56
women's status, women workers, attitudes, 7

gender preference
contraception, abortion, sterilization, sexually transmitted diseases, AIDS, female genital mutilation, women's rights, 192

gender roles
agricultural development, women's status, women workers, development planning, 142
AIDS, ethics, human rights, contraceptive usage, 213
AIDS, urban poverty, 177
AIDS, women's status, non-governmental organizations, 275
cultural and social anthropology, AIDS, 215
development models, women's status, 42
development planning, gender discrimination, women-in-development, 79
disaster preparedness, disaster prevention, disaster relief, women-in-development, 65
economic analysis, development, economics, 123
family, population policy, 189
family planning, decision-making, marriage, demographic analysis, 190
family planning, fertility, men, women, 187
feminism, information management, women-in-development, development planning, 18
fisheries, women workers, customs and traditions, 135
gender division of labour, households, labour market, gender discrimination, rural areas, 141
gender division of labour, women in agriculture, 21
group relations training, women-in-development, women's status, community development, manuals, 102
horticulture, urban areas, agricultural workers, women, land use, 125
informal sector, women's status, 143
interpersonal communication, decision-making, family planning, 216
kinship, family, social change, 41
livestock industry, animal husbandry, bibliographies, 249
Muslim women, women's status, social movements, 4
population policy, women's rights, 214
primary health care, maternal welfare, 191
refugees, women's status, gender division of labour, 30
risk, AIDS, sexually transmitted diseases, 212
risk, health, 164
sexual behaviour, women's status, women's rights, AIDS, sexually transmitted diseases, 197
small industry, women workers, shoe industry, 111
social change, social values, cultural values, 55
time-use statistics, grain processing, technological innovations, women's status, 110
transport, appropriate technology, women in agriculture, 114
women, agricultural workers, employment security, agricultural extension, 153
women-in-development, 23, 91
women-in-development, gender division of labour, human geography, feminism, 36
women-in-development, education, development planning, 78
women-in-development, structural adjustment, 133
women-in-development, development, 37
women-in-development, social movements, 39
women-in-development, women's status, social conditions, feminism, social policy, 89
women workers, community participation, social development, economic development, 150
women workers, women's status, gender division of labour, agriculture, cross-cultural analysis, 147
women's advancement, development planning, 101
women's status, AIDS, health education, 173
women's status, democracy, community participation, international relations, 38
women's status, health, family health, use studies, 209

women's status, health services, health policy, 201
women's status, feminism, history, 17
women's status, feminism, subsaharan literature, 40
women's status, population policy, family planning programmes, 163
women's status, sexual behaviour, disease prevention, AIDS, 180
women's status, women-in-development, 67
women's status, women-in-development, political aspects, economic aspects, 11
women's status, women workers, gender division of labour, attitudes, 7

girls
education, school attendance, 245
epidemiology, disease prevention, AIDS, women, 202
family budget, gender discrimination, household surveys, 44
prostitution, women's status, public health, AIDS, reference materials, 194
school attendance, public schools, private schools, women's status, attitudes, 71

grain processing
gender roles, time-use statistics, technological innovations, women's status, 110
technological innovations, women, 152

group relations training
women-in-development, gender roles, women's status, community development, 102

health
disease prevention, bacteriology, family planning, breast-feeding, female genital mutilation,
    teaching materials, health personnel, 267
gender roles, risk, 164
health services, medical care, women, 188
human reproduction, family planning programmes, contraceptives, women, recommendations,
    research, 238
human reproduction, research and development, international cooperation, 205
women, 251
women, morbidity, social aspects, 228
women-in-development, programmes of action, WHO, 226
women's rights, treaties, health legislation, 13
women's status, family health, gender roles, use studies, 209
women's status, living conditions, rural population, support (domestic relations), 10

health care delivery
women's status, social conditions, nutrition, attitudes, family planning, 161
women's status, women-in-development, 178

health conditions
maternal and child health, mortality, morbidity, economic aspects, social aspects, 199
women, basic needs, environmental health, occupational health, 264

health education
AIDS, health programmes, sexually transmitted diseases, women, economic indicators, 246
curriculum development, teaching materials, women, family planning education, project evaluation,
    77
disease prevention, AIDS, family planning programmes, 207
gender roles, women's status, AIDS, 173
mothers, small groups, 103

health information
AIDS, women, sexual behaviour, 234
child health, maternal health services, questionnaires, guidelines, manuals, 247

health legislation
health, women's rights, treaties, 13

health personnel
disease prevention, bacteriology, family planning, breast-feeding, female genital mutilation,
    teaching materials, health, 267

health policy
AIDS, demographic analysis, women, 171
women's status, gender roles, health services, 201

health programmes
AIDS, health education, sexually transmitted diseases, women, economic indicators, 246

health services
abortion, mortality, pregnancy, adverse health practices, 229
AIDS, women, epidemiology, 186
health, medical care, women, 188
mortality, maternal welfare, economic indicators, 220
women, gender discrimination, 225, 193
women, gender discrimination, mortality, morbidity, 196
women's status, gender roles, health policy, 201
health services research
human reproduction, sexually transmitted diseases, contraception, women, population policy, 176
higher education
women, educational systems, social aspects, cultural aspects, educational policy, 69
horticulture
urban areas, agricultural workers, women, land use, gender roles, 125
household surveys
family budget, gender discrimination, girls, 44
households
gender division of labour, labour market, gender discrimination, rural areas, 141
women-in-development, feminism, sexual behaviour, birth control, population policy, 22
women workers, public enterprises, employment, social aspects, 155
human reproduction
family planning, 250
family planning, maternal health services, bibliographies, 256
family planning programmes, contraceptives, health, women, recommendations, research, 238
health, research and development, international cooperation, 205
sexually transmitted diseases, contraception, women, population policy, health services research, 176
human rights
AIDS, ethics, contraceptive usage, gender roles, 213
epidemiology, disease prevention, AIDS, women's status, 181
Palestine question, women's rights, declarations, UN, 52
violence, right to development, 50
women's rights, 15

illiteracy
literacy, women, 70
ILO
women workers, technical cooperation, women-in-development, population, occupational safety,
     treaties, 257
income
national accounts, time-use statistics, women workers, informal sector, family responsibilities,
     statistical methodology, 137
income sources
entrepreneurship, women, small enterprises, development assistance, 121
indigenous populations
women's status, minorities, 45
informal sector
entrepreneurship, vocational training, women, business management, training programmes,
     cost-benefit analysis, 90
gender roles, women's status, 143
national accounts, time-use statistics, women workers, income, family responsibilities, statistical
     methodology, 137
women-in-development, women workers, 32
women workers, labour market, domestic workers, data collection, statistics, 112
women workers, trade unions, 118
information dissemination
motherhood, maternal health services, teaching materials, reference materials, 166
information management
feminism, women-in-development, development planning, gender roles, 18
information sources
women in agriculture, data collection, statistical data, data bases, 243

women-in-development, water supply, sanitation, project activities, community participation, data collection, guidelines, reference materials, 270

inheritance and succession
customary law, rural areas, parent-child relations, econometrics, 47
women, marriage customs, violence, death, marriage, marriage law, 66

institution-building
women's status, project evaluation, project implementation, employment creation, community participation, 8

interagency cooperation
population policy, conferences, recommendations, 258

international cooperation
human reproduction, health, research and development, 205
maternal health services, programmes of action, maternal welfare, project activities, 221

international instruments
girls, women-in-development, child development, 3
treaties, gender discrimination, women's rights, UN, 12
violence, public health, women's rights, adverse health practices, recommendations, 19
women-in-development, international decades, women's status, conferences, UN, meeting records, development strategies, 48, 49

international relations
women's status, gender roles, democracy, community participation, 38

interpersonal communication
decision-making, gender roles, family planning, 216

Islam
Muslim women, women's status, feminism, social conditions, 2

Islamic countries
women's rights, treaties, Islamic law, 53

Islamic law
women's rights, treaties, Islamic countries, 53
women's rights, women's status, family law, women, 43

kinship
family, gender roles, social change, 41

labour
women, development, education, gender discrimination, 154

labour market
gender division of labour, gender roles, households, gender discrimination, rural areas, 141
women, living conditions, structural adjustment, social conditions, women workers, urban areas, 157
women, structural adjustment, school attendance, labour mobility, microeconomics, 117
women-in-development, social conditions, women workers, 31
women workers, domestic workers, informal sector, data collection, statistics, 112
women workers, privatization, women's status, urban areas, 140
women workers, public administration, attitudes, management, 26
women workers, salaries, gender discrimination, 145, 146
women workers, wages, gender division of labour, comparative analysis, 233
women's status, employment, structural adjustment, women workers, 25

labour mobility
labour market, women, structural adjustment, school attendance, microeconomics, 117

labour relations
domestic workers, women workers, trade unions, 115

labour statistics
employment, unemployment, women, data collection, statistical data, 253

land rights
women in agriculture, farming systems, gender division of labour, 116
women-in-development, agrarian reform, women's rights, women in agriculture, rural-urban migration, legislation, women's status, 151
women's rights, gender division of labour, women's status, women in agriculture, 56

land use
horticulture, urban areas, agricultural workers, women, gender roles, 125

law
women-in-development, community development, 95
laws and regulations
women workers, breast-feeding, maternity leave, child care services, 59
legislation
women-in-development, agrarian reform, women's rights, women in agriculture, rural-urban migration, land rights, women's status, 151
literacy
educational policy, women, rural education, 75
illiteracy, women, 70
women-in-development, 86
women-in-development, literacy programmes, 72
literacy programmes
literacy, women-in-development, 72
livestock industry
animal husbandry, gender roles, bibliographies, 249
living conditions
mortality, women, 204
rural poverty, women, 144
women, structural adjustment, social conditions, labour market, women workers, urban areas, 157
women's status, health, rural population, support (domestic relations), 10

male contraception
contraceptive usage, 206
sexual behaviour, men, contraceptive usage, 208
malnutrition
nutritional diseases, maternal welfare, 259
management
women workers, public administration, attitudes, labour market, 26
management development
business, entrepreneurship, women, women-in-development, manuals, 84
women workers, universities and colleges, promotion, 85
manpower statistics
manpower, women workers, data collection, statistical data, 106
marketing
attitudes, contraceptives, contraceptive usage, men, family planning, cross-cultural analysis, 222
marriage
abortion, attitudes, fertility decline, family planning, 169
family planning, decision-making, gender roles, demographic analysis, 190
sexually transmitted diseases, risk, sexual behaviour, AIDS, 170
women, marriage customs, violence, death, marriage law, inheritance and succession, 66
marriage customs
women, violence, death, marriage, marriage law, inheritance and succession, 66
marriage law
women, marriage customs, violence, death, marriage, inheritance and succession, 66
married women
family planning programmes, attitudes, contraceptive usage, men, 175
mass media
women, public opinion, 6
maternal and child health
mortality, morbidity, health conditions, economic aspects, social aspects, 199
pregnancy, childbirth, motherhood, pre-natal care, maternal health services, 182
maternal health services
child health, questionnaires, health information, guidelines, manuals, 247
family health, primary health care, family planning, bibliographies, WHO, 231
family planning, human reproduction, bibliographies, 256
motherhood, information dissemination, teaching materials, reference materials, 166
pregnancy, childbirth, motherhood, pre-natal care, maternal and child health, 182
programmes of action, maternal welfare, project activities, international cooperation, 221
statistical data, 237

maternal welfare
abortion, mortality, fertility decline, 165
child survival, fertility, motherhood, 198
maternal health services, programmes of action, project activities, international cooperation, 221
mortality, health services, economic indicators, 220
nutritional diseases, malnutrition, 259
primary health care, gender roles, 191
women's status, family planning programmes, economic aspects, 185
maternity leave
women workers, breast-feeding, child care services, laws and regulations, 59
medical care
health, health services, women, 188
men
attitudes, contraceptives, contraceptive usage, marketing, family planning, cross-cultural analysis, 222
attitudes, family planning, 262
family planning, attitudes, 183
family planning, fertility, gender roles, women, 187
family planning, attitudes, 179
family planning programmes, attitudes, contraceptive usage, married women, 175
family planning programmes, attitudes, contraceptive usage, urban areas, 219
family planning programmes, attitudes, contraceptive usage, evaluation, 200
sexual behaviour, AIDS, disease prevention, 195
sexual behaviour, male contraception, contraceptive usage, 208
women, attitudes, women-in-development, guidelines, UNDP, reference materials, 260
minorities
women's status, indigenous populations, 45
moral aspects
sexual behaviour, AIDS, 230
morbidity
health, women, social aspects, 228
health services, women, gender discrimination, mortality, 196
maternal and child health, mortality, health conditions, economic aspects, social aspects, 199
mortality
abortion, maternal welfare, fertility decline, 165
abortion, pregnancy, health services, 229
health services, women, gender discrimination, morbidity, 196
maternal and child health, morbidity, health conditions, economic aspects, social aspects, 199
maternal welfare, health services, economic indicators, 220
women, living conditions, 204
motherhood
maternal health services, information dissemination, teaching materials, reference materials, 166
maternal welfare, child survival, fertility, 198
pregnancy, childbirth, pre-natal care, maternal health services, maternal and child health, 182
mothers
health education, small groups, 103
Muslim women
women's status, feminism, Islam, social conditions, 2
women's status, nationalism, national liberation movements, religious behaviour, Palestine question, 35
women's status, gender roles, social movements, 4
women's status, social conditions, economic conditions, social change, 34

national accounts
time-use statistics, women workers, informal sector, income, family responsibilities, statistical methodology, 137
national liberation movements
women's status, nationalism, religious behaviour, Muslims, Palestine question, 35
nationalism
women's status, national liberation movements, religious behaviour, Muslims, Palestine question, 35

non-formal education
women's advancement, manuals, 87
non-governmental organizations
AIDS, women's status, gender roles, 275
women, social groups, development policy, 122
women's status, UN, women's rights, development strategies, women's advancement, conferences, 61
nutrition
health care delivery, women's status, social conditions, attitudes, family planning, 161
nutritional diseases
malnutrition, maternal welfare, 259

occupational health
women, health conditions, basic needs, environmental health, 264
occupational safety
women workers, technical cooperation, ILO, women-in-development, population, treaties, 257
operational activities
women-in-development, World Bank, 255

parent-child relations
inheritance and succession, customary law, rural areas, econometrics, 47
plantations
women workers, agricultural workers, project evaluation, 138
political economy
women-in-development, feminism, 131
political participation
women workers, trade unions, 109
political systems
women's status, democracy, 51
population
women workers, technical cooperation, ILO, women-in-development, occupational safety, treaties, 257
population education
education, women's rights, population aspects, guidelines, 76
women, manuals, teaching materials, 248
population policy
conferences, recommendations, interagency cooperation, 258
development models, women's status, environmental policy, political aspects, women's advancement, 20
family, gender roles, 189
family planning, women's status, 265, 184
human reproduction, sexually transmitted diseases, contraception, women, health services research, 176
women-in-development, feminism, sexual behaviour, households, birth control, 22
women's rights, gender roles, 214
women's rights, women-in-development, 232
women's status, gender roles, family planning programmes, 163
poverty
structural adjustment, economic policy, women, 107
women, structural adjustment, urban areas, 139
women-in-development, development policy, 46
women-in-development, social conditions, structural adjustment, 149
pregnancy
abortion, mortality, health services, 229
childbirth, motherhood, pre-natal care, maternal health services, maternal and child health, 182
pre-natal care
pregnancy, childbirth, motherhood, maternal health services, maternal and child health, 182
primary health care
family health, family planning, bibliographies, WHO, maternal health services, 231
maternal welfare, gender roles, 191

private enterprises
   financing, credit, savings, women workers, financial institutions, financial assistance, 129
private schools
   school attendance, girls, public schools, women's status, attitudes, 71
privatization
   women workers, labour market, women's status, urban areas, 140
programmes of action
   AIDS, disease prevention, women's status, women's rights, attitudes, sexual behaviour, 274
   maternal health services, maternal welfare, project activities, international cooperation, 221
   women-in-development, WHO, health, 226
project activities
   maternal health services, programmes of action, maternal welfare, international cooperation, 221
   small enterprises, women-in-development, World Bank, financial institutions, 113
   women-in-development, water supply, sanitation, community participation, data collection,
       guidelines, information sources, reference materials, 270
project evaluation
   curriculum development, teaching materials, women, health education, family planning education, 77
   women-in-development, rural development, 126
   women workers, agricultural workers, plantations, 138
   women's status, project implementation, institution-building, employment creation, community
       participation, 8
project implementation
   credit, women-in-development, guidelines, manuals, 240
   women's status, project evaluation, institution-building, employment creation, community
       participation, 8
promotion
   management development, women workers, universities and colleges, 85
prostitution
   criminal law, domestic violence, gender crimes, abortion, sterilization, women's rights, 64
   girls, women's status, public health, AIDS, reference materials, 194
public administration
   women workers, attitudes, management, labour market, 26
public enterprises
   women workers, employment, social aspects, households, 155
public health
   prostitution, girls, women's status, AIDS, reference materials, 194
   violence, women's rights, adverse health practices, recommendations, international instruments, 19
   women's status, economic conditions, women-in-development, women workers, 63
public opinion
   women, mass media, 6
public schools
   school attendance, girls, private schools, women's status, attitudes, 71

refugees
   women's status, gender division of labour, 30
regional development
   women-in-development, self-reliance, rural development, 136
religious behaviour
   women's status, nationalism, national liberation movements, Muslims, Palestine question, 35
research and development
   human reproduction, family planning programmes, contraceptives, health, women,
       recommendations, 238
   human reproduction, health, international cooperation, 205
right to development
   violence, human rights advancement, 50
rights of the child
   female genital mutilation, women's rights, 172
rural areas
   gender division of labour, households, labour market, gender discrimination, 141
   inheritance and succession, customary law, parent-child relations, econometrics, 47

rural development
    women-in-development, abstracts, bibliographies, tropical areas, 271
    women-in-development, development planning, 93
    women-in-development, project evaluation, 126
    women-in-development, regional development, self-reliance, 136
    women-in-development, women workers, women's status, family welfare, rural employment,
        fertility, demographic analysis, family planning, 105
rural education
    literacy, educational policy, women, 75
rural employment
    women-in-development, rural development, women workers, women's status, family welfare,
        fertility, demographic analysis, family planning, 105
rural population
    social change, family planning, women in agriculture, 16
    women's status, living conditions, health, support (domestic relations), 10
    women's status, women in agriculture, women-in-development, bibliographies, abstracts, 252
rural poverty
    women, living conditions, 144
rural water supply
    community participation, water resources, sanitation, women-in-development, bibliographies, 254
rural-urban migration
    women-in-development, agrarian reform, women's rights, women in agriculture, land rights,
        legislation, women's status, 151

salaries
    women workers, labour market, gender discrimination, 145, 146
sanitation
    community participation, women-in-development, water supply, teacher training, manuals, 96
    rural water supply, community participation, water resources, women-in-development,
        bibliographies, 254
    women-in-development, water supply, project activities, community participation, data collection,
        guidelines, information sources, reference materials, 270
savings
    financing, private enterprises, credit, women workers, financial institutions, financial assistance, 129
school attendance
    education, girls, 245
    girls, public schools, private schools, women's status, attitudes, 71
    labour market, women, structural adjustment, labour mobility, microeconomics, 117
science and technology
    women scientists, women's status, economic development, social conditions, 88
secondary education
    women-in-development, population aspects, 98
self-reliance
    women-in-development, regional development, rural development, 136
sexual behaviour
    AIDS, disease prevention, women's status, attitudes, programmes of action, 274
    AIDS, men, disease prevention, 195
    AIDS, moral aspects, 230
    AIDS, sexually transmitted diseases, 167
    AIDS, social research, 174
    AIDS, women, disease prevention, 203
    AIDS, women, health information, 234
    attitudes, sexually transmitted diseases, AIDS, contraceptive usage, 224
    culture, disease prevention, AIDS, 210
    gender roles, women's status, disease prevention, AIDS, 180
    gender roles, women's status, women's rights, AIDS, sexually transmitted diseases, 197
    men, male contraception, contraceptive usage, 208
    sexually transmitted diseases, risk, AIDS, marriage, 170
    social systems, history, AIDS, geographical distribution, 235
    women-in-development, feminism, households, birth control, population policy, 22

sexually transmitted diseases
    AIDS, health programmes, health education, women, economic indicators, 246
    contraception, abortion, sterilization, gender preference, AIDS, female genital mutilation, women's
       rights, 192
    gender roles, risk, AIDS, 212
    human reproduction, contraception, women, population policy, health services research, 176
    risk, sexual behaviour, AIDS, marriage, 170
    sexual behaviour, AIDS, 167
    sexual behaviour, attitudes, AIDS, contraceptive usage, 224
    sexual behaviour, gender roles, women's status, women's rights, AIDS, 197
shoe industry
    small industry, gender roles, women workers, 111
small enterprises
    credit, women, family responsibilities, 159
    entrepreneurship, women, 119
    entrepreneurship, women, income sources, development assistance, 121
    entrepreneurship, women-in-development, training programmes, manuals, 241
    women, technological innovations, development aspects, technology transfer, 108
    women-in-development, project activities, World Bank, financial institutions, 113
small industry
    gender roles, women workers, shoe industry, 111
social aspects
    health, women, morbidity, 228
    higher education, women, educational systems, cultural aspects, educational policy, 69
    maternal and child health, mortality, morbidity, health conditions, economic aspects, 199
    women workers, public enterprises, employment, households, 155
social change
    family planning, women in agriculture, rural population, 16
    gender roles, social values, cultural values, 55
    kinship, family, gender roles, 41
    Muslim women, women's status, social conditions, economic conditions, 34
social conditions
    health care delivery, women's status, nutrition, attitudes, family planning, 161
    Muslim women, women's status, economic conditions, social change, 34
    Muslim women, women's status, feminism, Islam, 2
    science and technology, women scientists, women's status, economic development, 88
    women, living conditions, structural adjustment, labour market, women workers, urban areas, 157
    women-in-development, structural adjustment, poverty, 149
    women-in-development, women workers, labour market, 31
    women-in-development, women's status, gender roles, feminism, social policy, 89
social development
    women workers, community participation, gender roles, economic development, 150
social groups
    women, non-governmental organizations, development policy, 122
social movements
    Muslim women, women's status, gender roles, 4
    women-in-development, gender roles, 39
social planning
    women-in-development, 57
social policy
    women-in-development, women's status, social conditions, gender roles, feminism, 89
social research
    sexual behaviour, AIDS, 174
    women, women's status, bibliographies, 269
social systems
    sexual behaviour, history, AIDS, geographical distribution, 235
social values
    social change, gender roles, cultural values, 55
socio-economic indicators
    women's status, demographic statistics, reference materials, 242

women-in-development, development strategies, 9

soil conservation

women in agriculture, water conservation, bibliographies, 268

statistical data

employment, unemployment, women, data collection, labour statistics, 253

manpower, women workers, data collection, manpower statistics, 106

maternal health services, 237

women in agriculture, data collection, information sources, data bases, 243

statistical methodology

national accounts, time-use statistics, women workers, informal sector, income, family responsibilities, 137

sterilization

contraception, abortion, gender preference, sexually transmitted diseases, AIDS, female genital mutilation, women's rights, 192

criminal law, domestic violence, gender crimes, abortion, prostitution, women's rights, 64

structural adjustment

economic policy, poverty, women, 107

economic policy, women in agriculture, women-in-development, 127

labour market, women, school attendance, labour mobility, microeconomics, 117

women, living conditions, social conditions, labour market, women workers, urban areas, 157

women, poverty, urban areas, 139

women-in-development, gender roles, 133

women-in-development, social conditions, poverty, 149

women workers, feminism, 156

teacher training

community participation, women-in-development, water supply, sanitation, manuals, 96

teaching materials

curriculum development, women, health education, family planning education, project evaluation, 77

disease prevention, bacteriology, family planning, breast-feeding, female genital mutilation, health personnel, health, 267

motherhood, maternal health services, information dissemination, reference materials, 166

population education, women, manuals, 248

women-in-development, training programmes, manuals, 92

technical cooperation

women workers, ILO, women-in-development, population, occupational safety, treaties, 257

technological innovations

gender roles, time-use statistics, grain processing, women's status, 110

grain processing, women, 152

women, small enterprises, development aspects, technology transfer, 108

technology transfer

women, small enterprises, technological innovations, development aspects, 108

time-use statistics

gender roles, grain processing, technological innovations, women's status, 110

national accounts, women workers, informal sector, income, family responsibilities, statistical methodology, 137

trade unions

domestic workers, women workers, labour relations, 115

political participation, women workers, 109

women workers, informal sector, 118

women workers, workers' education, domestic workers, working conditions, 134

training programmes

entrepreneurship, small enterprises, women-in-development, manuals, 241

entrepreneurship, vocational training, women, informal sector, business management, cost-benefit analysis, 90

women in agriculture, women-in-development, environmental management, manuals, 273

women-in-development, 81, 94

women-in-development, cooperatives, manuals, 82

women-in-development, teaching materials, manuals, 92

transport

appropriate technology, gender roles, women in agriculture, 114

UN

Palestine question, women's rights, declarations, human rights, 52

treaties, international instruments, gender discrimination, women's rights, 12

women-in-development, international decades, women's status, conferences, meeting records, international instruments, development strategies, 48, 49

women's status, women's rights, development strategies, women's advancement, non-governmental organizations, conferences, 61

UNDP

women, men, attitudes, women-in-development, guidelines, reference materials, 260

unemployment

employment, women, data collection, labour statistics, statistical data, 253

universities and colleges

management development, women workers, promotion, 85

urban areas

family planning programmes, attitudes, contraceptive usage, men, 219

horticulture, agricultural workers, women, land use, gender roles, 125

women, living conditions, structural adjustment, social conditions, labour market, women workers, 157

women, poverty, structural adjustment, 139

women workers, labour market, privatization, women's status, 140

urban poverty

AIDS, gender roles, 177

violence

conflict, women, 14

gender discrimination, women, cross-cultural analysis, 54

human rights advancement, right to development, 50

public health, women's rights, adverse health practices, recommendations, international instruments, 19

women, marriage customs, death, marriage, marriage law, inheritance and succession, 66

vocational training

entrepreneurship, women, informal sector, business management, training programmes, cost-benefit analysis, 90

wages

women workers, gender division of labour, labour market, comparative analysis, 233

water conservation

women in agriculture, soil conservation, bibliographies, 268

water resources

rural water supply, community participation, sanitation, women-in-development, bibliographies, 254

water supply

community participation, women-in-development, sanitation, teacher training, manuals, 96

women-in-development, sanitation, project activities, community participation, data collection, guidelines, information sources, reference materials, 270

WHO

family health, primary health care, family planning, bibliographies, maternal health services, 231

women-in-development, programmes of action, health, 226

women

agricultural workers, gender roles, employment security, agricultural extension, 153

AIDS, 162, 227

AIDS, demographic analysis, health policy, 171

AIDS, disease prevention, sexual behaviour, 203

AIDS, epidemiology, health services, 186

AIDS, health programmes, health education, sexually transmitted diseases, economic indicators, 246

AIDS, sexual behaviour, health information, 234

business, entrepreneurship, management development, women-in-development, manuals, 84

conflict, violence, 14

credit, credit policy, 120
curriculum development, teaching materials, health education, family planning education, project evaluation, 77
development, labour, education, gender discrimination, 154
disease prevention, AIDS, 218
educational systems, educational policy, 97
employment, bibliographies, 244
employment, unemployment, data collection, labour statistics, statistical data, 253
entrepreneurship, income sources, small enterprises, development assistance, 121
entrepreneurship, small enterprises, 119
entrepreneurship, vocational training, informal sector, business management, training programmes, cost-benefit analysis, 90
epidemiology, AIDS, 217
epidemiology, disease prevention, AIDS, girls, 202
family planning, fertility, men, gender roles, 187
feminism, gender roles, 33
health, 251
health, health services, medical care, 188
health, morbidity, social aspects, 228
health conditions, basic needs, environmental health, occupational health, 264
health services, gender discrimination, 193, 225
health services, gender discrimination, mortality, morbidity, 196
higher education, educational systems, social aspects, cultural aspects, educational policy, 69
horticulture, urban areas, agricultural workers, land use, gender roles, 125
human reproduction, family planning programmes, contraceptives, health, recommendations, research, 238
human reproduction, sexually transmitted diseases, contraception, population policy, health services research, 176
labour market, structural adjustment, school attendance, labour mobility, microeconomics, 117
literacy, educational policy, rural education, 75
literacy, illiteracy, 70
living conditions, structural adjustment, social conditions, labour market, women workers, urban areas, 157
marriage customs, violence, death, marriage, marriage law, inheritance and succession, 66
mass media, public opinion, 6
men, attitudes, women-in-development, guidelines, UNDP, reference materials, 260
mortality, living conditions, 204
population education, manuals, teaching materials, 248
poverty, structural adjustment, urban areas, 139
rural poverty, living conditions, 144
small enterprises, credit, family responsibilities, 159
small enterprises, technological innovations, development aspects, technology transfer, 108
social groups, non-governmental organizations, development policy, 122
social research, women's status, bibliographies, 269
structural adjustment, economic policy, poverty, 107
technological innovations, grain processing, 152
violence, gender discrimination, cross-cultural analysis, 54
women's status, 28

women in agriculture
data collection, information sources, statistical data, data bases, 243
economic policy, structural adjustment, women-in-development, 127
farming systems, land rights, gender division of labour, 116
gender division of labour, 21
social change, family planning, rural population, 16
soil conservation, water conservation, bibliographies, 268
transport, appropriate technology, gender roles, 114
women-in-development, agrarian reform, women's rights, rural-urban migration, land rights, legislation, women's status, 151
women-in-development, environmental management, training programmes, manuals, 273
women workers, women's status, gender division of labour, cross-cultural analysis, 74, 147

women's rights, gender division of labour, women's status, land rights, 56

women's status, women-in-development, rural population, bibliographies, abstracts, 252

women-in-development

agrarian reform, women's rights, women in agriculture, rural-urban migration, land rights, legislation, women's status, 151

business, entrepreneurship, management development, women, manuals, 84

cooperatives, training programmes, manuals, 82

communication media, 27

community development, community participation, women's status, 5, 68, 100

community development, law, 95

community participation, water supply, sanitation, teacher training, manuals, 96

credit, 130

credit, project implementation, guidelines, manuals, 240

declarations, 104

development strategies, women's advancement, socio-economic indicators, 9

directories, 261, 239

disaster preparedness, disaster prevention, disaster relief, gender roles, 65

economic development, 60

economic policy, structural adjustment, women in agriculture, 127

education, 99

education, employment, women's status, development policy, World Bank, 124

entrepreneurship, small enterprises, training programmes, manuals, 241

feminism, sexual behaviour, households, birth control, population policy, 22

fisheries, women workers, bibliographies, 266

gender division of labour, human geography, feminism, 36

gender roles, 91, 23

gender roles, development, 37

gender roles, development planning, gender discrimination, women's advancement, 79

gender roles, education, development planning, 78

girls, child development, international instruments, 3

group relations training, gender roles, women's status, community development, manuals, 102

health care delivery, women's status, 178

informal sector, women workers, 32

international decades, women's status, conferences, UN, meeting records, international instruments, development strategies, 48, 49

inventories, 272

literacy, 86

literacy, literacy programmes, 72

operational activities, World Bank, 255

political economy, feminism, 131

population policy, women's rights, 232

programmes of action, WHO, health, 226

poverty, development policy, 46

regional development, self-reliance, rural development, 136

rural development, abstracts, bibliographies, tropical areas, 271

rural development, development planning, 93

rural development, project evaluation, 126

rural development, women workers, women's status, family welfare, rural employment, fertility, demographic analysis, family planning, 105

rural water supply, community participation, water resources, sanitation, bibliographies, 254

secondary education, population aspects, 98

small enterprises, project activities, World Bank, financial institutions, 113

social conditions, structural adjustment, poverty, 149

social conditions, women workers, labour market, 31

social planning, 57

structural adjustment, gender roles, 133

training programmes, 81, 94

training programmes, teaching materials, manuals, 92

water supply, sanitation, project activities, community participation, data collection, guidelines, information sources, reference materials, 270

women, men, attitudes, guidelines, UNDP, reference materials, 260
women in agriculture, environmental management, training programmes, manuals, 273
women workers, 128
women workers, technical cooperation, ILO, population, occupational safety, treaties, 257
women's advancement, education, women's status, 83
women's advancement, feminism, information management, development planning, gender roles, 18
women's advancement, gender roles, social movements, 39
women's rights, family, 58
women's rights, women's advancement, 24, 62, 80
women's status, economic conditions, public health, women workers, 63
women's status, gender roles, 67
women's status, gender roles, political aspects, economic aspects, 11
women's status, social conditions, gender roles, feminism, social policy, 89
women's status, women in agriculture, rural population, bibliographies, abstracts, 252

women in politics
women managers, biography, 132

women managers
career development, women's status, civil service, 160
women in politics, biography, 132

women scientists
science and technology, women's status, economic development, social conditions, 88

women workers
agricultural development, gender roles, women's status, development planning, 142
agricultural workers, plantations, project evaluation, 138
breast-feeding, 158
breast-feeding, maternity leave, child care services, laws and regulations, 59
community participation, gender roles, social development, economic development, 150
domestic workers, labour relations, trade unions, 115
financing, private enterprises, credit, savings, financial institutions, financial assistance, 129
fisheries, gender roles, customs and traditions, 135
labour market, domestic workers, informal sector, data collection, statistics, 112
labour market, privatization, women's status, urban areas, 140
management development, universities and colleges, promotion, 85
manpower, data collection, manpower statistics, statistical data, 106
national accounts, time-use statistics, informal sector, income, family responsibilities, statistical methodology, 137
political participation, trade unions, 109
public administration, attitudes, management, labour market, 26
public enterprises, employment, social aspects, households, 155
salaries, labour market, gender discrimination, 145, 146
small industry, gender roles, shoe industry, 111
structural adjustment, feminism, 156
technical cooperation, ILO, women-in-development, population, occupational safety, treaties, 257
trade unions, informal sector, 118
wages, gender division of labour, labour market, comparative analysis, 233
women, living conditions, structural adjustment, social conditions, labour market, urban areas, 157
women-in-development, 128
women-in-development, fisheries, bibliographies, 266
women-in-development, informal sector, 32
women-in-development, rural development, women's status, family welfare, rural employment, fertility, demographic analysis, family planning, 105
women-in-development, social conditions, labour market, 31
women's status, economic conditions, women-in-development, public health, 63
women's status, labour market, employment, structural adjustment, 25
women's status, gender division of labour, attitudes, 7
women's status, gender division of labour, women in agriculture, cross-cultural analysis, 147
workers' education, domestic workers, trade unions, working conditions, 134

women's advancement
development models, women's status, population policy, environmental policy, political aspects, 20
development planning, gender roles, 101

education, 73
gender roles, development planning, gender discrimination, women-in-development, 79
non-formal education, manuals, 87
women's status, development strategies, 148
women's status, UN, women's rights, development strategies, non-governmental organizations, conferences, 61
women's status, women's rights, feminism, 29

women's rights
AIDS, disease prevention, women's status, attitudes, sexual behaviour, programmes of action, 274
contraception, abortion, sterilization, gender preference, sexually transmitted diseases, AIDS, female genital mutilation, 192
criminal law, domestic violence, gender crimes, abortion, prostitution, sterilization, 64
education, population aspects, guidelines, population education, 76
family, women-in-development, 58
female genital mutilation, rights of the child, 172
gender division of labour, women's status, women in agriculture, land rights, 56
health, treaties, health legislation, 13
human rights, 15
Palestine question, declarations, human rights, UN, 52
population policy, gender roles, 214
population policy, women-in-development, 232
sexual behaviour, gender roles, women's status, AIDS, sexually transmitted diseases, 197
treaties, international instruments, gender discrimination, UN, 12
treaties, Islamic law, Islamic countries, 53
violence, public health, adverse health practices, recommendations, international instruments, 19
women-in-development, agrarian reform, women in agriculture, rural-urban migration, land rights, legislation, women's status, 151
women-in-development, 24, 62, 80
women's status, Islamic law, family law, 43
women's status, UN, development strategies, women's advancement, non-governmental organizations, conferences, 61
women's status, women's advancement, feminism, 29

women's status
agricultural development, gender roles, women workers, development planning, 142
AIDS, 168
AIDS, disease prevention, women's rights, attitudes, sexual behaviour, programmes of action, 274
AIDS, gender roles, non-governmental organizations, 275
contraceptive usage, family planning, economic indicators, credit policy, 211
democracy, political systems, 51
development models, population policy, environmental policy, political aspects, women's advancement, 20
development models, gender roles, 42
development strategies, women's advancement, 148
economic conditions, women-in-development, public health, women workers, 63
epidemiology, disease prevention, AIDS, human rights, 181
family planning, population policy, 184, 265
family planning programmes, economic aspects, maternal welfare, 185
gender roles, AIDS, health education, 173
gender roles, democracy, community participation, international relations, 38
gender roles, feminism, history, 17
gender roles, feminism, subsaharan literature, 40
gender roles, health services, health policy, 201
gender roles, population policy, family planning programmes, 163
gender roles, sexual behaviour, disease prevention, AIDS, 180
gender roles, time-use statistics, grain processing, technological innovations, 110
gender roles, women-in-development, 67
group relations training, women-in-development, gender roles, community development, manuals, 102
health, family health, gender roles, use studies, 209
health care delivery, social conditions, nutrition, attitudes, family planning, 161

health care delivery, women-in-development, 178
indigenous populations, minorities, 45
informal sector, gender roles, 143
labour market, employment, structural adjustment, women workers, 25
living conditions, health, rural population, support (domestic relations), 10
Muslim women, feminism, Islam, social conditions, 2
Muslim women, gender roles, social movements, 4
Muslim women, social conditions, economic conditions, social change, 34
nationalism, national liberation movements, religious behaviour, Muslims, Palestine question, 35
project evaluation, project implementation, institution-building, employment creation, community participation, 8
prostitution, girls, public health, AIDS, reference materials, 194
refugees, gender roles, gender division of labour, 30
school attendance, girls, public schools, private schools, attitudes, 71
science and technology, women scientists, economic development, social conditions, 88
sexual behaviour, gender roles, women's rights, AIDS, sexually transmitted diseases, 197
social research, women, bibliographies, 269
socio-economic indicators, demographic statistics, reference materials, 242
UN, women's rights, development strategies, women's advancement, non-governmental organizations, conferences, 61
women, 28
women in agriculture, women-in-development, rural population, bibliographies, abstracts, 252
women-in-development, agrarian reform, women's rights, women in agriculture, rural-urban migration, land rights, legislation, 151
women-in-development, community development, community participation, 100
women-in-development, education, 83
women-in-development, education, employment, development policy, World Bank, 124
women-in-development, international decades, conferences, UN, meeting records, international instruments, development strategies, 48, 49
women-in-development, rural development, women workers, family welfare, rural employment, fertility, demographic analysis, family planning, 105
women-in-development, gender roles, political aspects, economic aspects, 11
women-in-development, social conditions, gender roles, feminism, social policy, 89
women managers, career development, civil service, 160
women workers, gender division of labour, attitudes, 7
women workers, gender division of labour, women in agriculture, cross-cultural analysis, 147
women workers, labour market, privatization, urban areas, 140
women's rights, gender division of labour, women in agriculture, land rights, 56
women's rights, women's advancement, feminism, 29

workers' education
women workers, domestic workers, trade unions, working conditions, 134

working conditions
women workers, workers' education, domestic workers, trade unions, 134

World Bank
small enterprises, women-in-development, project activities, financial institutions, 113
women-in-development, education, employment, women's status, development policy, 124
women-in-development, operational activities, 255

Geographical index

(figures refer to abstract numbers)

Afghanistan
women's status, nationalism, national liberation movements, religious behaviour, 35
Africa
AIDS, demographic analysis, women, health policy, 171
AIDS, women's status, gender roles, non-governmental organizations, 275
female genital mutilation, 223
female genital mutilation, rights of the child, women's rights, 172
gender roles, women, risk, AIDS, sexually transmitted diseases, 212
higher education, women, educational systems, social aspects, cultural aspects, educational policy, 69
management development, women workers, universities and colleges, promotion, 85
maternal and child health, mortality, morbidity, health conditions, economic aspects, social aspects, 199
sexual behaviour, AIDS, moral aspects, 230
women, credit, credit policy, 120
women in agriculture, women-in-development, environmental management, training, manuals, 273
women-in-development, credit, 130
women-in-development, declarations, 104
women-in-development, development strategies, women's advancement, socio-economic indicators, 9
women-in-development, structural adjustment, gender roles, 133
women workers, public enterprises, employment, social aspects, households, 155
women workers, trade unions, informal sector, 118
women's advancement, education, 73
women's rights, 15
Africa South of Sahara
abortion, marriage, attitudes, fertility decline, family planning, 169
agricultural development, gender roles, women's status, women workers, development planning, 142
AIDS, ethics, human rights, contraceptive usage, gender roles, 213
economic policy, structural adjustment, women in agriculture, women-in-development, 127
education, girls, school attendance, 245
family planning, men, attitudes, 183
gender roles, women-in-development, 23
primary health care, maternal welfare, gender roles, 191
science and technology, women scientists, women's status, economic development, social conditions, 88
sexual behaviour, social systems, history, AIDS, geographical distribution, 235
sexually transmitted diseases, risk, sexual behaviour, AIDS, marriage, 170
transport, appropriate technology, gender roles, women in agriculture, 114
women in agriculture, farming systems, land rights, gender division of labour, 116
women in agriculture, women-in-development, environmental management, training programmes, manuals, 273
women-in-development, rural development, women workers, women's status, family welfare, rural employment, fertility, demographic analysis, family planning, 105
women-in-development, training programmes, 81
women's status, gender roles, feminism, subsaharan literature, 40
Algeria
women's status, nationalism, national liberation movements, religious behaviour, Muslims, 35
Americas
AIDS, women, epidemiology, health services, 186
Argentina
women-in-development, social conditions, structural adjustment, poverty, 149

Asia
  human reproduction, family planning programmes, contraceptives, health, women, research, 238
  social planning, women-in-development, 57
  women's advancement, education, 73
  women's status, indigenous populations, minorities, 45
Asia and the Pacific
  literacy, educational policy, women, rural education, 75
  population education, women, manuals, teaching materials, 248
  poverty, women-in-development, development policy, 46
  women, socio-economic indicators, women's status, demographic statistics, reference materials, 242
  women-in-development, directories, focal points, 239
  women-in-development, fisheries, women workers, bibliographies, 266
Bangladesh
  abortion, mortality, maternal welfare, fertility decline, 165
  contraceptive usage, women's status, family planning, economic indicators, credit policy, 211
  human reproduction, family planning programmes, contraceptives, health, women, research, 238
  manpower, women workers, data collection, manpower statistics, statistical data, 106
  women, family planning, women's status, population policy, 265
  women-in-development, community development, law, 95
  women-in-development, rural development, development planning, 93
  women-in-development, gender division of labour, human geography, feminism, 36
  women's status, nationalism, national liberation movements, religious behaviour, Muslims, 35
Barbados
  attitudes, contraceptive usage, men, marketing, family planning, cross-cultural analysis, 222
Benin
  women, social groups, non-governmental organizations, development policy, 122
Bolivia
  communication media, women-in-development, 27
  violence, gender discrimination, women, cross-cultural analysis, 54
  women-in-development, rural development, project evaluation, 126
  women-in-development, gender division of labour, human geography, feminism, 36
  women-in-development, social conditions, structural adjustment, poverty, 149
Brazil
  AIDS, women, urban poverty, gender roles, 177
  communication media, women-in-development, 27
  contraception, abortion, sterilization, gender preference, sexually transmitted diseases, AIDS,
    female genital mutilation, women's rights, 192
  gender roles, women's status, sexual behaviour, disease prevention, AIDS, 180
  sexual behaviour, AIDS, social research, 174
  violence, gender discrimination, women, cross-cultural analysis, 54
  women, AIDS, women's status, gender roles, non-governmental organizations, 275
  women-in-development, gender division of labour, human geography, feminism, 36
  women-in-development, social conditions, structural adjustment, poverty, 149
Burkina Faso
  contraception, abortion, sterilization, gender preference, sexually transmitted diseases, AIDS,
    female genital mutilation, women's rights, 192
  women-in-development, rural development, project evaluation, 126
Cameroon
  school attendance, girls, public schools, private schools, women's status, attitudes, 71
  women's status, women, 28
Caribbean region
  women-in-development, community development, law, 95
  women-in-development, informal sector, women workers, 32
  women's status, gender roles, health services, health policy, 201
Central America
  informal sector, gender roles, women's status, 143
Chile
  contraception, abortion, sterilization, gender preference, sexually transmitted diseases, AIDS,
    female genital mutilation, women's rights, 192
  violence, gender discrimination, women, cross-cultural analysis, 54

women-in-development, agrarian reform, women's rights, women in agriculture, rural-urban
    migration, land rights, legislation, women's status, 151
China
women's status, gender roles, women, feminism, history, 17
Colombia
women-in-development, agrarian reform, women's rights, women in agriculture, rural-urban
    migration, land rights, legislation, women's status, 151
women-in-development, informal sector, women workers, 32
women-in-development, gender division of labour, human geography, feminism, 36
Costa rica
women, poverty, structural adjustment, urban areas, 139
Dominican Republic
women-in-development, agrarian reform, women's rights, women in agriculture, rural-urban
    migration, land rights, legislation, women's status, 151
East Asia
small enterprises, women-in-development, project activities, World Bank, financial institutions, 113
Ecuador
women, poverty, structural adjustment, urban areas, 139
women-in-development, social conditions, structural adjustment, poverty, 149
Egypt
contraception, abortion, sterilization, gender preference, sexually transmitted diseases, AIDS,
    female genital mutilation, women's rights, 192
curriculum development, teaching materials, women, health education, family planning education,
    project evaluation, 77
health, women, morbidity, social aspects, 228
women workers, public administration, attitudes, management, labour market, 26
Ethiopia
contraception, abortion, sterilization, gender preference, sexually transmitted diseases, AIDS,
    female genital mutilation, women's rights, 192
family planning programmes, attitudes, contraceptive usage, men, urban population, 219
Fiji
curriculum development, teaching materials, women, health education, family planning education,
    project evaluation, 77
Gambia
gender roles, time-use statistics, grain processing, technological innovations, women's status, 110
technological innovations, grain processing, women, 152
women-in-development, gender division of labour, human geography, feminism, 36
Ghana
attitudes, contraceptive usage, men, marketing, family planning, 222
contraception, abortion, sterilization, gender preference, sexually transmitted diseases, AIDS,
    female genital mutilation, women's rights, 192
family planning, human reproduction, maternal health services, bibliographies, 256
family planning programmes, attitudes, contraceptive usage, men, married women, 175
structural adjustment, economic policy, poverty, women, 107
women, poverty, structural adjustment, urban areas, 139
women-in-development, community development, law, 95
women-in-development, informal sector, women workers, 32
women-in-development, gender division of labour, human geography, feminism, 36
women workers, public administration, attitudes, management, labour market, 26
Guatemala
women-in-development, agrarian reform, women's rights, women in agriculture, rural-urban
    migration, land rights, legislation, women's status, 151
Guinea-Bissau
sexual behaviour, AIDS, social research, 174
women-in-development, rural development, development planning, 93
Guyana
women, poverty, structural adjustment, urban areas, 139
Haiti
women, AIDS, women's status, gender roles, non-governmental organizations, 275

Honduras
  women-in-development, agrarian reform, women's rights, women in agriculture, rural-urban migration, land rights, legislation, women's status, 151
  women-in-development, social conditions, structural adjustment, poverty, 149
Hong Kong
  women-in-development, gender division of labour, human geography, feminism, 36
India
  communication media, women-in-development, 27
  contraception, abortion, sterilization, gender preference, sexually transmitted diseases, AIDS, female genital mutilation, women's rights, 192
  employment, unemployment, women, data collection, labour statistics, statistical data, 253
  gender roles, women, risk, health, 164
  human reproduction, family planning programmes, contraceptives, health, women, research, 238
  manpower, women workers, data collection, manpower statistics, statistical data, 106
  maternal welfare, child survival, fertility, motherhood, 198
  sexual behaviour, AIDS, social research, 174
  social research, women, women's status, bibliographies, 269
  violence, gender discrimination, women, cross-cultural analysis, 54
  women, agricultural workers, gender roles, employment security, agricultural extension, 153
  women, family planning, women's status, population policy, 265
  women, marriage customs, violence, death, marriage, marriage law, inheritance and succession, 66
  women, poverty, structural adjustment, urban areas, 139
  women, women's status, living conditions, health, rural population, support (domestic relations), 10
  women-in-development, community development, law, 95
  women-in-development, rural development, development planning, 93
  women-in-development, rural development, project evaluation, 126
  women-in-development, gender division of labour, human geography, feminism, 36
  women workers, breast-feeding, maternity leave, child care services, laws and regulations, 59
  women workers, public enterprises, employment, social aspects, households, 155
Indonesia
  attitudes, contraceptive usage, men, marketing, family planning, cross-cultural analysis, 222
  human reproduction, family planning programmes, contraceptives, health, women, research, 238
  social change, family planning, women, women in agriculture, rural population, 16
  women-in-development, cooperatives, training programmes, manuals, 82
  women-in-development, rural development, development planning, 93
Iran
  women's status, nationalism, national liberation movements, religious behaviour, Muslims, 35
Iraq
  women workers, public enterprises, employment, social aspects, households, 155
Ivory Coast
  entrepreneurship, vocational training, women, informal sector, business management, training programmes, cost-benefit analysis, 90
  family budget, gender discrimination, girls, household surveys, 44
  sexual behaviour, AIDS, social research, 174
  structural adjustment, economic policy, poverty, women, 107
  women workers, public administration, attitudes, management, labour market, 26
  women's status, women, 28
Jamaica
  communication media, women-in-development, 27
  disease prevention, AIDS, health education, family planning programmes, 207
  small enterprises, credit, women, family responsibilities, 159
  structural adjustment, economic policy, poverty, women, 107
  women-in-development, social conditions, structural adjustment, poverty, 149
Kenya
  entrepreneurship, vocational training, women, informal sector, business management, training programmes, cost-benefit analysis, 90
  entrepreneurship, women, income sources, small enterprises, development assistance, 121
  gender division of labour, households, labour market, gender discrimination, rural areas, 141
  horticulture, urban areas, agricultural workers, land use, gender roles, 125
  sexual behaviour, AIDS, social research, 174

social change, gender roles, social values, cultural values, 55

women-in-development, gender roles, gender division of labour, human geography, feminism, 36

women workers, public administration, attitudes, management, labour market, 26

women's status, gender roles, democracy, community participation, international relations, 38

women's status, women workers, gender division of labour, attitudes, 7

Kuwait

Muslim women, women's status, gender roles, social movements, 4

Latin America

criminal law, domestic violence, gender crimes, abortion, prostitution, sterilization, women's rights, 64

disease prevention, AIDS, health education, family planning programmes, 207

domestic workers, women workers, labour relations, trade unions, 115

educational systems, educational policy, women, 97

mortality, women, living conditions, 204

women, health care delivery, women's status, women-in-development, 178

women-in-development, political economy, feminism, 131

women-in-development, social conditions, women workers, labour market, 31

women workers, salaries, labour market, gender discrimination, 145

women workers, salaries, labour market, gender discrimination, 146

women's advancement, education, 73

women's rights, gender division of labour, women's status, women in agriculture, land rights, 56

women's status, democracy, political systems, 51

women's status, gender roles, health services, health policy, 201

women's status, gender roles, population policy, family planning programmes, 163

women's status, women's rights, women's advancement, feminism, 29

Lesotho

entrepreneurship, small enterprises, women, 119

Malawi

family planning, fertility, men, gender roles, women, 187

Malaysia

violence, gender discrimination, women, cross-cultural analysis, 54

women-in-development, gender division of labour, human geography, feminism, 36

women managers, career development, women's status, civil service, 160

women workers, public enterprises, employment, social aspects, households, 155

Maldives

health education, mothers, 103

Mali

women workers, public administration, attitudes, management, labour market, 26

Mexico

AIDS, health programmes, health education, sexually transmitted diseases, women, economic indicators, 246

violence, gender discrimination, women, cross-cultural analysis, 54

women-in-development, community development, law, 95

women-in-development, social conditions, structural adjustment, poverty, 149

Middle East

Muslim women, women's status, feminism, Islam, social conditions, 2

Muslim women, women's status, social conditions, economic conditions, social change, 34

Morocco

attitudes, contraceptive usage, men, marketing, family planning, cross-cultural analysis, 222

communication media, women-in-development, 27

women workers, public administration, attitudes, management, labour market, 26

Nepal

national accounts, time-use statistics, women workers, informal sector, income, family responsibilities, statistical methodology, 137

prostitution, girls, women's status, public health, AIDS, reference materials, 194

women, family planning, women's status, population policy, 265

Nigeria

health, women, 251

sexual behaviour, AIDS, men, disease prevention, 195

sexual behaviour, AIDS, social research, 174

sexual behaviour, gender roles, women's status, women's rights, AIDS, sexually transmitted diseases, 197
sexual behaviour, social systems, history, AIDS, geographical distribution, 235
women-in-development, gender division of labour, human geography, feminism, 36
women workers, public administration, attitudes, management, labour market, 26
women workers, public enterprises, employment, social aspects, households, 155
women's status, gender roles, women, feminism, 40
women's status, women, 28

Oceania
fisheries, women workers, gender roles, customs and traditions, 135

Pakistan
contraception, abortion, sterilization, gender preference, sexually transmitted diseases, AIDS, female genital mutilation, women's rights, 192
manpower, women workers, data collection, manpower statistics, statistical data, 106
structural adjustment, economic policy, poverty, women, 107
violence, gender discrimination, women, cross-cultural analysis, 54
women, family planning, women's status, population policy, 265
women workers, public enterprises, employment, social aspects, households, 155
women's rights, women's status, Islamic law, family law, 43

Peru
communication media, women-in-development, 27
curriculum development, teaching materials, women, health education, family planning education, project evaluation, 77
living conditions, structural adjustment, social conditions, labour market, women workers, urban areas, 157
women-in-development, agrarian reform, women's rights, women in agriculture, rural-urban migration, land rights, legislation, women's status, 151
women-in-development, community development, law, 95
women-in-development, gender division of labour, human geography, feminism, 36

Philippines
human reproduction, family planning programmes, contraceptives, health, women, research, 238
inheritance and succession, customary law, rural areas, parent-child relations, econometrics, 47
women, mass media, public opinion, 6
women, poverty, structural adjustment, urban areas, 139
women-in-development, community development, law, 95
women-in-development, rural development, development planning, 93

Sahel, Africa
family planning, men, attitudes, 183

Samoa
women-in-development, gender division of labour, human geography, feminism, 36

Senegal
sexual behaviour, AIDS, social research, 174
technological innovations, grain processing, women, 152
women, AIDS, women's status, gender roles, non-governmental organizations, 275
women workers, public administration, attitudes, management, labour market, 26

South Africa
entrepreneurship, small enterprises, women, 119
women, poverty, structural adjustment, urban areas, 139

South Asia
kinship, family, gender roles, social change, 41
small enterprises, women-in-development, project activities, World Bank, financial institutions, 113
women workers, women's status, gender roles, gender division of labour, women in agriculture, cross-cultural analysis, 147
women's status, women-in-development, gender roles, political aspects, economic aspects, 11

South East Asia
women managers, women in politics, biography, 132

South Korea
contraception, abortion, sterilization, gender preference, sexually transmitted diseases, AIDS, female genital mutilation, women's rights, 192

Southern Africa
  sexual behaviour, social systems, history, AIDS, geographical distribution, 235
  women, feminism, gender roles, 33
Sri Lanka
  interpersonal communication, decision-making, gender roles, family planning, 216
  violence, gender discrimination, women, cross-cultural analysis, 54
  women, small enterprises, technological innovations, development aspects, technology transfer, 108
  women-in-development, community development, law, 95
  women-in-development, gender division of labour, human geography, feminism, 36
Sudan
  sexual behaviour, AIDS, social research, 174
  violence, gender discrimination, women, cross-cultural analysis, 54
  women workers, public administration, attitudes, management, labour market, 26
Swaziland
  entrepreneurship, small enterprises, women, 119
Taiwan
  women-in-development, gender division of labour, human geography, feminism, 36
Tanzania
  contraception, abortion, sterilization, gender preference, sexually transmitted diseases, AIDS, female genital mutilation, women's rights, 192
  cultural and social anthropology, gender roles, AIDS, 215
  entrepreneurship, vocational training, women, informal sector, business management, training programmes, cost-benefit analysis, 90
  women-in-development, regional development, self-reliance, rural development, 136
  women workers, agricultural workers, plantations, project evaluation, 138
Thailand
  contraception, abortion, sterilization, gender preference, sexually transmitted diseases, AIDS, female genital mutilation, women's rights, 192
  violence, gender discrimination, women, cross-cultural analysis, 54
  women-in-development, rural development, development planning, 93
  women's status, gender roles, women-in-development, 67
Tunisia
  women-in-development, informal sector, women workers, 32
  women workers, public administration, attitudes, management, labour market, 26
Turkey
  women's status, economic conditions, women-in-development, public health, women workers, 63
Uganda
  political participation, women workers, trade unions, 109
  sexual behaviour, AIDS, social research, 174
  sexual behaviour, attitudes, sexually transmitted diseases, AIDS, contraceptive usage, 224
  sexual behaviour, men, male contraception, contraceptive usage, 208
  women, social groups, non-governmental organizations, development policy, 122
  women-in-development, community development, law, 95
  women-in-development, gender division of labour, human geography, feminism, 36
  women's status, women, 28
Vietnam
  women workers, labour market, privatization, women's status, urban areas, 140
Zaire
  sexual behaviour, AIDS, sexually transmitted diseases, 167
  sexual behaviour, AIDS, social research, 174
  sexual behaviour, culture, disease prevention, AIDS, 210
  sexual behaviour, gender roles, women's status, women's rights, AIDS, sexually transmitted diseases, 197
Zambia
  women, development, labour, education, gender discrimination, 154
  women's status, women, 28
Zimbabwe
  AIDS, women, 227
  entrepreneurship, small enterprises, women, 119
  family planning programmes, men, attitudes, contraceptive usage, evaluation, 200

refugees, women's status, gender division of labour, 30
violence, gender discrimination, women, cross-cultural analysis, 54
women, poverty, structural adjustment, urban areas, 139
women, small enterprises, technological innovations, technology transfer, 108
women-in-development, community development, law, 95
women-in-development, directories, 261
women-in-development, women workers, 128

Author index

(figures refer to abstract numbers)

About the authors

Marguérite Appel studied psychology and management at the University of Amsterdam, the Netherlands. Since 1989 she has been employed by the Women and Development Training Programme at the Royal Tropical Institute where she is responsible for the development, coordination and organization of workshops and training courses on issues related to women, gender and development. She has undertaken consultancies for international agencies and NGOs in Egypt, Indonesia, Tanzania, Thailand, USA, Zambia and Zimbabwe. Prior to joining KIT, Marguérite undertook group therapy and counselling for drug addicted women, as well as managing multidisciplinary teams in health and development institutes.

Maria de Bruyn, a medical anthropologist specializing in HIV/AIDS health promotion/education, works in the Information, Library and Documentation Department of the Royal Tropical Institute. Manager of the AIDS Coordination Bureau (the secretariat and resource centre of the Dutch AIDS Coordination Group), she is also executive editor of the *AIDS/STD Health Promotion Exchange*. She has undertaken consultancies in Chile, Tanzania and Zambia for international organizations and NGOs.

Anita Hardon has a doctorate from the University of Amsterdam, the Netherlands, where she now works as research coordinator of the research and networking project Gender, Reproductive Health and Population Policies. Under the umbrella of this project, studies are being conducted in Bolivia, India, the Netherlands, the Philippines and Zimbabwe. She is an assistant professor in the Medical Anthropology Unit of the University of Amsterdam, where she has also been involved in research on the use and provision of medicines in primary health care, and where she currently coordinates the Unit's research programme.

Maaike Jongepier studied cultural anthropology at Leiden University, the Netherlands. As a project officer, she worked in the Asia Department of the co-financing organization, CEBEMO. She is currently working as an education specialist with the Centre for Education in Developing Countries, The Hague. Her experience includes identification, monitoring and evaluation of formal and non-formal education in Indonesia, Pakistan and Uganda. Among her main topics of interest are gender issues in relation to education, population education and participatory processes.

Loes Jansen studied sociology at the University of Utrecht, the Netherlands. Over the past 15 years she has undertaken both project management and external project evaluation in many developing countries for a variety of development organizations. She is currently employed by the Enterprise Development Department of the Royal Tropical Institute. Her interests include small enterprise development and women-in-development.

Neil Thin graduated in social anthropology from the University of Cambridge, UK, and was awarded his PhD with a thesis on the Irula forest people of southern India by the University of Edinburgh in 1990. Since 1983 he has worked as a social development consultant for various NGOs and development agencies in India, Indonesia, Kenya and Tanzania. In 1985 he won the Sunday Times Kenneth Allsop Conservation Essay Prize. Since 1990, he has been a lecturer in the Department of Social Anthropology, University of Edinburgh, combining teaching and research with consultancy work.

Wilma Wentholt studied human geography of developing countries at the University of Utrecht, the Netherlands. She has worked as a rural sociologist for projects in Burkina Faso, Benin and Indonesia. Previously employed as the Women and Development specialist at the International Institute for Land Reclamation and Improvement, Wageningen, Wilma is currently gender specialist in agricultural development at the Royal Tropical Institute. She provides advice to the Dutch Ministry of Development Cooperation and the Dutch Embassy in New Delhi, India, on gender issues and institutional development in land and water projects.

Annelies Zoomers studied human geography of developing countries at the University of Utrecht, the Netherlands. She gained her PhD from the University of Nijmegen in 1988. Since then, Annelies has worked as a project economist at the Netherlands Economic Institute and at the Royal Tropical Institute. She is currently a senior researcher at the Centre for Latin American Research and Documentation. Research and consultancies have been undertaken in the field of small enterprise development, rural development and employment generation.